Tarot

Pronunciation: tăr´ō

Function: noun

Etymology: Middle French, from Italian *tarocchi* (plural)

Date: circa 1623

Meaning: Any of a set of usually 78 playing cards, including 22 pictorial cards, used for fortunetelling

Diva

Pronunciation: dē´və

Function: noun

Etymology: Italian, from Latin *diva*, goddess, feminine of *divus*, god

Date: 1883

Meaning: An usually glamorous and successful female performer or personality; a fashion diva

LA PAPESSA LA PAPESSE · II · THE HIGH PRIESTESS LA SACERDOTISA

DIE HOHEPRIESTERIN · DE HOGEPRIESTERES

The Moon

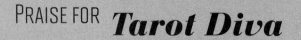

PRAISE FOR *Tarot Diva*

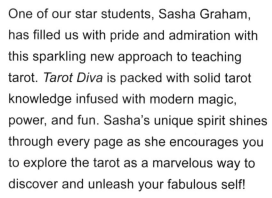

One of our star students, Sasha Graham, has filled us with pride and admiration with this sparkling new approach to teaching tarot. *Tarot Diva* is packed with solid tarot knowledge infused with modern magic, power, and fun. Sasha's unique spirit shines through every page as she encourages you to explore the tarot as a marvelous way to discover and unleash your fabulous self!

— **Ruth Ann and Wald Amberstone,**
directors of the Tarot School

Tarot needs to be dragged out of its museum now and again, given some new clothes and a makeover, and allowed to speak in contemporary language. Sasha Graham's *Tarot Diva* does just that, via a novel and fun approach that results in a greater understanding and interaction with tarot's rich imagery.

—**Ciro Marchetti, creator of**
The Gilded Tarot and
Legacy of the Divine Tarot

About the Author

Sasha Graham teaches tarot classes and produces tarot events at New York City's premier cultural institutions, including the Metropolitan Museum of Art. She has appeared on film, television, and radio, and in the *Wall Street Journal*. She resides in New York City.

Visit her online at http://www.sashagraham.com.

TAROT
Diva

SASHA GRAHAM

Keep making
magic!
Sasha
Graham

Llewellyn Publications · WOODBURY, MINNESOTA

Ignite Your Intuition · Glamourize Your Life · Unleash Your Fabulousity!

First Printing, 2011
FIRST EDITION

Book design by Rebecca Zins
Cover design by Ellen Lawson
Cover image by Image Source/PunchStock

Card illustrations from Fairy Tale Tarot by Lisa Hunt, Gilded Tarot by Ciro Marchetti, Golden Dawn Ritual Tarot by Chic and Tabatha Cicero, Legacy of the Divine Tarot by Ciro Marchetti, Llewellyn Tarot by Anna-Marie Ferguson, Mystic Faerie Tarot by Linda Ravenscroft, Robin Wood Tarot by Robin Wood, Rumi Tarot by Nigel Jackson, Sacred Circle Tarot by Anna Franklin, Shadowscapes Tarot by Stephanie Pui-Mun Law, and Shining Tribe Tarot by Rachel Pollack are reproduced by permission of Llewellyn Publications. Card illustrations from the Egyptian Tarot, Sola-Busca Tarot, Universal Tarot by Robert de Angelis, Tarot of Marseilles, and Visconti Tarot are reproduced by permission of Lo Scarabeo. Further reproduction is prohibited.

Rider Tarot card illustrations are based on those contained in *The Pictorial Key to the Tarot* by Arthur Edward Waite, published by William Rider & Son Ltd., London, 1911.

Tree of Life illustration on page 187 by Llewellyn Art Department.

Llewellyn is a registered trademark of Llewellyn Worldwide Ltd.

Cover model used for illustrative purposes only and may not endorse or represent the book's subject.

Library of Congress Cataloging-in-Publication Data

Graham, Sasha.
  Tarot diva: ignite your intuition, glamourize your life, unleash your fabulousity! /
Sasha Graham.—1st ed.
      p.   cm.
  Includes bibliographical references and index.
  ISBN 978-0-7387-2604-5
  1. Tarot. 2. Self-actualization (Psychology)—Miscellanea. I. Title.
  BF1879.T2G657 2011
  133.3'2424—dc22

                                                                          2011002369

Llewellyn Worldwide Ltd. does not participate in, endorse, or have any authority or responsibility concerning private business transactions between our authors and the public.
  All mail addressed to the author is forwarded, but the publisher cannot, unless specifically instructed by the author, give out an address or phone number.
  Any Internet references contained in this work are current at publication time, but the publisher cannot guarantee that a specific location will continue to be maintained. Please refer to the publisher's website for links to authors' websites and other sources.

Llewellyn Publications
A Division of Llewellyn Worldwide Ltd.
2143 Wooddale Drive
Woodbury, MN 55125-2989
www.llewellyn.com

Printed in the United States of America

For Isabella...

It is choice, not chance, that
determines your destiny.

Jean Nidetch

Note to Reader

Embarking upon the path of becoming a tarot diva is exciting and profound. You will be asked to venture deep within yourself to seek your intuition, wisdom, and inner grace. No part of this book is meant to replace a licensed physician, therapist, or professional counselor.

The author and publisher assume no responsibility for consequences that result from the use of this book, including but not limited to last-minute trips to Paris, bodacious behavior, pestering paparazzi, and an urge to profess self-love each and every day.

TABLE OF Contents

The Star

The word *diva* to me means doing something supernatural with something natural.

❝ **Patti LuPone**

> The thing that is really hard, and really amazing, is giving up on being perfect and beginning the work of becoming yourself.
>
> **Anna Quindlen**

Lead me not into temptation.
I can find the way myself.

Rita Mae Brown

Breathe in experience, breathe out poetry.
Muriel Rukeyser

The secret of staying young is to live honestly, eat slowly, and lie about our age.

 Lucille Ball

A true diva's heart is open and she's ready to play
by her own rules, rules that are gentle and kind.

Jenifer Lewis

Beauty is in the eye of the beholder, and it may be necessary from time to time to give a stupid or misinformed beholder a black eye.

Miss Piggy

LIST OF *Cards*

XXI *The World*

The cards reproduced in this book are from the following decks:

- Egyptian Tarot (Lo Scarabeo)
- Fairy Tale Tarot by Lisa Hunt
- Gilded Tarot by Ciro Marchetti
- Golden Dawn Ritual Tarot by Chic and Tabatha Cicero

- Legacy of the Divine Tarot by Ciro Marchetti
- Llewellyn Tarot by Anna-Marie Ferguson
- Mystic Faerie Tarot by Linda Ravenscroft
- Rider Tarot
- Robin Wood Tarot by Robin Wood
- Rumi Tarot by Nigel Jackson
- Sacred Circle Tarot by Anna Franklin
- Shadowscapes Tarot by Stephanie Pui-Mun Law
- Shining Tribe Tarot by Rachel Pollack
- Sola Busca Tarot (Lo Scarabeo)
- Universal Tarot by Robert de Angelis (Lo Scarabeo)
- Tarot of Marseilles (Lo Scarabeo)
- Visconti Tarot (Lo Scarabeo)

List of Cards by Page

We don't see things as they are,
we see them as we are.

Anaïs Nin

Let's face it: I want it all—just like you and everybody else. It may not be in the cards, but the prospect is so dazzling that I have to try.

Lauren Bacall

Foreword

Now and then, people interview me for a magazine or radio show and at some point, usually at the end, they almost always ask, "What will happen next with tarot?" or "Where is tarot going?" It's probably the effect of a new century, or maybe it's the excitement of the flood of apps, tweets, and "friends" that suggest everything is different now in the new millennium, so tarot should be as well.

Now, you would think that as a tarot reader and sometime science fiction writer, I would be well set to predict the future. But the fact is that aside from asking the cards themselves, I really have little idea of what will happen with tarot. Predictions are always based on right now, which is why readings are more like a mirror than a newspaper of the future (albeit a mirror that can show what is under the surface). Over a decade ago, when we were all worried that Y2K computer implosions would doom civilization, who could have predicted that politicians would spend their days tweeting their fans?

But if we cannot say just what will happen to tarot, we can, in fact, say what it needs. And what tarot needs—right now, at the start of the second decade of the twenty-first century—is Sasha Graham.

Okay, let's put that a little more broadly. It's time for tarot to open up, to find a new audience, and especially to become part of the larger society without losing its long tradition as a tool for self-knowledge and a program of spiritual transformation. *Tarot Diva* and its author bring tarot into our world now, showing us how to weave the cards through our lives so that tarot becomes almost a part of our DNA. This book covers everything—the meaning of the cards but also intuition, intimacy, art, clothing, romance, family, food—life itself. We learn how to use tarot for everyday spells geared to particular cards, and we learn to identify our own styles through consideration of the tarot archetypes. This delightful book even gives us recipes to make tarot part of our diet—in a sense, to literally take the cards into our bodies.

Sasha is always practical. After giving us a capsule history of the Hermetic Order of the Golden Dawn, the famous "secret society" that defined tarot for the last century (with an interesting argument that links the Golden Dawn to Modernism), Sasha suggests we start our own secret society. What a wonderful idea.

Tarot became popular in the 1960s and '70s (half a century ago!) because it seemed to match the hippie spirit of those times, just as another half-century earlier, the mysteries of the cards were taken up by the poet T. S. Eliot and the surrealists. More recently, however, tarot seems to have become the domain of specialized groups. Its image today is part "gypsy" fortuneteller, part hippie, part witch, and part mysterious psychic.

> *Tarot Diva* brings tarot into the present … by embracing the image of our times, the diva.
> **Rachel Pollack**

Tarot Diva brings tarot into the present, into the age of Lady Gaga (and whoever will come after her), by embracing the image of our times, the diva. We can use the cards to live large, to speak and act with all our energy and love. Tarot is, in fact, a great tool for such a life, because its great variety of images allows each of us to see our own way. The book does not simply take a diva slant to tarot or graft an attitude onto existent knowledge and approaches. More exciting, it shows us, in very real and practical ways, how we can use tarot to open up who we are.

In the nineteenth century, tarot became viewed as the secret path of great mages removed from the world. No doubt most of the great occultists would consider the diva approach a kind of indulgence. But in a way, *Tarot Diva* is a fresh version of the nineteenth-century concept, from Paul Christian, that tarot forms a course of spiritual magic, a training system to transform our lives and consciousness. Sasha Graham also wants us to rise to our highest level, the most we can be. She just recognizes that this power should be there in our daily lives. How else can the cards bring us to "massive internal growth, revealing the directions our hearts want us to follow"?

Rachel Pollack

Acknowledgments

This book is a result of intense love and support from my friends and family. Allow me to take a moment to thank the souls upon whose shoulders I rested this laptop: Mia Borrelli and Holly Buzeck for holding me accountable; Susan Weinthaler for barging in with a printer; Karl Giant, whose talent leaves me breathless; Laurie Knoop, goddess of food and fine taste, for help with the recipes; Sindi Bauer, the fashionista of Madison Avenue, for martini advice on fashion archetypes; Jim Steward, my ambassador of punctuation; Lisa Finander for telling me I am a writer; Corrine Kenner, who sensibly suggested I write an outline; Barbara Moore, heaven-sent author's guardian angel and acquisitions editor at Llewellyn; and Ruth Ann and Wald Amberstone for profound Monday evening tarot teachings and without whose tutelage *Tarot Diva* would not have been possible.

Warren Etheredge for challenge, guidance, and reaching for corners you could not see but felt from so many miles away—and for writing my favorite book fifteen years before our paths were to cross. My grandmother Mimi, essence of woman, who showed me what it means to be a diva. My sister, Juniper, the Snow White to my Rose Red, forever my champion and very best friend. Mom, for your awesome love, an endless supply of Nancy Drew books, naming me after Tolstoy's daughter, and everything else. My husband, Bill, the Magician, for believing in me when I didn't have the strength to do it for myself; you *knew*. The artists, mavericks, and ghosts of my family in whose footsteps I gingerly tread. The awesomely gifted tarot community for their inspiration, ideas, and support.

Above all, I would like to thank my clients for trusting and sharing their beautiful lives, hopes, and dreams with me as I walked, skipped, stumbled, and flew down the tarot pathway.

Thank you.

You only live once, but if you do
it right, once is enough.

Mae West

How to Use *Tarot Diva*

THE UNIVERSE

My heartfelt belief is that tarot is meant to do two things in our lives: one, tarot—more than a deck of cards—is an experiential formulation meant be lived and breathed; and two, tarot can be used as an instrument of massive internal growth, revealing the directions our hearts want us to follow.

To foster an active tarot practice in your life, the pages of this book contain tarot musings, meditations, journeys, card explanations, exercises, recipes, spells, and charms.

Tarot Meditations: Read each meditation carefully. Some readers may want to read through and then imagine what I have described in their meditative space. Others may read aloud and record or have a trusted friend read to them while in a meditative state. The meditations are a jumping-off point for your imagination. Where you venture when my words cease is entirely up to you.

Card Explanations: Each tarot card carries an infinite well of interpretation and understanding. I've offered up some textbook definitions and a few perhaps you haven't heard before. Like the meditations, they offer a jumping-off point. Dive in—attach your own personal meaning.

Exercises: Scattered thoughout *Tarot Diva* are exercises inspired by the energy of the cards. Performing these exercises, you'll become a living embodiment of tarot.

Recipes: The smattering of recipes included are connected to some Major Arcana cards. Cook and enjoy. Use them in conjunction with the energy of the assigned card to whip up magic in your kitchen.

Spells: Magical spells are your intention put into action. Tarot contains a treasure trove of energy you can use to weave enchantment into your life. These simple spells may be performed by anyone, anywhere.

Charms: Charms are magically charged items that aid you in attaining a specific goal. Discover how to charm a card, then harness its power all day.

Invoking: I talk often about invoking a card's energy. To invoke tarot energy is to access the card's vitality, apply it to yourself, and receive a power boost.

Weaving the magic of tarot to life, connecting the cards to your words and actions, empowering yourself and others, you'll become a true tarot diva, sprinkling stardust wherever you step.

Find out who you are and do it on purpose.

Dolly Parton

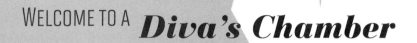

WELCOME TO A *Diva's Chamber*

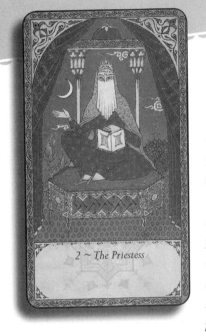

2 ~ The Priestess

A full moon beckons in a bruised black and purple evening sky. Icy wind tickles your hair and neck as you walk toward a looming stone mansion. The mansion is set aside jagged cliffs and overlooks a lusty ocean. Dancing shadows leap, flying before your feet, paving passage as you move forward. Walking to the mansion door, you notice it is wooden, with strange engravings. You knock softly. It slips open with a sigh. Leaving raw twilight behind, you enter a yawning great room. It is illuminated with flickering candles and dark, hidden spaces. Instinctively (you've been here before?), you make your way down a corridor to the library where I sit. "Hello and welcome," I say. "Take a seat. I've been waiting for you. The cards are on the table; you've pulled yourself quite a hand. The fire is blazing, the blinds are drawn, it's just us two, and I've got so much to tell you…"

Wouldn't it be wonderful to have your own personal fortuneteller—someone you could chat with whenever you needed insight or guidance, a sage you could check with when you are unsure of the future? We've all faced confusion and uncertainty. Wouldn't it be helpful to find the person who could see the truth of your life and know what is best for you and how things will wind up?

Magic in You

Darling reader, I am here to tell you that you already have this intuitive psychic/witch/oracle/wise woman in your life. She's not hidden away in a castle or meditating in a desert cave. In fact, she's been with you since the day you were born. She's watched you, cared for you, and been with you every step of the way. She's right there in front of you. Don't see her yet? If you are having trouble, walk in front of the closest mirror and take a nice long glance. Do you see that beautiful person in the looking glass? That is your sage. She is *you*.

I'm going to let you in on a little secret I learned from tarot master Pattie Canova. This secret has been known by fortunetellers through the ages, but most of them would rather you didn't know it. It's a secret that just may change your life…

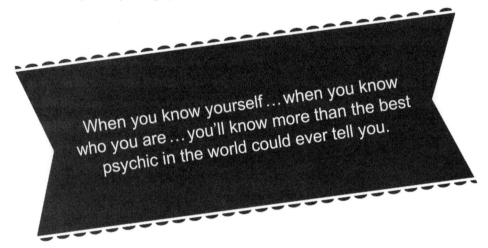

When you know yourself…when you know who you are…you'll know more than the best psychic in the world could ever tell you.

It is important to remember that we all have magic inside us.

J. K. Rowling

In tune with your higher self and intimate with your hopes and dreams, you will make gestures to invoke those dreams and walk with kindness toward yourself and others. You will become the weaver of your destiny. You will work magic in the world and sprinkle delight all around you.

Do you see the tarot deck spread upon the table? Those seventy-eight cards resonate with magic, mystery, esoteric information, secret codes, religious dogma, symbolic images, and reserves of miraculous power. But the cards are useless on their own. They need a power source: you. You are that source. They need you. You are full of such unbelievable potential. You are a cascading fountain of power, light, magic, and wisdom.

We seek out tarot readers and psychics because we want to be seen by another. We want confirmation, someone to recognize and understand us. There is an assumption when you step into a reader's chamber that they can "see" you and your life's events unfolding before them—things you cannot see for yourself. What's more, they will tell you what they see. A reader taps into the cards and unseen forces to garner knowledge about you.

Reading tarot, I meditate, open energetic channels, and tell clients what I see. Often, profound and valuable advice is given. Guess what? I'm no different than you are. I didn't descend from a long line of witches (no matter how much I wish I did), and I wasn't struck by a lightning bolt, awakening my super psychic powers. I work with tarot to guide me, to kindle the magic and intuition that lives inside me. This same magic is thriving in you this very moment!

Nestled between the pages of this book is all the information you will ever need to begin a fantastic journey with a legendary and mysterious pack of cards. Consider this book the dusty old grimoire you've uncovered in the attic—a book of secrets. Dare to open these pages, and you set off on an exciting path to becoming a certified tarot diva.

Viva la Diva

A tarot diva works with tarot the same way an herbalist works with herbs or a crystal healer works with gems and stones. A tarot diva releases the power and magic of tarot into her life, and everyone asks: "What's different?"

Tarot Diva offers more than mere definitions and instructions on how to read tarot for yourself and others. Inside this book, you will be given the keys to turning on parts of yourself—to switching on your inner light. The exercises, meditations, recipes, and musings are meant to be interactive and inspiring. You see, tarot cards are so much more than pictures on cards. Tarot is meant to be lived and experienced. And when you can see the deck as a living, breathing entity and expression of yourself, you'll become a certified tarot diva.

What Exactly *Is* a Diva, Anyway?

The origin of the word *diva* comes from the Latin term meaning "goddess" and is a derivative of the word *divine*, or *divus*, meaning "god" or "godlike." In Italian, a diva is a distinguished female opera star and celebrated singer. The term *diva* made its way into English language in the late nineteenth century, coincidentally around the same time Arthur Edward Waite and Pamela Colman Smith began collaboration on a tarot deck that would become our modern standard of tarot: the Rider-Waite deck.

The word *diva* evolved in American culture to describe women of outstanding talent in the world of theater, film, and popular music. The gay culture embraced the term *diva* to describe fabulousness. We now use *diva* to describe any woman of unusually glamorous and successful talent. You can attach the word *diva* to anything you are passionate about: a fashion diva, a food diva, and, here and now, a tarot diva.

> Remember, Ginger Rogers did everything Fred Astaire did, but she did it backwards and in high heels.
>
> **Faith Whittlesey**

What goddesses do we worship in today's modern culture? Well, if the ancient Greeks and Romans were transplanted to a modern supermarket shopping aisle or were sitting on the couch next to us watching the telly or flipping through a magazine, chances are they would say we worship the cult of celebrity. The women who command the stage and screen fascinate us. Our modern-day goddesses transform themselves and float down red carpets. We watch with delight, glimpsing the drama of their private lives unfolding before us. We become these divas when we are transported by their films or their music. We judge, idolize, knock them down, built them back up, and use them for inspiration.

Diva definition has crossed over from singers and entertainers to describe anyone who exhibits fierce, fabulous behavior—anyone who walks the walk, talks the talk, knows what she wants and will get it. A diva could be a writer, a nurse, a teacher, even your mother. Apart from the talent a diva possesses is the idea that a diva can write her own ticket. What a diva says goes. If she wants cream-colored pillows, vanilla candles, and calla lilies in her dressing room, that's exactly what she gets. A diva is not to be crossed or messed with.

However, the darker side of divahood—bad behavior or hissy fits—is not what we are interested in. We are not encouraging behavior that shuts other people out, knocks people down, or creates negativity in the world. And let's not go down the long road of double standards—a man can say or do as he pleases and he's being assertive, but a woman is pushy or bitchy if she does the same. We are interested in a diva who stands up for herself and what she wants and who reaches out to the miraculous—a diva who is authentically true to herself.

Now, let's take the term *diva* and not only apply it to the Arethas, Angelinas, and JLos of the world but to ourselves as well. What would it mean to take possession of our marvelous abilities to live an incredible and enriched life? What would it mean if we became a fully realized version of ourselves? Can you write your ticket? Yes! I know you can. Tarot provides a perfect blueprint, a roadmap with which to get started on the road to divahood. Let's use the term *diva* to unleash the inner goddess of ourselves and to help mine our inner talents, personality, and glamour!

To become a tarot diva is to use tarot as a tool to unlocking your true self and igniting your intuition. When your authentic self walks hand in hand with your intuition, you'll find life unfolding in amazing ways. A tarot diva uses the tarot to release her creative potential and let her inner beauty shine. Then you really can reach for the things you want. Most importantly, you'll find great satisfaction in yourself and in life.

At the end of the day, when a tarot diva is true to herself, the lights go down, a hush falls over the audience, and there you are: standing in a pool of brilliance, in touch with your intuition, you shimmer with beauty like the Star card.

XVII The Star

How Does Tarot Help Me Unleash My Inner Diva?

Easy. I'll let you in on another little secret:

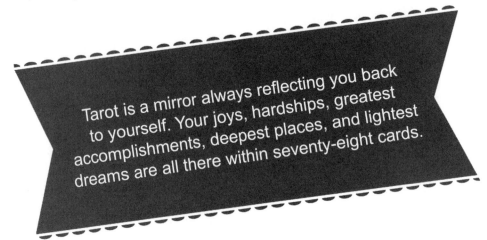

Tarot is a mirror always reflecting you back to yourself. Your joys, hardships, greatest accomplishments, deepest places, and lightest dreams are all there within seventy-eight cards.

Tarot will always show you your greatest potential. That is because the deck of cards shows a complete picture of you! So when you are looking at a tarot card, what you really are looking at is yourself. Even more extraordinary, tarot demonstrates you operating at your fullest potential. Imagine yourself for a moment, working with what you love, content in your body, satisfied in your relationships, knowing you are moving forward and not back.

To understand exactly how a tarot card reflects you, let's look at artfulness unbound: the Empress card. The Empress represents utter creativity. She is reflecting you in the light of your most creative self. Since you are unique, your creative potential will be different than your best friend's or mother's creative potential. The cards reflect different scenarios for different people. The Magician represents you at your most enigmatic level, the Devil represents you at your most fiendish and devilish self, and so on. Once you begin to understand each card as a different facet of yourself, you can then put various cards together. Multiple-card spreads create your story, your situation, and the narrative of your life.

Besides representing your ideal self, tarot cards contain:

✦ Advice

✦ Role models

✦ Situations

- ✦ Solutions

- ✦ Energy

A tarot diva understands that tarot can be used in a number of different ways. Tarot cards can be used for:

- ✦ Honing intuition

- ✦ Making decisions

- ✦ Creative endeavors

- ✦ Meditations

- ✦ Cooking

- ✦ Entertainment

- ✦ Storytelling

- ✦ Magic

Unlike dreams, tarot has the virtue of being a mirror that we can hold in our hands and look at whenever we want.

Elinor Greenberg

Dissecting Divaness

Here's another secret about famous divas. It's easy to flick through glossy magazines or see footage of a star rushing though an airport incognito and think to yourself, "Boy, do they have the life!" I'll let you in on something I've observed in my years of working in and around show biz. Divas work extremely hard on themselves and their careers. Madonna didn't just wake up with her muscular body and sweet dance moves. She works at it! Janet Jackson didn't coast on the notoriety of her famous family to be an endearing musical sensation for the last thirty years. No one works harder than Beyoncé when she releases a CD. She sweats, struts, and works her butt off to promote, sell, and publicize her CDs and concerts.

I'm not suggesting you suddenly begin a three-hour daily workout regimen and embark on a worldwide promotional tour. What I am suggesting is that to become a tarot diva requires slow and consistent work with tarot. Remember that all great changes in life are made up of a series of small steps—baby steps, baby changes. The exercises in *Tarot Diva* are precisely the steps you'll want to be taking.

At first, it can be overwhelming to learn the meanings of 78 cards—156, if you count reversals. *Tarot Diva* makes it easy and fun to work with tarot, no matter how far you've traveled down the tarot path. You'll experience the cards via meditation, writing, and play. You needn't sit and memorize meanings by rote—this isn't a calculus class, it's a ticket to a richer life. The amount of effort is entirely up to you. The truth is, the more time and effort you spend working with tarot, the more you will get back. You'll reap exactly what you sow, and baby, you deserve it all.

So, repeat out loud after me, diva:

> I am gorgeous.
> I deserve it all.
> I shine like a star.
> I know what is best for me.
> I do good in the world.

Now that you understand more about what a tarot diva is, we are off and running. Stay with me. I have so much to tell you, and we get along so well. Take my hand, and let's journey together...

THE *Tarot Test*

My tarot fascination blossomed at twelve years old, turning into a full-time career after the birth of my daughter. There I was, doling out advice, telling anyone who listened what I saw in their cards. One day it dawned on me. A client sat across from me, pining for answers … but was I using this magical deck of cards for myself? People were paying *me* for insight, but could I find the answers *I* so desperately needed?

You know the old joke—a lady walks into a gypsy's shop and asks if she may have a reading. "Of course," says the gypsy. "I knew you were coming."

Imagine for a moment you are a professional fortune-teller. Doesn't it stand to reason that if you could glean information about others' lives from tarot, then you should use it to discern the fabric of your own life? Wouldn't you be a big hypocrite telling others what was best for them and turning a blind eye to yourself? Isn't the assumption that a fortuneteller holds *all* the answers?

Well, yes; in a way, they do. But divine knowledge belongs not only to fortunetellers and psychics. We have all of the answers we need locked inside ourselves. We must find a way to unearth them, and a deck of tarot cards makes the loveliest of excavation kits.

I had uncovered a principle that would become the core of *Tarot Diva*: the tarot test. I would become as good a sage to myself as I was for others. You, my dear, can do the exact same thing. You can examine your life through the lens of tarot. You can apply tarot to every aspect of your decision making and all the facets of your life. After all, what good is an oracle if you are not going to use it, right? Well, wouldn't you know it, the most extraordinary thing happened when I did this for myself: my life began to change in wonderful ways. Before taking the tarot test, you must ask yourself:

Do you believe?

Do you believe tarot represents you? Do you believe a single card can address any question, any issue, at any time? Do you believe that tarot creates the perfect picture of you, from your most ravishing to your most dreaded state? Do you believe the cards represent the world around you and the universe thriving inside of you—that each card is a facet of yourself reflected like a diamond, dazzlingly bright?

If you can acknowledge that you believe in the cards and in the archetypes, scenarios, and situations depicted there, then you must ask yourself an even more important question:

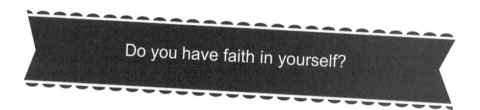

Do you have faith in yourself?

Do you have faith in the honesty and integrity of the answers you arrive at when looking at tarot? Do you take responsibility for the choices you've made, both good and bad, which brought you to this moment? Think of the roads you have traveled—your trials, tribulations, efforts, failures, and successes. If you are reading *Tarot Diva*, it means there is some glimmer of hope that tarot will provide you with answers. Tarot will give you all the answers you've ever wanted. Do you have faith tarot will empower you? Can you trust yourself? Do you have faith in your intuition?

If you can answer yes to any of the above questions, then fasten your seat belt, my dear, sweet diva. You are in for the ride of your life.

The Tarot Test

Answer the questions below to discover how you feel about tarot:

+ Do I believe the Fool represents myself, open to new opportunities and new adventures? The Fool believes each moment carries an opportunity for something new. Do you?

+ Do I believe, like the Magician, that I have all the tools before me to create the life and the outcomes I desire—that the Magician represents my body and soul operating as a conduit to the Divine?

+ Do I believe the High Priestess is my intuition, the secreted parts of myself where inner wisdom resides? Do I believe I already possess the answers I seek?

+ Do I believe the Empress is me at the height of creativity, beauty, fertility, and sumptuousness?

+ Do I believe the Emperor is me creating structure in my world? That the Emperor is me when creating and cementing my habits and routines?

+ Do I believe that the Hierophant is me, both student and teacher, and is the gateway to higher wisdom? Do I believe I learn something new each day?

+ Do I believe the Lovers represent the choices, passion, and sexual energy I use as a springboard for creating and manifesting my life?

+ Do I believe the Chariot is me moving forward, taking control, and having a solid hand in creating my own destiny?

+ Do I believe Strength is the delicate power and control I exert over issues both large and small?

+ Do I believe the Hermit is me soul searching, meditating, and contemplating in order to receive higher wisdom? Will I become a walking example to those around me?

+ Do I believe that the Wheel of Fortune represents the energy and forces around me in the universe—that the Wheel is the movement of life and synchronicity at play?

+ Do I believe the Hanged Man is a moment's pause, enabling my ability to see my life from a different perspective?

◆ Do I believe Justice is my work? Do I believe the quality of effort I put forth affects the quality of what I receive back?

◆ Do I believe Death is the destruction of what is known and comfortable so I may begin afresh and start again? Do I believe my task is to break new ground?

◆ Do I believe the Devil represents my power and control issues?

◆ Do I believe Temperance is my ability to balance life's ups and downs, honing my innate talents and skills?

◆ Do I believe the Tower represents things I cannot control and my ability to bounce back from the unimaginable?

◆ Do I believe the Star is beauty, inspiration, and freshness operating inside myself at all times?

◆ Do I believe the Moon represents cycles, strangeness, my dreams, and moments when things are not as they seem?

◆ Do I believe the Sun is abundance, glory, energy, and growth?

◆ Do I believe Judgement is me standing at the precipice of a new life and knowing I can never return to what once was?

◆ Do I believe the World is me captivated by the beauty of life, freely participating in the dance—effortless, free, in the moment, and fully realized?

Tarot readings help us develop
confidence in our own perceptions.
Rachel Pollack

Time to Suit Up

If you believe in the Major Arcana, then you must ask yourself if you believe in the qualities of the four suits:

✦ Do I believe pentacles represent the body, my objects, my money, people, places, and things?

✦ Do I believe cups represent my emotions, feelings, joys, fears, laughter, and tears?

✦ Do I believe swords represent my mind, thoughts, and ability to communicate?

✦ Do I believe wands represent my passion, sexuality, life force, spirituality, and ever-flowing energy?

If you can answer yes to the questions posed above, then you have passed the tarot test. You may now use the deck of cards to answer any question, fill you with inspiration, and provide hope in the darkness. You now have a tool in your possession to help you create exactly the life you desire.

Now, an even more important question:

What do you want?

To really ask is to open the door to the whirlwind. The answer may annihilate the question and the questioner.

Anne Rice

DIVA *Power Questions*

You agree that power lies within tarot, and more importantly that power resides in you. Where shall you start? How to begin?

The most powerful thing you can do is to start asking yourself the right questions. What do I mean by "right questions"? Often, people come to tarot readers in hopes of quick answers. Typical fortunetelling questions include, "Will I lead a long and happy life? Will I meet my soul mate? How many children will I have? Will I be rich, wealthy, and travel the world?" These are all perfectly appropriate questions to ask at a quickie carnival reading. But aren't you interested in transforming your life into something extraordinary?

People sometimes seek a fortuneteller or psychic because their life is at a crisis point. They need answers, quick reassurance. "Will I get the job? Is my husband cheating on me? Is this recession ever going to end?" Crisis questions are understandable in the moment, but a tarot diva is interested in evolution and creating long-lasting change. You can't just show up and expect the cards to give you answers to everything when your life's gone to pot. Work with tarot should continue through life's ups and downs.

Before you start randomly asking questions of tarot, I want you to do three things:

1. Acknowledge the role you play in your future.

2. State your desired outcome.

3. Construct your power question.

Let's take a closer look at what makes a power question.

Acknowledge the Role You Play in Your Future

Every action and intention we set forth creates a wave of effects in our lives. Apart from random acts of chaos, we are solely responsible for the events of our adult lives. Our lives are the result of the choices we've made. Our lives are a result of actions taken or not taken. Once we acknowledge the role we play in our future, we can add the fun part—our heart's desire.

State Your Desired Outcome

This is what you want: your dream, ambition, wish; what you are working toward and what you are hoping for. I suggest you reach for the stars here. After all, a diva knows anything is possible.

Construct Your Power Question

Do this carefully and with thought. Here's an example. Say you are wondering when, if ever, you will meet your true love. You ask tarot impatiently, "Will I find a soul mate?" Chances are, when you flip the card, it will give you a general yes or no answer. What will you do if the answer is no? Will you stop asking, searching, and yearning for love? Do you really believe the answer to such a question is so cut and dried? The interesting thing about you is that even if the answer is no, you'll probably keep asking until you get the answer you want. You are nothing if not tenacious.

The question "Will I find a soul mate?" thrusts us firmly into the hands of fate, thus removing our own responsibility. And a tarot diva knows she can work with the energies of the universe to manifest anything she wants. So, let's ask the same question in a more creative, helpful manner: "What can I do to attract a loving and healthy relationship into my life?" Aha! Notice the question acknowledges your responsibility *and* your desired outcome. Now you'll arrive at an answer that gives you something you can play with.

Sometimes questions are more
important than answers.

Nancy Willard

Say the Nine of Wands appears to answer your soul mate question. The Nine of Wands means picking yourself up by the bootstraps and breaking new ground. Your answer could be to look where you haven't before and not to lose hope. Be brave in what you ask the universe for. Say the Nine of Cups appears. It looks like you are on the right track. Keep up the good work—love is indeed heading your way.

Let's look at a money question: "Will I be rich?" You'll probably arrive at an answer, which is either a yes or a no. But why not a more helpful question: "How can I make more money while working less?" Once again, this question acknowledges your responsibility and states a desired outcome. Now you've got something you can really work with. The Six of Cups appears to answer your money question. The Six of Cups is about giving. Perhaps you could hand over some of your working responsibilities to other people. The gentleman walking away in the background of the card signifies there may be a financial endeavor you should walk away from.

There is a particular magic that occurs in asking the right sort of questions…

Your mind will start working to find the appropriate answers.

I speak my mind. I just speak my heart.
I will not turn away from any question.

Jessica Hahn

TAROT *Intuition*

POLISENA

The absolute number-one important, fantastic gift tarot offers is the delicate, careful cultivation of your intuition. Your intuition is as unique as your soul—in fact, it's part and parcel of it, an intrinsic part of yourself. Your intuition is precisely the part of yourself where your fortuneteller, your sage, your inner witch resides, the beacon guiding you to this very moment. Your intuition is operating all the time, active like a heartbeat, a breath, whether you are aware of it or not. Intuition is the superhighway to tarot divahood.

Intuition is the ability to sense or know something immediately, without reasoning: a quick and ready insight, an immediate apprehension or cognition. We know our intuition is working because we can feel it. Think of the first time you locked eyes with the person you would go on to have a major romantic relationship with. I bet dollars to donuts you knew at that moment something important was happening. Your intuition tells you when something feels deliciously right or when something feels horribly wrong. Think of a moment when you made an excellent decision. You knew, with every ounce of your body, it was right. That was your intuition backing you up. By the same token, we often make wrong decisions while we feel our intuition screaming out *no*. We so desperately and intellectually want what we want, we ignore our intuition and wind up paying the price later.

As children and into our tumultuous teen years, we feel our way through the world. We may be told our intuition is wrong by peers or family. We act on our intuition, our gut instincts, and we are quieted, shushed, or made fun of. In abusive situations, children raise their voice in objection and are silenced by adults who supposedly know better. Our childhood intuition is stuffed down, ignored, or suppressed. When you lie to a child, you send the message that their intuition is worthless and unreliable. This same child grows and greets adulthood questioning and doubting themselves. They don't trust their decisions and actions because they were told their instinctive reactions were wrong. As an adult, one of the most empowering things you can do is to start to heal, trust, and cultivate your intuition. If you are reading this book, you have the ability to reignite that candle inside yourself. You can reclaim your intuitive facilities. To do so is your birthright.

Damaged or not, whether or not you place your attention on it, your intuition is operating every second. Intuition is uniquely you, and therein lies its beauty. No one else experiences the world through your eyes; no other person feels your feelings. Your intuition is succinct, distinct, and carries its own unique character.

The gift of working with tarot is that it exercises and strengthens your intuition. Reading the cards, intuition guides your interpretations. As you venture deeper into the cards, you soon realize that each tarot card holds a bottomless well of meanings, images, and ideas for you to grasp. Your intuition selects what meanings and which symbols hold importance.

Tarot readings teach us many things. One of the most valuable is this necessary balance of objective and subjective, action and intuition.

Rachel Pollack

As trust in tarot intuition grows, the most phenomenal thing will happen. You will find that the trust in yourself with the cards spills into your regular everyday life. Soon, your decisions are made with clarity, you begin trusting yourself more, and you find life flowing with ease. You'll gain confidence in your tarot work, and synchronistic happenings will amaze you.

Synchronicity is two or more unrelated events occurring at the same time. Say you are thinking about your favorite college professor, whom you haven't seen in years. You bump into him on the street. You are listening to your favorite recording artist, reveling in adoration. The phone rings. A friend informs you the musician is playing a concert, and she's surprising you with tickets. Synchronicity is intuition in action.

Intuition versus Psychic Ability

Working with tarot will also increase your psychic ability. Psychic faculties are a much different animal than our intuitive faculties, although the two words are often used to explain the same phenomenon. You can understand the difference between intuition and psychic phenomena by discriminating where the information is coming from. Intuition is deep knowledge, a certainty within yourself. Psychic information comes to us from the outside world and can rarely be controlled. Our intuition is a constant current of energy, a river, a flow, while our psychic ability comes and goes. I call psychic flashes "pops" due to the way the information suddenly pops into your body or mind. Pops can happen very quickly. The typical psychic pop example is knowing who is on the other end of a ringing phone. It happens in a split second: the phone rings, and before glancing at the caller ID, you know who it is. You answer—only to find out you were correct. How many times has that happened to you?

Psychic information can be very specific and doesn't always make sense. It is important when you feel a psychic pop, especially if it doesn't make sense, to say what you hear out loud or write it down. You must confirm if the information is right or wrong. You may get psychic pops that seem silly or inconsequential, but you must validate them when it happens. The day you get a psychic pop that says there is a gas leak in the stove, you'll want to be listening. You'll soon be on the road to trusting those psychic gems as an added gift to your intuitive facilities.

> True intuition is subtle and graceful and will leave you secure if you listen.
> **Sonia Choquette**

Cultivating your intuition and trusting psychic pops will provide a richer context for your life. The reason importance is placed on intuition building is because the truth and beauty of your life springs from your intuition. When you open yourself up, are free, and don't pass judgment on what you feel, life begins to flow. Life becomes a dance, with you on center stage, graceful and effortless.

Reading tarot sharpens your intuition in a very specific way. Setting yourself up mentally to read the cards, you open up intuitive channels on an energetic level. You are literally acknowledging your intuition is there and actively asking it for guidance. Think of your intuition like a flowing wellspring. Setting up for a tarot reading, you literally sit down next to the spring. As you turn over the cards and interpret the symbols, you are now navigating the water. You see what floats to the surface and what mysteries lie beneath. You will learn to trust what you see. Since no intuition is alike, no tarot reading is alike either. Here, in front of the cards, is where you seek the truth to your life.

Piercing the Veil

Come a step closer to reclaiming your intuition with the following guided meditation, where you'll meet a major archetype of tarot. Approaching the tarot for guidance and accessing our intuition, we are attempting to lift the veil between unseen and seen reality; the veil between this world and the other; the veil that hangs before the world of our imagination, our unconscious, the world of untapped possibility, the spiritual, and the supernatural. We reach beyond the boundaries of a natural, explainable world. We can look at the image of a veil and understand this is the veil between day and night, between the living and the dead, between our conscious and our unconscious. Working with tarot, we attempt to raise, peek, and pierce this veil.

A Helping Hand from the High Priestess

Here is a meditation for you to embark on. The High Priestess represents the most highly intuitive and sensitive part of yourself. She is of invaluable aid to the tarot reader. Many tarot readers feel most akin to the High Priestess because she guards a veil of secrets. There is a belief that the most auspicious day for divining the future is on Halloween; on October 31, this veil between the living and dead is the thinnest. On this evening, spirits wander, sprites play, ghosts haunt, and fortunes are unraveled.

Notice the High Priestess sits in front of a veil, obscuring the waterscape behind her. The water is your unconsciousness, and the High Priestess is the guardian of what lies in the wellspring of your intuition. The High Priestess is associated with water and the moon. See the crown upon her head? This crown marks the phases of the moon cycles, from waxing (growing bigger, toward a full moon) to waning (growing smaller, toward a new moon). An additional yellow moon is woven within the folds of her dress, symbolizing an active energy.

The High Priestess can assist you in your readings, reminding you of the strength of intuition. An additional quality of the High Priestess is silence. Even if you can't articulate an answer, somewhere deep down the answer is forming and will be revealed.

Look at the veil that hangs behind the High Priestess. Direct your gaze to the immense water pictured beyond, your intuition and the places where answers are found. The High Priestess is the guardian of this place. You need only ask for admittance and it shall be granted.

Close your eyes and clear your mind. Work your way through your body to find relaxation. Release any tension you feel.

You are sitting upon a beach in the moonlight. Amidst the seascape, you hear waves crashing and feel the sea foam. You smell the salty air, and it tickles your nose. The sand is cool and wet beneath your feet. You see a figure approaching. Mysterious, not at all threatening, she approaches you, blue and white robes flapping in the wind. She raises her hand and beckons you to follow. You follow for some distance down the length of the beach. She seems to glow with an otherworldly illumination.

In a moment, you are sitting across from her. She rests on a throne, a pillar flanking either side, a veil suspended behind them. Her skin is milky white, eyes sparkling violet. "You are divine," she says without speaking. She is communicating directly into your mind. "What lies here belongs to you. You possess all the answers that have somehow been lost. When you learn something new, you do not acquire knowledge but uncover what was already resting in your soul. The tarot will help you to remember. Your journey begins here."

She stands up, and the pillars next to her slip away. She walks toward you, dissolving into you like a shadow. The veil that hung behind her dissipates in an array of muted colors and twinkling white points of light. You are behind the veil. White steps descend to a large, flowing river. You walk to the water with care. This is a hallowed place. Water rolls along softly. You see a beautiful face reflected on its surface. You are sublime.

You touch the water, inundated with feelings and emotion. Happiness and joy pulse through you. The pleasure of living moves in and out with each breath. You step into the water up to your waist. Venture deeper. You begin to float with the river. The night sky is alive and bright as you float, consumed with the passions that have created your life. You are one with the water, an open channel, and you begin to understand you must follow your instincts and emotions. Your instincts will not lead you astray. You trust your intuition. You trust your intuition. You trust your intuition.

When you are ready, slowly come back to this world, trusting yourself more than you did before.

Follow your instincts. That's where true wisdom manifests itself.

Oprah Winfrey

Choosing *Your Deck*

The Fool

0

Let's be honest: to a fresh-faced new tarot student, seventy-eight cards can appear vast and overwhelming. Choosing a deck that captures your imagination—a deck that begs you to return again and again to gaze, study, and contemplate it—is essential to your tarot studies. Besides your own beautiful vision, the deck is your most treasured tool.

Many of us are actively engaged in a tarot practice. At times, as in any relationship, we need to spice things up and break out of a slump. A tarot artist's fresh perspective and new tarot deck can work wonders on your tarot work. New decks reveal additional layers of meaning and offer exciting new intuitive leaps.

Some tarotists become avid deck collectors, amassing deck after deck of beautiful cards like book, stamp, or shoe collectors. Other tarotists use only one or two decks for their practice. Old decks become weighty and heavy with time and use, as if the souls of all who have been read have somehow left their imprint on the cards.

A Classic Deck

Each and every student of tarot must own a classic deck. A classic deck is a traditional Rider-Waite deck or a clone deck. A Rider-Waite clone is a deck pattered very closely after the Rider-Waite. Why is it important to have a classic deck in your possession? There is an underlying structure to tarot that must be respected and adhered to if there will be a common order in the tarot world. Yes, each and every tarot card has an endless well of potential meaning and interpretation.

But like musical notation, you can't create a symphony without first knowing what the notes truly mean and what they sound like. The Rider-Waite deck is the common denominator for tarot.

Many modern decks take liberties by changing cards and suits. There is nothing wrong with this practice, but it can cause confusion among new tarot students. Tarot makes use of archetypes. Imagine the original Rider-Waite as the archetype for the variety of decks on the market today.

A Signature Deck

A signature deck is a deck whose artistic sensibility captivates you long enough to bring you back again and again. A signature deck is the deck you fall in love with. The journey to tarot is a long and time-consuming one, and a signature deck makes the learning process fun and rewarding because you are so in love with the images, you never tire of it. Your signature deck is an extension of your personal style.

How do you know when you've discovered your signature deck? Stumbling across your signature deck is quite akin to the act and sensation of falling in love. The deck will look familiar, though you've never seen it before. Something inside of you clicks the moment it is in your hand. It *feels* right. You may sense an uncanny, strange waver inside—a glimmer deep down. You'll find yourself thinking about the deck when it is not in front of you. You'll want to pull it out again and again, shuffling, flipping, and fingering through it. You won't tire of looking at it; in fact, you'll be drawn back again and again for more. You'll become connected on a soul level to your deck. This is how you know you've found your signature deck.

Don't be surprised if, at first, your signature deck is the classic Rider-Waite deck. There's nothing wrong with that at all. But with all the marvelous deck choices on the market, you should be able to discover a deck that suits your personality and taste perfectly.

Finding Your Deck

An old wives' tale states you may not buy or purchase your own tarot deck—that your deck must be given to you as a gift. Nothing could be further from the truth. For a lucky few, the deck chooses us. We are given a gorgeous deck as a gift or inherit one from a relative. If a deck has already found you, consider yourself lucky and gifted with its presence. If not, then enjoy the process of finding your signature deck. Hopefully, I can make your selection process a touch easier by narrowing it down.

Discovering Your Tarot Aesthetic

Lucky for us, a massive variety of tarot decks are on the market. With thousands of decks and a few brick-and-mortar stores to browse in, how can you find the deck just right for you? In order to facilitate your search for a signature deck, I've complied a list of decks you might enjoy based on your particular aesthetic. Your aesthetic is your own personal sense of what you find beautiful, your taste and style. I've connected each deck aesthetic to an archetype of one of the Major Arcana cards. Begin your search by looking at your favorite Major card and seeing what decks are suggested. The decks suggested are not a comprehensive list but merely a jumping-off point in your search for a signature deck.

The most comprehensive online collection of browsable cards can be found at http://www.aeclectic.net/tarot/.

The Fool

The Fool represents the openness and optimism of youth, a fresh start, the beginning of a journey. The Fool is reminiscent of childhood. If you revel in the innocence and optimism of your younger days, one of these decks might be for you:

Children Tarot by Lele Luzzati

Whimsical Tarot by Dorothy Morrison and Mary Hanson-Roberts

The Fairy Tale Tarot by Lisa Hunt

The Magician

The Magician is a conduit of spiritual energy, and he represents mastery and control. He's the ultimate ceremonial magician. If you find yourself grooving on his supernatural vibe, you'll enjoy these decks that have been inspired or created by the magicians of the Golden Dawn:

Aleister Crowley Thoth Tarot by Aleister Crowley and Frieda Harris

Golden Dawn Magical Tarot by Chic Cicero and Sandra Cicero

Initiatory Tarot of the Golden Dawn by Giordano Berti and Patrizio Evangelisti

The High Priestess

The High Priestess represents the psyche, divine intuition, and your deepest, wisest self. She is the source of ultimate feminine power. If you crave female divinity and goddess power, shower your celestial glow on the following decks:

Goddess Tarot by Kris Waldherr

Universal Goddess Tarot by Antonella Platano and Maria Caratti

Mythical Goddess Tarot by Sage Holloway and Katherine Skaggs

The Empress

The Empress represents pure and utter unabashed creativity. She is artistry and originality in motion. If fine art and day tripping to a museum curls your toes, feast your eyes on these decks inspired by the work of famous artists:

Da Vinci Tarot by A. Atanassov and I. Ghiuselev

Dali Universal Tarot by Juan Llarch and Salvador Dali

Golden Tarot of Klimt by A. Atanassov

Touchstone Tarot by Kat Black

The Emperor

The Emperor, representing order, is a stickler for the rules and a strict, old-school fellow. He is the constant, controlled traditionalist. If structure suits you and you are ready to travel back in time, check out these pre-Golden Dawn decks:

Ancient Tarot of Marseilles by Conver

Visconti-Sforza Tarot (by an unknown artist)

Ancient Minchiate Etruria Tarot by Pietro Alligo

The Hierophant

The Hierophant represents a great teacher and spiritual authority. He's the pope, professor, and advisor. His wealth of knowledge is yours for the taking when you pick up one of these beguiling historical decks:

Victorian Romantic Tarot by Alex Ukolov and Karen Mahony

Golden Tarot of the Renaissance by Giordano Bert and Jo Dworkin

Da Vinci Enigma Tarot by Caitlin Matthews

The Lovers

The Lovers represent love, lust, romance, and choice. The Lovers are the life force. If issues of affection, devotion, and amour are overriding themes in your life, you might cozy up with one of these decks:

Heart Tarot by Maria Distefano

Lover's Path Tarot by Kris Waldherr

Tarot of Sexual Magic by Laura Tuan and Mauro De Luca

The Chariot

The Chariot represents speed and being in the driver's seat. The Chariot moves fast, and so do our winged friends, the fairies. If fairy magic and art helps your soul take flight, race toward the nearest fairy deck:

Mystic Faerie Tarot by Barbara Moore and Linda Ravenscroft

Fey Tarot by Mara Aghem and R. Minetti

Fairy Ring Oracle by Anna Franklin and Paul Mason

Strength

The Strength card represents mental and physical stamina, courage and energy. While gently holding the lion, the woman proves subtle power presides over brute force. If roaming free through animal kingdoms and running with the wolves is your idea of fun, check out these zoological-themed decks:

Animals Divine Tarot by Lisa Hunt

Fantastical Creatures by D. J. Conway and Lisa Hunt

Tarot for Cats by Kipling West and Regen Dennis

The Hermit

The Hermit represents solitude and silence. The Hermit embarks on a spiritual quest, then shares his wisdom with others. If Holy Grail and Arthurian legend–questing captures your fancy, seek out these fine decks:

Grail Tarot by John Matthews and Giovanni Caselli

Legend: Arthurian Tarot by Anna-Marie Ferguson

Magdalene Legacy Tarot by Casey DuHamel and Deborah L. Shutek-Jackson

The Wheel of Fortune

The Wheel of Fortune is a reference to life's cycles and the ups and downs of luck, chance, destiny, and fate. The symbolism of the wheel, a circle, reminds you all is connected eternally. Should you care to embrace the circular, cyclical nature of life, you may do so with these circle-shaped cards:

Tarot of the Cloisters by Michelle Leavit

Motherpeace Tarot by Karen Vogel and Vicki Noble

Circle of Life Tarot by Maria Distefano

Justice

The Justice card represents work, fairness, and the effort you place into your endeavors, both personal and professional. The Justice card maintains a sense of equality. If you have an entrepreneurial spirit and want tarot inspiration for work, check out these enterprising decks:

Bright Idea Deck by Mark McElroy and Eric Hotz

Silicon Valley Tarot by Thomas Scoville

Management Tarot by Korai Peter and Ute Stemmann

The Hanged Man

The Hanged Man represents a pause, momentary suspension, and seeing things in a new light. The Hanged Man hangs upside down and is able to view life with a new set of eyes. If you enjoy trippy, surreal visuals that carry you to altered states of reality, plunge yourself into these mind-bending cards:

Phantasmagoric Theater Tarot by Graham Cameron

Tarot of Metamorphosis by Massimiliano Filadoro and Luigi di Giammarino

Dante Tarot by Andrea Serio and Giodano Berti

Death

The Death card represents destruction followed by regeneration. Death stamps out the old so new growth may occur. If the eerie, grotesque, and gothic ignites yummy chills underneath your leather bra, put down the black lipstick and pick up one of the following decks:

Deviant Moon Tarot by Patrick Valenza

Bohemian Gothic Tarot by Alex Ukolov and Karen Mahony

Gothic Tarot by Joseph Vargo

Temperance

Temperance represents blending, honing, and transferring energy. The deity on the card is Michael the archangel, working diligently to achieve balance. If radiant, heavenly angels dapple your universe and color your sense of sacred, then descend upon these angelically themed decks:

The Angels Tarot by Robert Place and Rosemary Guiley

Dark Angels Tarot (by an unknown artist)

Shining Angels Tarot by Giuditta Dembech and Federico Penco

The Devil

The Devil represents excess, enslavement, and a rip-roaring good time. The Devil is often tied to the occult. If profound, esoteric matters keep you up late at night, peruse these occult decks:

B.O.T.A. Tarot by Paul Foster Case

Hermetic Tarot by Godfrey Dawson

Tarot of the Sephiroth by Dan Staroff

The Tower

The Tower represents a major shakeup, streak of insight, and shocking new reality. Landscapes of stone towers and fortresses summon dragons to mind at once. If you've a soft spot for these scaly fire breathers, you've plenty of decks to choose from:

Celtic Dragon Tarot by D. J. Conway and Lisa Hunt

Dragon Tarot by Peter Pracownik

Dragon's Tarot by Manfredi Toraldo and Severino Baraldi

The Star

The Star represents rejuvenation and clarity after the drama of the preceding cards. The Star is inspiration from within and above. If you have a knack for astrology, can forecast fate in the heavens, and would enjoy cards linked with astrological information, look no further:

Celestial Tarot by Kay Steventon and Brian Clark

Elemental Tarot by Caroline Smith and John Astrop

Zodiac Tarot by Lee Bursten and Luca Raimondo

The Moon

The Moon represents sleep, our unconscious, wild dreams, and hidden truth. The Moon is our lunar landscape, and there is one creature that ventures into it while the rest of us sleep … the vampire! If your pulse quickens at the thought of fang bangers and blood-sucking vamps, check out these drippingly delicious decks:

Vampire Tarot by Robert Place

Gothic Tarot of Vampires by Ricardo Minetti and Emiliano Mammucari

Vampire Tarot of the Eternal Night by Barbara Moore and Davide Corsi

Tarot of Vampyres by Ian Daniels

The Sun

The Sun represents regeneration, fertility, and abundance. The Sun is glowing good health and the prosperity of nature. If you live in sync with the seasons, have a gardener's touch, and worship mother earth, you'll find a happy companion in any of the following nature-themed decks:

Gaian Tarot by Joanna Powell Colbert

Shining Tribe Tarot by Rachel Pollack

Spirit of the Flowers Tarot by Antonella Castelli and Laura Tuan

Judgement

Judgement is the wake-up call and the transformation card. Once you pass through Judgement, you are at the point of no return. If cutting-edge, outside-the-box, new, and modern ideas help to propel you forward, check out these amazing decks:

Transparent Tarot by Emily Carding

International Icon Tarot by Robin Ator

Legacy of the Divine Tarot by Ciro Marchetti

The World

The World heralds success, completion, euphoria, and travel. The World represents the end of a journey and the beginning of a new one. With that in mind, here is a selection of some of the most popular, eclectic decks ever created that have found worldwide acclaim:

Maat Tarot by Julia Cuccia-Watts

Osho-Zen Tarot by Ma Deva Padma and Osho

DruidCraft Tarot by Stephanie Carr-Gromm, Philip Carr-Gromm, and Will Worthington

Robin Wood Tarot by Robin Wood

Creating *Sacred Space*

o The Fool

Something you should do, if you don't already, is set yourself up for success. Establishing beneficial habits that become second nature is a great gift to yourself. In the same way you establish excellent eating habits, brush your teeth, and maintain healthy exercise regimens or daily writings in gratitude journals, you can create successful tarot habits. Tarot habits become a welcome part of life. It begins with pulling a card a day, but it goes further when creating your tarot space. Set your readings up for success by taking some time to create a lovely tarot environment. This is also a chance for you to get super creative and have some fun.

The Importance of Ritual

The importance of creating tarot ritual for yourself cannot be underestimated. When you set the stage for a tarot reading, a bit of care goes a long way in cultivating deep and meaningful readings. As your tarot habits become ingrained, your unconscious and intuition unfold on their own. Every religious practice, from Christianity to Judaism to Buddhism, is grounded in ritual and rite. This is no accident. By creating a ritual, selecting your tarot accessories, and opening sacred space, you are giving your subconscious clues that you are opening up in a magical way. Ritual activates our sensory perception, alerting us, awakening us.

Creating a Tarot Environment and Sacred Space

Ever notice the energy shift when you step into a church, theater, or yoga studio? Do you sense the calmness, the reverence? This is because the environment is a sacred space. The collective energy of the people who've come to pray, worship, and meditate creates a palpable electricity. You can even sense the energy shift on a palpable level when walking into different departments of a university. Think of the energetic difference between the math department and the dance department, or the difference between the art studios and the anthropology labs at any college. The energy is affected by the type of work taking place.

Sacred spaces can be created in any environment.

Christy Turlington

You can discover naturally occurring sacred space outdoors. Locations like Stonehenge or Malibu are well known for the mystical, healing energy flowing there. Often, you can discover your own sacred spots in nature—a special grove, a spot beside a stream, a seat beneath a weeping willow. Seek out these places, and carry your cards with you when you visit them. You will want to encourage this same reverent energy wherever you read tarot.

Select a Spot

Select the space in your home where you'll perform regular readings. It may be tempting to just whip out the deck and read on your bed or any random place, but I advise you to pick a specific spot to read tarot and dedicate that space to readings. If you are fortunate to have an entire room for tarot, all the better. Create a tarot chamber—you can set up your tarot accessories, books, and decks all in one place. Don't fret if there's no extra room. Any space in your home can work well. It could be on your kitchen table, your desk, or in a special corner. You may already have a space where you meditate or journal, and you will find the energy there lends itself beautifully to creating your tarot space. Ultimately, it is your mindset, not your physical surroundings, that is important.

I am not implying you can't pull out your cards at the coffee shop or other locations. You certainly can. In fact, I usually travel with a deck of cards. I'm suggesting that you create a special area in your home where you will work with the cards as a home base—a place you can return to time and time again to work with tarot.

Tarot Accessories to Help You Pierce the Veil

The accessories offered below are not requirements, merely suggestions to include in your sacred tarot space. Some accessories can enhance the desired outcome of your readings. Look at them as power boosters to help you manifest your desires. None of these accessories are required for tarot reading. They will aid you in making your readings as powerful as possible. And remember…a tarot diva always sets herself up for success.

Candles

Candles are sacred objects. Candle magic is an ancient practice dating back thousands of years. It is no accident that candles and fire play a major role in every religion known to humanity. I find candles indispensable when reading tarot (or serving dinner, writing, playing a board game, or doing anything else, for that matter).

Light your candles. Use this act as a metaphor for igniting your intuition. As the candle flickers, grows, and glows, focus on it. Look for the heat waves emanating up. Imagine your inner fire glowing. As the candle sheds its light, so do you shed light on your current situation.

If you know ahead of time what the topic of your reading will be, you may choose a candle of a specific color to aid you in manifesting your desire:

White: Readings to do with good in all situations, purity, and protection

Red: Readings to do with strength, vitality, sex, and courage

Blue: Readings to do with peace, healing, and joy

Pink: Readings to do with love and friendship

Black: Readings to do with endings and banishing

Yellow: Readings to do with power, movement, and creativity

Purple: Readings to do with intuition and spirituality

Green: Readings to do with prosperity and money matters

> There are two ways of spreading light: to be the candle or the mirror that reflects it.
>
> **Edith Wharton**

Music

Music is powerful. It is mood altering, affects your heart rate, and can soothe and inspire you. You may choose an uplifting classical piece, a dramatic film score, techno or trance music … use whatever gets you in the mood, opens you up, and readies you to pierce that veil. Perhaps the music you use is the sound of the natural world around you—the sound of wind outside your windows or of birds chirping. For added drama, use the backdrop of a rolling thunderstorm to aid in your reading. Each time the thunder cracks, pull a card!

Incense and Aromatherapy

Incense and aromatherapy are wonderful ways to alert your unconscious and the universe as to your intentions. It puts you in the mood and alerts your senses that you are about to embark on a reading. Incense, along with candles, is another item commonly used in religious ceremonies, from the Vatican to Buddhist temples. This can be a wonderful sensory clue to your body that you are entering a sacred tarot space.

Light your incense with the same intention that you lit your candle with: ignite and imagine that you are accessing your higher self, your wisdom self.

Tea, Coffee, and Other Tasty Beverages

Tea is a comforting and nurturing drink. Reading tea leaves is a divinatory art in and of itself. If you are inclined to read tea leaves, you may drink loose-leaf tea while reading your cards, then look for an additional message in your cup. Besides being full of antioxidants, sipping your favorite herbal tea while reading cards is another clue to your body that you are opening up a sacred tarot space. You may also prepare yourself a refreshing water infusion. Choose a beverage to give yourself a magical power boost whilst reading:

Coffee: Insight and energy

Plain Black Tea: Courage

Cinnamon Tea: Increases intuition

Chamomile Tea: Peace

Blackberry Tea: Attracts money

Lavender Tea: Love and contentment

Mint Tea: Prosperity and safe travel

Cucumber Water: Fertility and healing

Lemon Water: Love, joy, and banishing bad habits

Important note: Do note consume alcohol before or during a reading. Never, ever mix tarot with booze, beer, wine, or drugs.

Fresh Flowers and Herbs

Fresh flowers and herbs contain a thriving energy of their own distinct character. This energy is often connected to their healing properties. Victorians created a language of flowers, where, like a tarot card, each bud carries a distinct message. Notice how a vase of fresh flowers brings your room or dining table to life? You may choose flowers and herbal bouquets the same way you choose colored candles or beverages. They are chosen for the magical intention of the reading. This is especially easy to do in the summertime, when fresh herbs and flowers grow in abundance and are widely available.

Daisies: Love

Mint: Success, motivation, and money

Roses: Love

Sage: Fresh starts

Basil: Love and protection

Bay Leaves: Victory and success

Snapdragons: Protection

Rosemary: Protection and memory

Thyme: Honor

Violets: Creativity

Parsley: Luck

Lavender: Specific answers

Foxglove: Thriving ambitions

Buttercups: Money

Table

Your reading table should be clean and clear. You wouldn't apply makeup on an unwashed face, you wouldn't eat dinner on last night's dirty dishes, and you should never, ever read cards on a messy table. If you do nothing else in the way of atmosphere, you should read on a clean, clear tabletop. You may also acquire beautiful and portable cloths reserved exclusively for reading the cards on. Perhaps you will find different colors and textures for varied readings: red velvet for love readings; sparkly, shimmery fabric for party readings; and so on.

Energy

Opening your sacred tarot space is an important and enjoyable moment before you begin reading cards. Sacred tarot space is the energy you open and surround yourself with when embarking upon a reading. Your sacred space is portable. It follows you everywhere, because you manifest the energy around yourself when you read the cards. This is your chance to open up and connect with the divine forces that surround you. It is also your opportunity to request help and guidance from higher sources.

You are always surrounded by your own unique energy. In addition to your words and actions, this energy is what attracts people and situations or repels them. Energy work is a fantastic area of study that you may want to investigate further.

The moment you decide to flip a card, actively fire up your intuition, and ignite your psychic abilities, you do the work of a true tarot diva. Treat yourself and your tarot space with respect and reverence. When you do, the information you receive will be powerful and profound.

When you really listen to yourself,
you can heal yourself.

Ceanne DeRohan

Center and Open Yourself

You've created your sacred space, and now is the moment to clear your mind and center yourself. A dancer would never start dancing without warming up and stretching her muscles. You, as a tarot diva, should also take the appropriate steps to ready your mind and body for the work you are about to embark upon.

Close your eyes and focus for a moment on your breath. Consciously make your exhales longer than your inhales. Briefly move through your body, looking for tension. Breathe and briefly move those tense places to release any pent-up energy. Forget about your responsibilities and tasks. Know you are perfect right where you are. Know the work you are about to do is important. Imagine a white light beginning to grow inside you. It brightens, whiter and stronger, and fills your body with a warm glow. It is now outside of your body, protecting you like a second skin. The white light continues to loom larger, forming a pyramid of power, with the point above your head. Now, open the top of the pyramid. Your body is surrounded by a cylinder, a column of light, filled with energy and radiance from above.

When you feel the moment is right, open your eyes. You may ask aloud for any helpful spirits or guides to assist you. You may also state aloud that your reading will be for you or your client's higher good.

You are now ready to perform your reading.

Closing Your Energy

When you are finished reading, you will want to close off this energy cone. Close your eyes again and imagine the great white light surrounding you. Consciously close off the top of the pyramid. You may allow the protective white light to stay with you. You might choose an additional grounding exercise after closing your energy. Thrust your hands into a bowl of smooth stones you have collected. Walk barefoot in the grass. Eat a handful of organic, unsalted nuts. However you choose, mark the closing of energy with as much clarity as possible.

What we really want to do is what we are meant to do. When we do what we are meant to do, money comes to us, doors open for us, we feel useful, and the work we do feels like play.

Julia Cameron

Tarot *Charms*

Invite the magic of tarot into your life on a daily basis with a tarot card-a-day practice. You will pull one card every morning and see how it applies to your day. This exercise develops a deep understanding and personal connection with each card. Slow and steady is the name of the game. If you are just laying a foundation for tarot, don't become impatient. Pulling one card a day will build your knowledge of the cards in a solid, stable way. To perform your card-a-day exercise, you'll need to:

✦ Have quick access to your tarot deck

✦ Keep a tarot journal

✦ Center yourself

✦ Perform enjoyable visualizations

Pulling a Random Card of the Day

You will select a random tarot card each morning. Your card should be selected with care, the same way you'd pick a bouquet of flowers for your home or choose a ripe, juicy apple from a farmer's market. In tarot, as in life, the more time you take, the better the results.

It is important to perform this exercise soon after rising from a night's sleep. We have a strong connection to our sleeping/dream state/unconscious mind for forty-five minutes after waking. We want easy access to deeper parts of our psyche for our card-a-day practice. Additionally, waking up and performing this meditative ritual liberates our day on a graceful, peaceful note.

If you are taking baby steps with tarot, I'd advise you not to work with reversed cards in your card-a-day practice. Reversal is the term used when the card is drawn upside down. People often read reversals as the polar opposite of the card's traditional upright meaning. Reading reversals is actually not such a cut-and-dried process. You will acquire the subtlety of reading reversals as you continue to study tarot (find more information about reversals on page 268). Integrating reversals is a separate area of tarot study and need not be applied to your card-a-day practice.

Your Tarot Journal

Your tarot journal is a repository of your thoughts and feelings on tarot. A three-ring binder works quite well. Divide your journal into five sections:

1} Card-a-Day

Here you will write and journal about your card of the day, listing your impressions of the card. Write thoughts in the morning and venture back later that night for an evening check-in.

2} Synchronicities

Synchronicities are coincidences that appear to be meaningfully related. You will write any synchronicities you experience. Working with tarot, synchronicities will increase. You'll want to be aware of their increasing frequency.

3} Psychic Popcorn

Just as with synchronicities, you want to make note of psychic pops. Confirmation is key. Affirm your pops, and you will not be so quick to disregard them.

4} Readings

You will want to write and record the readings you perform to look back and reflect upon.

5} Additional Notes

Mark extra space for other items you'll want to include. This could be your personal artistic renderings of the cards, your *Tarot Diva* writing exercises, or anything else that tickles your fancy.

Using a three-ring binder doesn't mean your tarot journal needs to look like it came straight from the office supply store. Sketch or glue a copy of your favorite tarot card on the front. Fill the journal with favored images cut from magazines, pressed flowers, glitter, or perfumed pages. Make your tarot journal as beautiful and unique as you are. For a marvelous resource on tarot notebooks and writing, see Corrine Kenner's book *Tarot Journaling*.

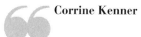

Ultimately, people who read tarot cards and people who keep journals are actively engaged in the creative process.

Corrine Kenner

Centering Yourself

Take a moment. Note how you are feeling before selecting your card. Have you awoken from a delicious dream or are you dragging your feet along the wrong side of the bed? Are you groggy? Excited? Energized? Enthused? Do you want to roll back into the soft comfort of your pillows? Look out the window. How does the weather make you feel? Is the sun sparkling or do rain clouds make you want to retreat?

Relax your body. Take a comfortable seat. Uncross your legs and arms. Slowly move through your muscles, scanning for areas of tension. Consciously relax those areas. Simply breathe into a tense spot and imagining the muscles softening. Consciously acknowledge and thank the relaxed, energized, healthy parts of yourself. Offer thanks to your good health.

Next, shuffle your deck while thinking about your day to come. Do you have a big meeting today? Are you heading to a tedious job or will you engage in work that feels like play? Will you spend the day with family, friends, or alone? Is it a sleepy Saturday with a lazy brunch planned?

Visualization

Performing a visualization is my favorite way to begin the day. After taking stock of your day, when it feels right, stop shuffling. For your visualization you must only close your eyes, concentrate, and imagine. Science has proven the power of conscious visualization. When we imagine or think about something, areas of our brain, our synapses, light up the same way as if that thing were actually happening. Since our imagination has such a strong effect on our physical body, I've created a divalicious scene set in a proper five-star hotel room.

Read through the scenario I've described below until you can adequately play out the scene in your mind, adding personal touches.

You have awoken in a bed of white linen, emerging from delicious, restful sleep. A dream of youthful love and a stolen first kiss lingers in your memory. You enjoy the sensation that anything is possible as you greet the day. Your nightgown falls to your feet as you slowly get off of your bed. Sunshine streams through the windows, and sheer curtains dance on the breeze effortlessly circulating across the room. The sound of water caresses your ears. A clawfoot tub sits in the corner, filling for your morning bath. The water is sprinkled with flower petals and lemon peels. A table has been set for you—fresh fruit, crisp toast, and hot steaming coffee. You walk over to the mirror, glancing at your reflection. You notice something lovely about yourself, a quality you've never seen before. On a table under the mirror, a tarot card has been placed out for you by the concierge.

Open your eyes.
Turn over your top card.
This is your card of the day.

Fill your visualization with any quality that makes you feel good. Replenish as your needs and desires evolve. Add items to your visualization you'd like to manifest in your day to come. Add someone wonderful snoozing in the bed next to you. Place a large check, your name on it, next to your bed. Your hotel can be set anyplace on earth you like. My hotel rooms rotate from tropical islands to Provence to Tuscany. Add your own unique, delightful touches. Tailor your visualizations. Make them divinely inspiring! Then examine your card of the day.

Focus on the Card

Take note of the strongest impressions you have about your card. Make sure to examine all aspects. Look at the foreground, background, objects, and characters:

✦ Does the suit or the number of the card resonate with you?

✦ Does a court card represent you or someone else?

✦ Where is your attention continually being drawn as you gaze at the card?

✦ What is your card saying about your day to come?

✦ Does your card offer a message?

✦ Does your card offer a lesson?

✦ Does your card offer advice?

✦ Is the card being prophetic?

✦ Does the card remind you of someone?

✦ Does the card confirm an experience you are going through?

✦ Does your card act as a mirror?

Scribble your observations, along with the title of your card of the day, in your tarot journal. Make careful note of your feelings.

Writing your impressions is of utmost importance. You may enjoy the act of writing and find yourself journaling away. You may only write one sentence. There is no right or wrong way to write about your card so long as you write something down. The moment you cast your attention to your card of the day, you are activating your intuition. In order to understand how well your intuitive facilities are operating, you must write them down. It is far too easy to disregard your intuition when it is correct. You can't ignore your wise insights when they are staring at you from a piece of paper. Additionally, you will need to refer to your musings for evening check-in.

After you have written down your impressions of the card, look up the traditional meaning in a tarot book. Look in *Tarot Diva* or any other tarot book on your shelf. This will give you extra card information to ponder as you glide through your day.

Evening Check-In

Later in the evening, note in your tarot journal how your card applied to your day. How did the card work out or reveal itself in the course of your day? Were you right on the money? Did the card predict a future event? Did the card remind you of someone you bumped into unexpectedly? Did the energy of the card reveal itself in a situation you encountered?

Don't worry about being right or wrong, and don't pass judgment on yourself. The card-a-day practice should never be used as ammunition against yourself if you were wrong. Card-a-day is a slow, steady, enjoyable approach to learning the cards and taking their meanings to a new and personal level. This is an exercise meant to deepen your relationship with the tarot and to engage your intuition.

> Whenever we begin a tarot journal, we are knowingly or unknowingly committing to studying and evolving ourselves.
> **Elinor Greenberg**

Using the power of card-a-day, I've reinvented the way I work with and interpret tarot meanings. The storm clouds on the Three of Swords once revealed themselves as a storm that knocked out the electricity in the house. The Tower card once revealed itself as a huge aha moment. The Six of Swords proved to be an unexpected guest. There is no end to the delight and surprise at your fingertips working with a card-a-day practice.

Note to beginners: If there are any cards that really freak you out or make you uncomfortable, feel free to remove them from the deck for your card-a-day practice. If the thought of drawing the Ten of Swords first thing in the morning makes you nervous, remove it at once. Reintegrate these cards when you feel ready and comfortable. Remember, you are in charge of your tarot experience. It should be an enjoyable one.

Diva Discernments

Learning tarot, you will formulate opinions about each card. You'll instinctively become drawn to or enamored of some cards, and perhaps leery and nervous of others. Our gut reactions are valuable. They put our intuition to the test and shower us with insights. Yet, sometimes our assumptions can lead us astray.

How often have you made judgment calls or speculations about someone you've just met—only to find out you were wrong? We'll make assumptions about strangers with a quick glance. Later, after chatting with them, you realize your first impression was wrong. You are surprised by how different they turn out to be. Assuming you know something is quite different than experiencing it intuitively. We don't want to make the same mistake with tarot.

Intuitive Reactions versus Associative Memory

Our assumptions and preconceived notions spring from our associative memory. Associative memory links our emotions to the things we learn. Our brains link objects and associations together. We see a green light; it means go. We see a red light and associate it with stop. This is a very helpful mechanism, yet it can sometimes stand in the way when interpreting a tarot card. The whole point of working with tarot is to see the world and yourself in an entirely different way.

While honing your intuition with tarot, you'll find there is a difference between an honest-to-goodness intuitive reaction and a reaction springing from a series of preconceived notions. An opinion based on preconceived notions is like the following: You once stayed up all night drinking peach-flavored schnapps when you were a teenager. You got horribly sick the next day. To this day, the smell of any peach-infused drink immediately fills you with revulsion.

The same set of preconceived notions and associative memory applies to people. Let's say your grandmother is a lovely, kind creature whom you adore with all your heart. She has a mane of white hair and is always stunning in her sterling silver jewelry and purple blouses. You spy a woman at the mall with white hair, a silver belt, and a purple dress. You immediately get a good feeling as she approaches you.

Let's also say you were bullied in grammar school. A mean girl with short black hair, a denim jacket, and horrid Oreo breath made your personal misery her seventh-grade mission. At the mall, you spy a girl with short black hair and a denim jacket approaching you. You instinctively want to run away.

But our preconceived notions can sometimes confuse us and rush us to quick conclusions. What if the white-haired woman in the mall was actually trying to lift your wallet while asking directions to the Orange Julius? What if the girl with short black hair in denim is walking over to return a twenty-dollar bill you accidentally dropped behind you?

Negatively, associative memory can even be a springboard for racism—a way of making quick assumptions. On the other hand, associative memory can be useful to us. As a preteen, I'd put on lipstick and passionately kiss posters of young John Travolta and Robby Benson. When I met the man who was to become my husband, what was the first thing I noticed? Why, I'll be darned if he wasn't the perfect blend of—who else?—John Travolta and Robby Benson!

The trick is in deciphering the difference between preconceived notion and intuitive reaction. Tricky, but with practice you'll become better at distinguishing between the two. You will also look at your world with a larger frame of vision. You can see more of what's in front of you when associative memory is kept at an arm's length, not clouding your perceptions. Try not to rush into a preconceived notion when examining a tarot card.

Many people instinctively become nervous of the swords cards because they depict sharp edges, figures that are blindfolded and bound, and images of distress. As you work with tarot, you discover these pictures represent allegories of the way the mind works. Swords represent our thoughts and words—the way we confuse ourselves, hold ourselves hostage, or, by the same token, free ourselves of mental constructs. When we look past our preconceived ideas of bondage and look beyond sharp, scary swords, then we uncover the truer, deeper message in the card.

Deciphering our fuzzy gray areas—differentiating between our wellsprings of intuition and our value judgments—is what will make us either so-so tarot divas or extraordinary tarot divas. And my intuition tells me you are extraordinary.

Total Tarot Empowerment with Conscious Choice

So, there I was, working with my card-a-day practice for years, learning about the cards, but I still felt like a creature enslaved by the hands of fate. I wanted to use tarot to improve, enrich, and empower my life. Certainly, cards appeared in my card-a-day practice that acted like power boosters. The Magician proved I'd be wildly enigmatic; the King of Wands reminded me I would teach my tarot class with authority; the Lovers promised a day of playful flirting; the World assured me that the ensuing day was to be my oyster. No matter how hard I tried to be objective, certain cards stuck out like favored children.

Working with clients and students, I explain how the future is fluid. Tarot can be an indicator of energies around an issue, but *you* have the power to influence how your future plays out. At the very least, you have a say in where your head will be at when the smoke clears. Think about it: you don't randomly choose a color of lip gloss; you select a shade that makes your mouth shimmer in the most delightful and alluring way. When you wake up, you don't reach into your closet with your eyes shut to randomly pull out an outfit to wear; you consider how you feel, how you want to look, the weather, your mood, and the message you want to send to those around you. You don't dress in flip-flops and a bikini to a business lunch, and you don't don flannel PJs when hosting a fancy dinner party. (Well, maybe you do. But that's another story…)

Point is, there is nothing wrong with having a favorite tarot card or actively choosing your card of the day and letting its energies aid you. In fact, actively choosing your card and utilizing its energy can be one of the most powerful agents for change in your life. Say you are nervous for an important meeting or interview in which you want to make a good impression; choose the Magician to fill you with his energetic, capable energy. Say you've got a hot date with someone you are really crazy about; choose the Queen of Wands, who saturates you with exciting, powerful sensuality. Perhaps you are trying to become pregnant; pull the Queen of Pentacles to fill you with fertility. Maybe you are already pregnant; pull the Sun for a healthy pregnancy. Tarot cards that make you feel good and cards you are strongly connected to will feed your actions and attitudes through the day.

It matters not what a person is born but who they choose to be.

J. K. Rowling

Tarot is sitting there, waiting for you to use it. The Wheel of Fortune is waiting for you to access its luck. The World card wants to remind you to live in the moment. The Fool prepares you for anything heading your way. Go ahead and access the power of the cards as you need it. When you do, you'll be a true tarot diva.

Creating a Tarot Charm

Want to know how to give your card of the day a super power boost? You can do this with a tarot charm. A charm is a verbal spell. In fact, the incantations or rhymes spoken by witches— "Bubble, bubble, toil and trouble!"—are charms. You might recall a charm we've all recited as children: "Starlight, star bright, first star I see tonight, I wish I may, I wish I might, have this wish I wish tonight." Perhaps you still find yourself saying it while gazing up at an evening sky.

You can fill any object with a short-term magical jolt by reciting a charm over it. Think of adorable charm bracelets or people who carry their "lucky charms." The idea is that the magic or luck is carried with you throughout the day.

You can charm a tarot card to invoke the card's energies and tap into the specific power you want to access. After you charm your card, you may place it somewhere special—on your nightstand, your desk, a shelf—or carry it with you in your bag (my preference). I enjoy seeing my tarot charm peeking and poking out during the day when I've forgotten about it. When I get home, I take the card out and place it where I can see it.

A tarot card is made into a charm by simply speaking or singing over it. You may create the rhyme yourself (always more effective) or use the example I have provided.

Select the card you wish to charm. Center yourself, hold your hands over the card, and recite the following:

> Wands, cups, swords, and pentacles play
> Let your magic fill my day.
> (Name of card), illuminate me with your powers
> Work this enchantment for 24 hours.

Below are suggestions for cards that make excellent charms. Remember, though: the more personal the card is to you, the more powerful the charm.

Charm	Cards
To induce love	The Lovers, Two of Cups, Ace of Wands
For hot sex	The Lovers, King of Wands, Queen of Wands
To glow with beauty	The Empress, Queen of Pentacles, Nine of Pentacles
To be magnetic	The Magician, Ace of Wands, Knight of Wands
Intuitive/psychic boost	The High Priestess, The Moon, Page of Cups, Queen of Cups
Peace of mind	Two of Swords, Four of Swords, The Hermit, The Star

Charm	Cards
Balance	Temperance, Two of Pentacles
Good health	The Sun, The World
Self-love	Queen of Pentacles
Rejuvenation	The Star
Deep spiritual insight	The Hermit, The Hanged Man, Judgement
Abundance	Ten of Cups, Ten of Pentacles, Seven of Pentacles
Friendship	Two of Cups, Three of Cups, Six of Cups
To invoke your imagination	King of Cups, Knight of Cups, Seven of Cups
Happy family	Ten of Cups, Queen of Pentacles
Joy and happiness	Three of Cups, Ten of Cups
To attract money	The Wheel of Fortune, Ace of Pentacles, Four of Pentacles
Good luck in business ventures	The Chariot, Justice, Three of Wands
Happiness in work	Three of Pentacles, Eight of Pentacles
Getting your work done	Two of Wands, Ten of Wands
Mastery over a situation	The Emperor, Strength, kings of any suit
Concise words and action	Queen of Swords, King of Swords, Page of Swords
Victory over a situation	Justice, Six of Wands, Seven of Wands
To invoke change	Death, The Tower, Judgement
Action and excitement	Knights of any suit, Five of Wands
For strength	Strength, The Sun

Charm	Cards
New beginnings	Ace of any suit, The Fool
Endings	Ten of any suit, The World
Stability	The Emperor, four of any suit
Good study habits	Page of Pentacles, Knight of Pentacles
Lightheartedness	Page of any suit
For charitable work	Six of Pentacles
Outrageous fun	The Devil
Stop something in its tracks	Ten of Swords
Good luck	The Wheel of Fortune, Nine of Cups
Speedy travel	The Chariot, Eight of Wands
Internal movement forward	Six of Swords, Eight of Cups, Nine of Wands

Extra Credit for Your Card-a-Day Practice

Did you know you can extend your card-a-day practice for other time periods? You can pull a card for the week, for the month, and even for the year. By the same token, you can pull a card to oversee a specific creative project or venture. You can pull a card for a move or the beginning of a new cycle in your life. You are limited only by your imagination!

Tarot's *Mysterious Past*

Imagine you've just begun dating someone fabulous. Are you wildly inquisitive? Do you research their name on the Internet, prod their friends to find out your new love's history, dig up their checkered past? I do; that may be just the Page of Swords in me. Certainly, value lies in knowing where and what certain people have been up to. You're falling in love with tarot, so let's find out what this beguiling deck has been up to for the last five hundred years or so. Then we'll be clear about the oracle you are using.

The origins of tarot are wrapped, shrouded, under the cloak of time. Truthfully, no one knows exactly when or where the very first deck of tarot was created. This is because, throughout history, most playing cards were disposable. The same way our Las Vegas casinos discard decks after they are played, ancient cards were tossed aside and destroyed. Ancient cards were created on flimsy, cheap paper that couldn't stand up to the ravages of time.

The Visconti-Sforza deck is the oldest tarot deck we have. It comes from Milan, Italy, at the height of the Renaissance, circa the year 1450. Reflecting its time period and the wealth of the family that commissioned it, the Visconti-Sforza Tarot is painted with gold leaf, each card a stunning piece of artwork. The wealthy Italians who commissioned this deck even had the court cards painted to reflect their own images. Imagine the Queen of Cups in your likeness. Perhaps, one day, you'll create your own deck and include yourself and those you love as some of the tarot characters. The Visconti-Sforza Tarot was treated as art, not as a disposable set of cards. This is why it survives in museums around the world today.

The Visconti-Sforza Tarot was probably not created as an oracle or fortunetelling device. Certainly, it was not a tool of personal empowerment. Most likely it was created for the Italian card-playing game *tarocchi* (where the term *tarot* derives), a game not unlike the modern version of bridge. Although no one can say when tarot divination began, one thing we do know about human nature is people have always sought the future in different ways. From scrying into water to the oracles at Delphi, reading clouds, palm reading, tea leaf reading, throwing dice, casting astrological charts, and reading regular playing cards, people have always sought guidance about future events. So, it was pretty much a no-brainer that sooner or later tarot would evolve from card game to fortunetelling device. What makes tarot so extraordinary and marvelous for divining, compared to regular playing cards, are the extra set of twenty-two images—the Major Arcana.

> Tarot cards were first invented as a game. Your work with them should be playful, not laborious.
>
> **Corrine Kenner**

Now, let's fast-forward out of the Renaissance and find ourselves smack-dab in the center of England circa 1900. Those cheeky Victorians were obsessed with the occult. Table tipping, mediums, occultism, and crystal balls were all quite the order of the day. Jack the Ripper was setting all of London afright. Gothic fiction such as *Dracula* and *Frankenstein* were all the rage. Charles Dickens, the Stephen King of his time, was igniting imaginations across Europe with his bone-chilling tales.

Simultaneously, in London and Paris, you have a potent mixture of artists igniting the art and literature world on fire with the emergence of Modernism. Modernism was a deliberate departure from the traditional, using innovative forms of expression. This expression distinguished the style of art and literature at the time. Picasso, Matisse, T. S. Eliot, D. H. Lawrence, Gertrude Stein, and Virginia Woolf were writing, painting, influencing, socializing, and drinking together in the evocative time period often coined "La Belle Époque." As art and literature marched forward into the twentieth century, so did arenas of occult thought. This Modernist movement would also produce a new deck of tarot cards that would become the basis for our modern decks—the Rider-Waite cards.

Amidst the intoxication and excitement of the turn of the century, on the outskirts of London, a group of eccentric upper-middle-class men and women gathered to form a secret magical society. This secret society was called the Hermetic Order of the Golden Dawn, and it would become the most influential magical society of its kind. The Golden Dawn's influences are still alive and well today. Its members included the poet W. B. Yeats; Florence Farr, a famed actress of the day; and the ever-controversial Aleister Crowley, known as "the wickedest man in the world." Among its members were Christian mystics, magicians, Freemasons, Rosicrucians, and Qabalists.

Tarot played a role in the magical work the Golden Dawn undertook. In fact, each member was to create his or her own unique tarot deck. Golden Dawn member Pamela Colman Smith took her painting instructions from member Arthur Edward Waite to create what eventually became the Rider-Waite Tarot deck. In 1909, Waite published the deck with the Rider Company, thus giving it its title. The Rider-Waite deck is viewed as the "traditional" tarot deck of today. It has been used in countless films and books and is the best-selling tarot deck of all time. There has been an explosion of new tarot decks in the last decade, and many are coined "Rider-Waite clones" because they follow the structure and imagery of the Rider-Waite deck.

Your key to unraveling the imagery of tarot is understanding where the symbols arose in the first place. It is important to understand that our modern tarot is a result of the mixing of many different mystical philosophies from the members of the Golden Dawn. These different philosophies are reflected in the imagery of tarot. Understanding this will help you to decipher the pictures in tarot. You'll unlock the secrets that fill the meanings of the cards. Because the Golden Dawn incorporated myriad philosophies to its own end, these philosophies are reflected in the images of tarot. Our modern decks are chock-full of themes that arise from Christianity, Qabalah, Freemasonry, and magical practice.

The Three of Pentacles Example

Nothing is more exciting than to discover a new symbol or meaning in a tarot card you have been looking at for years. To find a perfect example of the Golden Dawn's mixture of philosophies, look at the Three of Pentacles to discover a world of hidden symbolism:

Masonic Symbolism: See the stone worker with apron, hammer, and bench? It is a Masonic apron and a Masonic tool. Even his bench is a symbol of Freemasonry. The stone worker is, in fact, a Freemason.

Christian Symbolism: The Three of Pentacles is set within a medieval cathedral. We also see a Christian holy man pictured.

Qabalistic Symbolism: The triangle of three pentacles is arranged in the exact formation of the top of the Qabalistic Tree of Life. This is a direct reference to the tradition of mystical

Qabalah. The Tree of Life structure is discovered on many other cards upon close inspection. Look carefully to discover them for yourself.

Hermetic Magic: The pentacle itself is a magical symbol. The five-pointed star represents earth, air, fire, water, and spirit. The pentacle is a powerful magical symbol representing the element of earth.

Speaking of the Golden Dawn, I'll let you in on another secret. Look at the background of the image of the Ten of Swords in the Rider-Waite deck. You'll find a 'golden dawn' breaking across the horizon behind the man splayed upon the ground. Golden Dawn symbolism is everywhere in tarot once you know to look for it.

Multitudes of symbolism will continue to unfold before your very eyes as you continue in your tarot studies. Perhaps one of the most enjoyable aspects of studying tarot is finding secrets and symbols within the cards. Good luck hunting, my little diva detective!

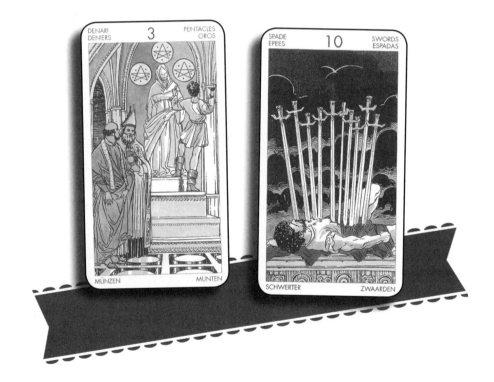

How You Play a Role in Tarot's Future

As far back as the 1970s, you'd be hard pressed to find a tarot deck. Few tarot books were in print, and if you stumbled into a dusty old bookstore that carried them, your selection was minimal at best. But take a look today at how not only tarot books but also tarot deck selection has exploded. You need only enter the word *tarot* online or check out your local chain bookstore to find a rich and vast selection of tarot books and decks to choose from. What does this tarot explosion mean? It means that tarot is moving into the future with new energy and vitality, and you are a vital part of its emergence into the future.

In the same way the painters and writers of the Modernist era changed the future of art and literature, when you shuffle a deck of tarot cards, you are also affecting tarot's future. We are using the tarot as a tool for not only fortunetelling but for personal growth—for magic, manifestation, and creation. Each time you sit and focus on the cards in a new and fresh way, you are helping to move tarot into the future.

Years ago, the Death card might have meant just that—literal death. But the New Age movement has reclaimed tarot as a tool of personal revelation and examination. Tarot continues to flourish, grow, and evolve. Each and every time you read the cards for yourself or others, you are participating in a movement that is vital, exciting, and evolving. Diva, isn't it wonderful to discover you are the postmodern face of tarot? You affect the way future generations read and experience the cards!

I love to see a young girl go out and grab
the world by the lapels. Life's a bitch.
You've got to go out and kick ass.

66 Maya Angelou

Don't wait around for other people to be happy for you. Any happiness you get you've got to make yourself.

Alice Walker

Super Sexy *Tarot Divas*

Queen of Wands

Come into my bedroom for a moment. Notice it is strewn with lacy underthings, feathers, and boas; the bed is rumpled, with silken sheets and dozens of pillows. In a dark corner, you spy a closet door peeping open. Slick leather straps, odd instruments, and chains glimmer at you subversively. Sexuality contains a spectrum of light and dark, just like my bedroom. Interesting opposites, dark and light collide in the world of your sensual imagination. We find this same set of opposites when examining what makes a tarot diva super sexy.

Harnessing the power of your sexuality is one of the most profound things you can do. Not only is sexuality a universally rewarding experience, but its power to motivate is surpassed perhaps only by the desire to eat, drink, and survive. You can channel sexual energy into whatever form you'd like it to take—use its power to attract another person or channel it to accomplish a project or a goal.

The first thing you'll notice about any famous diva is how sexy and magnetic they are. Sexiness, however, is a whole lot more than just looking hot in a pair of skinny jeans and more complex than writhing half-naked in a music video. In fact, sexiness has nothing to do with the size of your butt, what your facial features look like, or what clothes you are wearing. Sexiness is an aura that you project to the world when you are delighted with yourself. You fall in love with yourself, and the world cannot help but to follow suit.

Tarot encourages you to fall in love with yourself because work with tarot is an ever-evolving process of self-examination and discovery. You may use the cards to tackle any issue you grapple with. Conversely, you may use the cards to propel your creative ideas and dreams into fruition.

Most importantly, the use of tarot requires constant trust in your inner voice. This inner dialogue—probing to find answers, creating new questions—adds up to a self-aware, introspective, and curious creature: you.

Far from a purely narcissistic act, reading cards opens up the world in two distinct ways:

Number one: the more self-aware and trustful you become, the quicker you live a life of freedom. You participate with joy rather than wrestle with it. Ecstasy lies in front of your very eyes via the passing shadow of a bird, a strain of music, a breeze upon your face. But if you aren't paying attention to the world around you, you can't surrender to its beauty. Ecstasy thrives in every subtle act, and each passing moment is a chance to indulge your imagination, eyesight, taste buds, and sensory facilities. You must pay attention in order to cultivate this ability. Your body is a giant sensory organ created to feel, sense, listen, and experience your environment in any number of ways. But you can't savor ecstasy when distracted by chaotic thoughts. Focusing your attention outward, you become available to people and part of the solution, not the problem. When you turn your tarot curiosity to the incredible world that surrounds you, the world becomes a far more interesting place.

Number two: reading for others, you discover the divine subtext that thrives within another's life. It is your challenge as a reader to illuminate this subtext. Everyone's life is a novel, an adventure. Your delight as a tarot card reader is that you can hop in to read the pages of another's life and illuminate their subtext.

Sexiness contains an interesting set of opposites. Deeply kissing another, we close our eyes. Why do we do this? It is the interplay of light and dark, real and imagined, and fantasy and reality that come together in the midst of a kiss. Take a look at how tarot combines the intricacies of sensuality and throws them into an intoxicating mix…

Sex appeal is 50 percent what you've got and
50 percent what people think you've got.

Sophia Loren

The Darker, Shadier Side of Sensuality and Tarot

Intimacy Is Sexy

Reading tarot for another person creates immediate intimacy. Social niceties are thrown aside like clothes and you plunge into a heady level of communication as you open yourself up energetically to another person. Conversely, that person, eager to hear what you have to say about them, immediately opens up to you. They invite you in.

Reading tarot for another, you see them for who they really are. The beauty of tarot is it speaks in a symbolic language that can apply to anyone. It fosters trust and understanding between you and another. I don't know about you, but all I've ever wanted was to be understood, to be heard, and to be seen. Reading for another, you offer the gift of your subtle sight.

Secrets Are Sexy

Secrets exist on the darker, subversive side of sexiness. We all have secrets. What do you hide from the world? The stories, tales, and internal movie camera playing in your mind is delectably dangerous. No one can hop in to peek at the world through our eyes; it is impossible. We attempt the expression of ourselves via words, conversation, art, and metaphor. We connect our inner life to the outer world through these means. But who can really look inside of us? There is a back and forth, touch and go, between what you physically experience and the fantasy rolling inside your mind. This may be why when we kiss someone, we close our eyes.

When we use tarot as an examination of our deeper selves, we are reminded of the little nuggets we have tucked away. Sometimes, we don't even realize they are there. We harbor feelings and emotions we may not be able to articulate for ourselves until uncovered in a reading. Dig just a little deeper. What's behind your knowing smile? A juicy secret or two will always add interesting subtext to your life. Don't have any clandestine ideas? Use the tarot to help you come up with one! Start with the Lovers card…

When I'm good, I'm very good.
When I'm bad, I'm better.

Mae West

THE LOVERS

VI The Lovers

Whispers in the Dark Are Sexy

Tarot is always whispering to you. Tarot weaves truths, stories, secrets, and tales. All you need to do is slow down and listen.

Candlelight Is Sexy

Candlelight caresses our skin, smoothes out rough edges, flickers, and casts shadows. Candlelight is a connection to our past. Dim lights flicker. Do you know anyone who doesn't appear more alluring with the soft glow of a flickering candle caressing his or her face? Doesn't the figure in the Seven of Wands look like he's lighting a bunch of torches? Light a few tapers, flip a few cards, and take a closer look at yourself or someone you love.

Your Shadow Self Is Sexy

We all possess a deep, wet, emotional, unconscious well—similar to the pool pictured on the Moon card. It is out of this well that our deepest desires spring. If you keep accessing your shadow well and are brave in facing what you discover, you'll find depth and shades to your personality you never imagined existed. Self-discovery mixed with a tinge of darkness is sexy.

Out of darkness, candlelit romance, and stolen glances, look to the brighter, more transparent side of sexiness and tarot.

The Truth Is Sexy

Tarot creates a direct line to truth. How honest can we say we are with ourselves? With others? A peek into tarot demands, insists on truth—especially when we read for ourselves! Constant practice with tarot sharpens our internal bullshit detector. When you show the world you are a force to be reckoned with—when you call a spade a spade (or, in tarot, a sword a sword)—that is damn sexy.

Reaching for Your Higher Self Is Sexy

Reading tarot requires you to ask more from your intuition than you might ordinarily do in everyday life. You reach higher than you normally would. You ignite your intuition, and you realize there are parts of your psyche, higher parts of yourself, that you never imagined existed. As consciousness expands, your understanding of the world expands. You see more, experience more, and become enraptured by the beauty and the wonder of life. Caught in the moment, there is no room to judge yourself. When you stop judging yourself, that's sexy!

Trusting Your Instincts Is Sexy

Each tarot card has hundreds of potential meanings. With practice, you learn to trust your first instincts when interpreting a card or spread. You find, usually, your first instinct is correct. Trust with tarot will spill into your everyday life. Your split-second decision making becomes sharper and clearer. When you trust your gut, you make decisions authentic to your true self. You become confident, and confidence is sexy.

Knowing Who You Are Is Sexy

Knowingly, you toss your hair, dance through life with ease, laugh with abandon, and understand your desires and happily reach for them. You enjoy yourself and are a pleasure to be around. Tarot is a mirror always reflecting you back to you. Use tarot to gain greater knowledge about who you are and what you want—because when you know who you are, that is super sexy!

Do you really have to be the ice
queen intellectual or the slut whore?
Isn't there some way to be both?

Susan Sarandon

What Is An *Archetype?*

Sitting down to contemplate tarot, we find the word *archetype* scattered everywhere. But what is an archetype, and how do archetypes help us understand tarot? How does an archetype apply to our unconscious mind? How does an archetype make reading for others easier? An archetype is not a font style, nor is it a new software available to download, nor is it Marvel Comic's latest archvillain.

An archetype is a collective human idea. An archetype is the original model after which similar things are patterned—think of Adam and Eve as the original lovers. An archetype is a recurring symbol or motif in literature or painting—think of Romeo and Juliet as the original star-crossed lovers or the recurring images of Cupid to represent love.

In Jungian psychology, an archetype is an inherited pattern of thought or symbolic imagery derived from the past collective experience and present in the individual unconscious. How does this Jungian definition apply to your life? We can return to the image of Adam and Eve, the symbolism of a naked man and woman standing in a garden. One glance, and most Westerners gazing at a picture of Adam and Eve grasp the implication of love, sex, choice, opposites, and desire (the same implication of the Lovers card). The Adam and Eve image expresses these ideas without words. This is why an archetype is an innate psychic structure allowing expression. It is psychic because no words need be uttered. Recognition is immediate. The power of an archetype is it fosters the ability of human understanding through symbols. What appears throughout the tarot deck? The collective symbology of the human experience, which can be universally applied to anyone and everyone.

Some tarot archetypes are easier to grasp than others. It is simple to understand the kings of tarot as father archetypes and queens as mother archetypes. It is easy to grasp that the Fool archetype implies innocence and openness. It might take you some study and reflection to understand the Magician as an archetypal symbol of mastery, control, and self-expression. Once you begin to interpret and understand all the rich archetypal symbols contained within tarot, your unconscious will foster immediate recognition with one glance at the cards. Archetypes connect the unconscious to the conscious mind, and you are free to weave the story tarot tells you.

Unconscious versus Subconscious

Examining archetypes, it is worth taking a moment to understand the difference between the unconscious and the subconscious minds, especially because archetypes dwell within the unconscious mind. Subconscious and unconscious are vastly different terms often used to describe the same thing. They are, in fact, two completely different levels of the human mind. Let's probe the inner recesses of your mind for a moment to discover how you operate.

The subconscious mind is the information that lies under our conscious (normal thinking) mind and is easily accessible. Someone asks you to text them your address. Your address isn't just floating around your conscious mind, taking up space. You direct attention to your subconscious and easily access the information found there. In this way, the subconscious acts much like memory. Your subconscious contains all the easily accessible information we need. We wouldn't want all these facts, ideas, and thoughts clouding our conscious mind, so they are relegated to the subconscious.

Your unconscious (that well pictured on the Moon card) is that storage of collected information, memories, and desires that lingers way below the surface of your conscious mind. Our unconscious is not necessarily easily accessed. It may even drive or control the conscious mind on unseen levels. Someone asks you to describe the worst day of your life. You may be able to recall memories of that day, but the actual trauma or physical pain may be completely repressed within your unconscious. In this way, the unconscious works as a protector for us. This is also why to be knocked unconscious is to lack awareness and capacity for sensory perception. The unconscious mind exists without conscious control or awareness.

Intuition is the facility—the direct line, the highway—that links the unconscious to the subconscious to the conscious mind. You can easily understand this process by examining the first five cards of the Major Arcana and how they add up to waking consciousness.

You can read more about the intuitive process later in this book. For now, understand that the power of an archetype rests in its ability to reach into the depths of the unconscious and retrieve

Your Spirit + Intuitive Connection + Unconscious + Subconscious + Ordered Consciousness = YOU.
Natural State + Energy + Silent + Active + Ordered = YOU.

meaning via a symbol. A handsome boy offers you a folded piece of paper. You open it up to discover a red heart drawn upon it. You look up into his sparkling eyes with a shy smile. Message received.

You may also understand the use of archetypes in advertising. Advertisers and companies work very hard to create archetypal advertising. Think of the power of the Nike swoosh symbol, the Mercedes three-pointed star within a circle symbol, McDonald's giant yellow M. These companies have invested enough time, energy, and advertising dollars so their symbols are internationally recognized. More intriguing, in a glance, their symbols contain emotional implications. The Mercedes symbol implies luxury/status, while the McDonald's symbol implies fast food. A company able to convey its message within a symbol, without words, has struck an advertising gold mine. They express their messages, meanings, and associations without any words at all. Psychic advertising!

Awesome Archetypal Aid in Tarot Readings

An added benefit of archetypes comes to our aid when we read tarot for other people. Have you ever gone for a psychic, tarot, palm, or other reading and been disappointed and frustrated because the reader didn't truly grasp the scope of your situation, the gravity of your questions, or the nature of your life? The challenge of providing an excellent tarot reading is to understand the person sitting across from you. The problem is we each come equipped with our own personal filter—a filter through which we understand and view the world and other people. We sit down with preconceived notions that we inadvertently apply to the person sitting across the table from us. Our filter can diminish, distract, and mislead us in understanding our client. The only way to avoid making this mistake is to speak within the context of archetypes. Archetypes are universal and apply to each and every one of us regardless of our social, financial, or sexual standing.

Using archetypal language, you need not explain to your client what an archetype is, unless you feel compelled to. Simply apply the symbolic meaning of the card archetype that arrives in their tarot reading. The same way a horoscope will apply to anyone who reads it, your client will bring their own meaning to the table. Reading in this fashion, you needn't go out of your way to wow your client with details from your "psychic" abilities. Your job as a tarot reader is to stick to the archetypes, not zoom in too close to the client and inadvertently place your values or opinions upon them. For one client, "a trip" means venturing across state lines; to another client, a trip is three weeks in Thailand. Stick to the archetypal bones of a tarot reading and your client will walk away feeling understood.

The lasting benefit of understanding archetypal symbols within tarot is that, once you have a firm grasp, you can throw your tarot definition book away. Understanding archetypal symbols, you instantly access the meanings of the cards while adding your personal associations. It is the space offered between archetypal understanding and intuitive reasoning that, when combined, makes for a powerful, personal reading.

KNOW YOUR *Majors and Minors*

IV *The Emperor*

There are only twenty-two Major Arcana cards, while the remaining deck is composed of fifty-six Minor Arcana cards. So, what and where is the difference between major and minor? What is the difference between the Fool, who implies opportunity, and an ace, who offers opportunity as well? How does the Empress, who expresses creativity, carry more weight than the Three of Pentacles, which also expresses creativity?

The ability to distinguish the difference between a major and a minor card is an important one. Major Arcana cards represent major life lessons, soul issues, and turning points. The Minor Arcana cards speak of mundane, typical, day-to-day issues we encounter. Minor Arcana moments, combined together, add up to a Major Arcana experience.

Understand tarot as the Fool's journey. The Fool moves through the cards, one by one, gaining experience, learning lessons at each one, until he reaches the last card, the World. He then begins the cycle afresh, carrying his lessons learned.

High School: A Major Experience

There you are: fourteen years old, fumbling with your locker, hormones raging, hands sweaty, just ambushed by a social studies pop quiz, nervous for tonight's dance, embarrassed by your mother this morning, laughing at the note you were just passed, and…don't look behind you…the love of your life is *standing right there.*

We can understand the difference between the majors and the minors by examining a collective experience most of us have withstood: high school. High school is an excellent metaphor for the Fool's journey through tarot because it contains a definitive beginning (first day of ninth grade—the Fool) and an ending point (graduation—the World). You leave high school a completely different person than the one who entered it, thus echoing the Fool's journey of transformation.

Major Arcana moments are those big lessons and turning points. Major Arcana moments contain more than singular issues, often standing out as a result of lessons, learning, practice, and self-realization. Major Arcana cards have broad implications. Minor Arcana moments are daily activities, touch-and-go moments, things we encounter or do regularly. Look below to see if you can discern the difference between a major experience and a minor experience:

- ✦ Emotional anticipation of entering high school (the Fool) versus selecting your outfit for first day of school (Seven of Cups).

- ✦ Practicing and trying out for a team or squad (the Magician) versus performing as a team member (Five of Wands).

- ✦ Watching and waiting to see what the other kids are like (the High Priestess) versus meeting a new best friend (Two of Cups).

- ✦ Shining in the classes you love (the Empress) versus editing a term paper (Queen of Swords).

- ✦ Grappling with authority of teachers/parents (the Emperor) versus getting away with ditching a class (Seven of Swords).

- ✦ Teacher who inspires you to aim higher (the Hierophant) versus enjoying his or her class (Page of Pentacles).

- ✦ Your first love affair (the Lovers) versus locking lips with a cute boy (Ace of Wands).

- ✦ Practicing, studying, and acquiring your driver's license (the Chariot) versus nervousness on the night before the test (Nine of Swords).

- ✦ Standing up for yourself against a bully (Strength) versus how the bully makes others feel (Five of Swords).

- Daydreaming, plotting, and imagining the future from the privacy of your bedroom (the Hermit) versus writing an emotional poem (Page of Cups).

- Winning a scholarship for an exciting summer trip (the Wheel of Fortune) versus meeting new friends on the trip (Six of Cups).

- Esteem and responsibility of first part-time job (Justice) versus saving your money wisely (Four of Pentacles).

- Realizing the world is a much bigger place than you imagined (the Hanged Man) versus day of community service (Six of Pentacles).

- Parents getting divorced (Death) versus visiting your dad on the weekend (Eight of Cups).

- Recognition of innate talent and repeated practice (Temperance) versus a staged performance (Four of Wands).

- Walking the line of rebellion (the Devil) versus your first hangover (Five of Cups).

- Realizing your boyfriend's no angel (the Tower) versus a teen love triangle (Three of Swords).

- Feeling proud of yourself (the Star) versus acing a test (Six of Wands).

- Strange, confusing issues (the Moon) versus a bad breakup (Ten of Swords).

- The glory of summer vacation (the Sun) versus sunbathing and flirting with boys (Queen of Wands).

- Acceptance to the college of your dreams (Judgement) versus touring universities (Eight of Wands).

- Graduation day (the World) versus an awesome graduation present (Nine of Cups).

Notice how all the Major Arcana moments contain grand themes? Major Arcana moments are those you will remember long into adulthood, while the minor moments become hazy and fuzzy with time. In a reading, an abundance of Major Arcana cards indicate important, life-changing events. The Major Arcana is the broad spectrum, while the Minor Arcana represents slivers of time.

More Major versus Minor Examples

Dating: Imagine you are in a relationship and the object of your affection has a nasty habit: he stands you up on dates repeatedly. The random Friday night you get stood up is a Minor Arcana moment. But you grow sick and tired of this appalling treatment. The Friday night he stands you up and you end the relationship, kicking his ass to the curb, is an example of a Major Arcana moment.

Music: Imagine you are a music composer and conductor in Carnegie Hall. You stand before your musicians, audience seated behind you, breathlessly waiting the performance. You lift your wand to begin. Each player, each instrument—the horns, drums, the strings, piano—you gesture to play, all represent the Minor Arcana. Each note is a Minor Arcana card. The entire piece of music together—the chorus, the crescendo, the overall emotional feeling evoked by your work's composition—can be understood as a Major Arcana moment.

Painting: Imagine you are an artist, standing in your studio, fresh paint on your palette. The canvas stretches before you in possibility. Each brush stroke and every dash of color you place upon your canvas can be conceived as Minor Arcana. The final painting—the feelings and associations expressed and evoked gazing upon it—is Major Arcana.

Film: Imagine you are a movie director at the helm of a saucy independent film. Your assistant rushes to get you coffee, the star actress weeps in her trailer over tabloid gossip, costume designers barrage you with choices, background players await direction. All the elements coordinated to make a film can be understood as Minor Arcana elements. The final film as it premieres at the Sundance Festival—the work as a whole and the feelings it evokes—is a Major Arcana experience.

Food: You set out to bake a red velvet chocolate cake. You pull your ingredients together—sugar, flour, butter, etc. These are all examples of Minor Arcana elements. You combine them, bake it, and your gorgeous iced cake is an example of the Major Arcana.

The major moments of our lives are created by lots of minor experiences. Understand this difference and you'll understand how to distinguish between a major and minor card.

A deep lesson is echoed throughout the majors and minors. When you want to invoke a major change in your life—when you want to embrace a new way of being, whether it is to become healthier, happier, improve your finances, or completely reinvent yourself—do it in minor steps. Lots of minors add up to a major—that's a math equation you can't argue with.

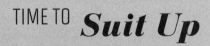

KNIGHT OF PENTACLES

I'm summoning you back into my parlor. You enter through lush red velvet curtains; a faint scent of cinnamon drifts in the air as a sense of secrecy surrounds the two of us. Candles blaze upon a table I've spread with tea, dark chocolate, and sweet treats. I want to explain the four suits of tarot. I want you to grasp their meaning with complete certainty. I want you to know exactly what they mean when they appear in a reading. But, to do so, you must trust me. Do you?

To deconstruct tarot is to understand the delicate interplay of the four suits of tarot—pentacles, swords, cups, and wands—and how these four suits apply to your life.

Allow me, for a moment, to become your guide, your personal assistant on a journey through the worlds of pentacles, cups, wands, and swords. By the time we are through, you'll understand exactly what each suit represents. Take my hand…

Pentacles

We approach a sparkling golden door with a five-pointed star emblazoned upon it: the world of pentacles. I open the door and gesture for you to enter. Your eyes are bright with excitement and curiosity. Spread before you are piles and piles of coins and cash. Sitting in front of the mountains of money is your investment banker. He grins, sifting, calculating, and counting out your riches.

Beyond the stacks of silver extend racks and racks of clothing—more sumptuous clothing than you could wear in a lifetime. Past leather shoes, crisp shirts, pants, and dresses extend more rooms.

Venturing in, you discover they contain furniture, appliances, and every imaginable convenience. Rooms splay to the side like wings of a museum. These are the rooms you have created in your life. Amazed, you walk into your childhood bedroom, your beloved toys strewn about it. Your teenage room, stacked with books, papers, and posters, sits next door. Your adult bedroom, living area, and assorted rooms of your current home lie before you. Laughing, you notice a parking lot through the window. It contains all the cars you have ever driven, the cars you have owned, lined up, waiting for the flag to drop.

You continue to explore room after room. An alcove contains all the art projects you have ever created. The ceramic ashtrays, the valentines, and every present you have ever wrapped and received. A delicious scent captures your attention, finding a chamber where every imaginable food has been laid out for your delight.

Circus music—strange, haunting—lingers up and down an eerie corridor. Wandering through the twists and turns, you enter a mirrored funhouse. The image of yourself a hundred times over dizzies your eyes. You, numbering in the thousands. The mirrors catch every angle of your body. Arms, legs, butt, chin, every piece of you is reflected. Haphazardly, you walk forward. Bumping here and there, you notice the mirrors are reflecting you closely. You are magnified. It is not just your hand tossed back from the glass, but your skin—close, elastic, etched, and stretched across your bones. Blood. Muscles. Tendons. Closer, molecules divide, dance, disappear, and reemerge.

Dashing into a dim room, something brushes the side of your nose. Strands of dangling DNA suspend from the ceiling. Soft tufts of hair follicles, trimmed and cut through the years, rise in piles before you. Buckets of sweat, running and playing sweat, scatter the floor. Nervously, you look at me, and I bring you to the final room. An audience is before you, alive, electric. A person in the front row catches your eye, looking familiar. It is a close friend. Relieved, you see all your friends are sitting in the front row. Your family sits behind them. This gathering contains every person you know and have ever met. Your jaw hangs open in amazement. Drawing you close to me, I explain:

> *Pentacles and the element of earth represent all of the things in your life you can touch, feel, and see: objects, people, money. It is the regenerative quality of earth that is the building block of your world. When a pentacle card appears in a reading, it suggests something about the material world.*

Cups

We walk toward a door with a cup etched upon it. I open it for you and we walk into an ample, sun-sparkling room. Wispy pockets of mist leave moisture, gathering in little droplets, on your cheeks. We walk toward a circular in-ground pool. The water ripples, incandescent in the shimmering light, a play of movement as if something live swims under the blue abyss. You bend down, caressing the water with your fingertips. Absently, you lick the water off your fingers, noticing it is salty. "This pool contains all the tears you have ever shed," I say.

Together, and as graceful as dancers, we dive into the pool. The moment your body is engulfed by rushing water, sadness wells within you. Deeper and deeper, your body descends to the depths. Each second your heart splinters and shatters into a million fragmented pieces. Your emotions rollercoaster as you move downward. Every second links a string of sensitivity. At one moment you feel the boredom of an endless lecture; the next, disgust at the behavior of a cruel person; confusion over what you saw your parents doing, red flush of embarrassment on your cheeks; seething anger in your trembling hands; jealous sting of envy; fear—tastes of copper on your tongue. You cannot bear to fall any deeper; you know what lies beneath. The sullen emptiness of the darkest point of your life. The very darkness you rejected so you could go on living is expanding before you. You've beaten it; how could it have appeared again? How can it lie right in front of you? To merge again means you will not return. Blackness. Gravity pulls you toward the void. Darkness. Despair.

You feel my hand jerk you upward. The darkness below you dissipates, receding into watery shadow as you move away. Helium lightness enters your heart. Reversed motion produces the opposite process of sensitivity strings. Happiness spreading with relief. Upward you move. You recall life is an adventure. The very thought fills you with excitement. You feel a tickling of laughter, the surprise of a birthday gift. Rolling affection and the warm embrace of a hug. The compassion of giving, curiosity spreading like raindrops on a leaf, the invigorating ecstasy of first love. The expansive euphoria of dreams realized. The gratitude of spirit connection to an infinite divine orbit. Knowing empathy, bathrobe-soft. Understanding and satisfaction of expression, delight in the world around you. You realize you extend far beyond the limitations of the physical body, too small to hold your spirit.

You break the surface of the pool with a gasp, only to discover a woman standing at the side of the pool—the woman whose body was your doorway to the world. It is your mother. She pulls you out of the water and dries you off with a soft white towel, tousles your hair, and hugs you in a generous embrace of tenderness. You look into her eyes and are met by a peaceful, steady gaze. Together, the two of you wander to an adjoining library. The library contains a collection of your favorite books, music, paintings, photographs, and films. At each object, the two of you stop to linger, sharing experiences and objects that have meant something to you, amused and moved you, throughout the years. Although you could stay in this library forever, it is now time to leave. I take your hand and explain:

> *Cups and the element of water represent your feelings, emotions, art, laughter, tears, and all shades in between. It is the fluid quality of water that allows your emotions to flow from one state to the next. When a cup card appears in a reading, it suggests something about the quality of your emotion.*

Wands

I place your hand upon a new door rising to meet us. You find it hot to the touch. It is a fire door, steel, thick, meant to contain flames until they can be quenched. We enter, and you discover yourself in the midst of a desert resort, dry sand beneath your feet. The air is hot yet devoid of humidity. Warmth fills your body, and the sun shines, illuminating brilliance as far as the eye can see. You feel your blood pumping beneath your skin, your heart pounding, processing, coursing your life force through your body. It is exhilarating.

Catching your breath, you collapse on a plush recliner, bruised, dappled with the shadows of a palm tree. A person appears and offers you a drink upon a tray. Looking up gratefully, you thank him. Startled, you realize with amazement who holds this tray: your first love, the man with whom you had your first romantic relationship, standing right in front of you. Passed years, shared history, slip like sand as you gaze into each other's eyes. Your body is at once electric; only a few inches separates the two of you. As awestruck as the moment before your first kiss, your stomach dips, rolls, falls, as if fastened to a roller coaster. Time melts away as you draw closer. You are at once young, innocent, and wide eyed, scared and excited, but the stirrings within you link to the maturity of a woman. Electric jolts of shock and desire race though your body as you stare. Your skin thrills as electricity surges back and forth between you. Soft touch of skin, he's reaching for your hand. His finger strokes the nape of your neck, plays at your hair, traces your lips. Trembling, your bodies connect; you feel every inch of him pressing upon your body. Your spine, now a conduit of tension.

Your lips, now an open pathway. Your palms seek softness, hardness. You embrace, deeper and deeper, melting together, forming an entity of two souls reunited. You cease to exist in singular form.

Moments, perhaps hours or days later, it is hard to tell, you open your eyes. Blinking into blindingly hot light, you find yourself alone on the recliner. Collecting your clothes, a pyramid in the distance catches your eye. You walk toward the pyramid, receiving the coolness offered within its cavernous interior with a sigh of relief. Hearing the melodic strain of a voice, you follow a stone corridor. You discover a person singing to himself while drawing on the vastness of a slate wall. His humorous, sparkling eyes meet your gaze, pausing, charcoal in hand: "Scribbling secrets and mysteries. Won't you help me out?" Nodding emphatically to this Yodalike creature, you pick up a piece of charcoal and begin working. You listen as him detail a philosophic, revealing nature of the universe. Drawing, you're enraptured in discussion, debating each point. The walls completely covered, he turns to you with a smile: "Now," he states, "you understand!" Thrilled, you possess the secret to life, all questions answered. You understand why we are here, where we go when we die, where we were before this life. It makes perfect sense. How did you not see it before? With a hug, you bid a giddy thanks and farewell. Sated with understanding, you exit the pyramid. Strangely, the moment you cross the threshold into hot, sandy air, you are unable to recall exact details of your discussion, the secrets and understanding falling away, slipping through your fingers. Rather than disappointment, you feel excited, inspired. There is a reason, an underlying equation…now if you could just remember what it was…

You move toward a striped cabana, peeking inside, only to discover it has been set up precisely for you. In fact, it's the workspace you've always dreamed of. Snappy computers sit on a desk and your business plan is laid next to a checkbook with a plump business account. An assistant sits patiently awaiting your instruction. Every imaginable object you could need for your work is placed there. The strings of your favorite song play in the background, and you immediately leap to work. It has never been so easy, so exhilarating. Pictures of people who inspire you scatter the room. You are doing the work you have always been meant to do, quickly and easily. Your creative juices flow; knowledge and all of the amazing things you are capable of are at your fingertips. Eventually, I poke my head through the curtain. You follow me outside where dusk has fallen. You and I, smudged silhouettes upon the desert horizon, stand before a bonfire. Flames leap and dance, and sparks fly into the air in a shower of flickering like fireflies dancing through the night. I take your hand and say,

Wands and the element of fire represent all the things you are passionate about, your sexual energy, your spiritual energy, and your work wattage. It is the combustive quality of fire that feeds your passions and fosters intensity. When a wand card appears in a reading, it suggests something about passion and work.

Swords

We walk to a door with a silver sword emblazoned upon it. Invigorated by your trip to hot desert sands, you are ready to face anything that waits for you on the other side. You push on the door but are met with resistance. A gust of cold air races through the crevices and cracks. You forge your way through and find yourself standing at the peak of a high mountain. Air rushes past, and your hair whips into your eyes. Clouds race overhead, but something else fills the air: grand statements, words and letters fill the sky like fighter planes—"I'm not good enough," "I can do this," "You are beautiful," "I don't deserve it," "I don't know," "I am nothing put potential"—all pass inches from your face.

Short, impactful words fly by: "No!" and "Yes!" and "Thank you!" Judgments linger like wandering ghosts: "Freak," "Lazy," "Goddess," "Girl," "Never happen for you," "Can do." You turn to me, yelling above the rushing air: "What is this place?" I respond above the wind: "This is the world of swords. Remove the *S* and you get *words*."

The wind dies to a whisper and words dissipate, falling like raindrops. A projected screen appears on the sky in front of us. An image flickers upon it: you, captured within a moment of childhood, a moment where you were harshly judged and criticized by a grownup you cared for. Accepting the words as gospel truth, you as a child believe them. Shocked from your adult perspective on this mountaintop, you watch, filled with sympathy for this child. You note the ridiculousness and carelessness of the adult whose thoughtless words and actions wounded you—words and actions you unintentionally integrated into your personality and personal viewpoint. With confusion, you look to me, and I explain: "You've been repeating this story, this moment, in your mind. This is how our internal monologue works, telling ourselves stories and weaving tales over and over again. The hurtful words and judgments lie there because you allow them to. To break through our mental constraints—to release ourselves from old patterns and old beliefs about ourselves and others—is the path to true freedom."

Stunned with feeling, you look down the side of the mountain. Hundreds of swords stick up from the ground. Curious, you reach for one, easily releasing it from the dirt. Your hand recoils in revulsion as blood drips from the end of its glimmering blade. The sword falls, sparkling with dark menace at your feet. "This is the sword that contains words you've used to hurt others," I say. "Pick up another." Gingerly, you select another sword reverberating with unseen energy. Brilliant, diamond-like, it feels good in your hand. "This sword contains the words you have used to empower others." You continue examining sword upon sword. Some contain decisions, others offer clear expression, some pain, some pleasure, some of reasoning, some of calculation. Here's the sword you used to ace your SATs.

Making your way to a large black sword, you find it sticky, wet, and heavy in your grasp. You feel a piercing in your heart, slitting into the shades of your soul. The world looms darker; your vision closes in; you can barely see a thing in front of you but for that damn black sword. "This is the sword you use to hurt yourself. Toss it away!" Using all your strength, you throw it hurtling down into the valley below. At once you feel lighter, freer. Clear vision returns. Endless mountains are spread before you, filled with glittering swords. They stretch to eternity, to the farthest horizons of vision where earth gives way to sky. "Those swords are the possibilities you have not yet considered, words you have not uttered, decisions you have yet to make."

A slight breeze picks up. You take note of a wispy cloud heading in your direction. I take your hand, saying:

> Swords and the element of air represent the mind, decisions, calculations, value judgments, and communication. It is the rapid quality of air that represents the mind. When a sword card appears in a reading, it suggests something about the way you think, express, and communicate.

Come back to my parlor. Leave the swords behind for now. Together, we sit once again. You may return to any of these worlds at will. You may explore them to your heart's content. You need only flip a tarot card and give yourself over to its essence to visit once again. Carry these images within you. Use them to inform your readings. Use them to heal yourself.

DIVALICIOUS *Definitions*

The High Priestess

Here you will find a quick reference to the meanings of all seventy-eight tarot cards. What to do with that pile of cards? Let's take a look ...

Major Arcana

The Fool is numbered zero because he precedes beginning. The Fool represents pure and utter potential. The Fool travels through tarot learning a lesson at each card. Can you recall a moment you stepped out into the abyss, into a new situation, trusting that you'd discover the answers as you plodded along? You are pure potential. Every moment of every day, you have the potential to do something amazing.

The Magician ignites energy into the tarot deck. He is a conduit who directs electric power from the spiritual world above him into the material ground beneath his feet. He has all four suits of tarot upon his table—a reminder that you always have everything you need before you. The Magician sparks things and is a master. You carry with you the same showmanship and energetic ability as the Magician. You are, in fact, full of magic!

The High Priestess is the guardian of your intuition. Behind her veil reside all the secrets you will ever need to know. She is silence and wisdom. The High Priestess represents the deepest parts of yourself, your psyche, and your inner state. She tells you your inner voice is never wrong and reminds you that the truth of your life and all answers lie inside yourself.

The Empress represents sheer creativity and regeneration. She is the eternal mother and represents the most creative aspect of yourself. Let the magic of the Empress surround your every gesture. You are full of unimaginable beauty. What would it mean to live out your creative potential?

The Emperor places order within the tarot deck and creates rules and structure. He reins in the unabashed creativity of the Empress who came before. Within you, he represents unwavering stability and commitment.

The Hierophant is a spiritual authority and your greatest teacher. Who was your most important teacher, your greatest mentor? How do you counsel others? Where do you go for special knowledge? What role has formal religion played in your life? What role does spirituality play?

The Lovers card represents love, lust, and romance—the life force. It also represents physicality, sensuality, and choice. What unions have you created in your life? Who can you bare your body and your soul to? Who and what have you chosen as the great passion of your life?

The Chariot represents speed, knowing where you are going and literally being in the driver's seat. You have the ability to choose a destination and arrive at it quickly. Set yourself goals and you will reach them. When you make up your mind, you are unstoppable. Where do you want to go?

Strength represents your slow, steady, and unwavering courage. There is no situation you cannot overcome. You are stronger than you ever imagined. You have inner resources you've yet to even tap. Dig deeper to discover how powerful you really are. What would you do if you were able to face your greatest fears?

The Hermit goes within to find inner wisdom and emerges to shine his light for all who would see it. What wisdom do you discover when you withdraw and spend time alone? What answers can you arrive at by yourself? How do you shine like a beacon for others?

The Wheel of Fortune is a reference to life's ups and downs. Can you roll with the punches? Can you accept the idea that your luck is about to change for the better? That life is a constant ride and you should hop on? That everything you know and hold dear could change tomorrow? That wheel pivots the gears of growth.

Justice represents events working out based on the quality of effort and work you have put in. Do you believe you reap what you sow? Does what goes around come around? Have you given yourself a fair shot, and, when you get called before those that matter, can you hold your own? What is the quality of your work?

The Hanged Man is suspended and inactive. He represents a moment's pause. Sometimes he represents sacrifice. Can you see your life from a new perspective? Can you look at the world with a new set of eyes? Can you imagine for a moment what is to come?

Death represents complete and utter change followed by new growth. They say those who would never commit suicide are those who are willing to let parts of themselves die. Can you let what is no longer useful perish behind as you move forward? Can you shake old habits and patterns to embrace something fresh and new?

Temperance represents transfers of energy back and forth. Life is never a constant stream or direct line—it floods and recedes, and you must adapt with it. How well do you work with others? How well can you adapt to a new situation? You have the ability to balance it all.

The Devil represents the things that enslave us—be they people, habits, or desires. Can we break free of the chains holding us captive or are we bound to make the same mistakes over and over while the cloven one laughs at us? Perhaps we don't allow ourselves enough devilish enjoyment in life. Regardless, the Devil wants you to indulge—but will you?

The Tower represents the complete shattering of illusions: a breakthrough. Sometimes the Tower is a flash of genius, and sometimes the Tower is the unexpected falling into our lap. What do you do with an aha moment? When you receive a flash of truth, what do you do with your knowledge?

The Star is the quiet after the storm: freshness after the darkness and drama of the cards who have come before. Did you know rejuvenation, inspiration, and hope live inside you at this very moment? The Star lets you know everything will be okay.

The Moon is a trip into our murky unconscious, the strangeness of dreams, and odd sleep. It is out of the well (pictured on the Moon card) that our deepest desires spring. If you're accessing your shadow self and are brave in facing what you discover, you'll find shade and depths to your personality you never imagined existed. Can you face the baser side of your personality? Can you look into your dark, strange side?

The Sun is in complete opposition to the Moon. The Sun represents joy, expansion, growth, and fertility. The Sun is the ability for you to evolve, to nurture others, and to broaden your horizons. When you do what you love, do you know how magnetic you become? How you shed light on those around you?

Judgement is a wake-up call. Things are changing. Your old way of life has gone by the way-side. Are you ready to experience joy and bliss? Judgement represents massive internal growth. Can you see an opportunity when it is staring you straight in the face? Are you ready for change?

The World card represents being alive in the moment: success, euphoria, and completion. You are the world dancer when you lose yourself, caught in the beauty of life. Can you laugh with abandon, experience joy, understand your desires and happily reach for them? This is what the World card represents. You are utter perfection right now, at this moment—transcendent just as you are. Can you accept this?

Minor Arcana

Below follows the Minor Arcana. In this section, you will find "tarot treats," which are quick and fun suggestions on how to invoke the quality of each card into your life. Indulge yourself as often as you wish!

Cups

The suit of cups is everything we feel—our emotions, empathy, psychic powers, laughter, and tears. If you are feeling it, if it makes you happy or sad, it relates to cups.

Ace of Cups is a new emotional beginning, an outpouring of feeling or being overcome with tears of happiness or sadness. Opening up a wellspring. The knowledge that your cup is always full. A fresh start.

✦ Buy a bottle of champagne, sparkling wine, or Prosecco. If you prefer a nonalcoholic drink, use ginger ale or orange juice. Pour into a champagne flute and toast yourself!

Two of Cups: Happy couple. Exchange of love. Marriage. The joining of two halves. Finding what makes you content. Coming together with ease. Recognition in another.

✦ Call your favorite person and treat them to coffee at your favorite cafe.

Three of Cups: Celebration. Glee. Fun with friends. Out for drinks. Having a grand time. Freedom with others. Throwing a party. Creativity and collaboration.

✦ Plan an impromptu party for a small group of friends. Have each guest write down a special quality about the other guests. Throw the qualities into a crystal bowl and read aloud.

Four of Cups: Emotionally closed off. Something is being offered; will you see the opportunity? You are on stable emotional ground but feeling low.

✦ Participate in a random act of kindness. Pay for the car behind you at the tollbooth. Leave an extra tip for the waitress. Open a door for the UPS guy. Surprise someone with an act of kindness and surprise yourself with how good you feel.

Five of Cups: Addiction issues. Depression. Sadness. Melancholia. Time to give something up.

✦ Think of a negative habit you'd like to be rid of. Write that habit down on a piece of paper and burn it!

Six of Cups: Childhood friends. Soul mates. Emotional give and take. People you feel as if you've known for a very long time. Gifts of the heart. Feeling at home.

✦ Purchase or make a small gift—a pack of gum or greeting card—and give it to someone you love.

Seven of Cups: Opportunities. Choices. Options. Preferences. A combination of favorable circumstances or situations. What will you select?

✦ Get a glossy fashion or home décor magazine or catalog and leaf through it for at least fifteen minutes. Dog-ear all the pages with something on it you would buy if money were no option.

Eight of Cups: Emotional journey. Onward and upward. A solid move forward. There is no going back now. Leaving behind what no longer serves you.

✦ Take yourself for a fifteen-minute walk. While doing so, let the images outside wash over you. What new direction would you like to take?

Nine of Cups: Your wish will come true! Genie in a bottle.

+ Write a wish list. When finished, circle one wish that is certain to come true. Put it into an empty bottle and toss it into the ocean the next time you stand upon sandy shores. Write your wish one more time upon the sand with a sea stick.

Ten of Cups: Joyous family. Contentment. Celebration. The "happily ever after" card!

+ Select your favorite fairy tale or movie. Spend fifteen minutes rewriting the ending so that it includes you.

Page of Cups: Childlike delight in what you love. Play. Pay attention to your psychic pops and intuition. Messages. Youthful energy.

+ Drink some loose-leaf tea. When you are finished, look at the pattern of remaining tea leaves at the bottom of your cup. Predict what you think it means.

Knight of Cups: Enthusiasm for what feels good. Lost in emotion. Momentary pause while examining how you feel. Contemplating your emotions.

+ Rent or watch a film that either makes you laugh hysterically or cry uncontrollably—or both.

Queen of Cups: Extremely empathetic woman. Deep understanding. The ideal tarot card reader. Understanding others and using your compassion to make the world a better place. A woman deeply connected to water.

+ Find a friend who appreciates or is interested in tarot. Offer to do a reading for them.

King of Cups: Extremely creative man. Wildly imaginative and able to see projects through to completion.

+ Think about the one creative act or project you've always wanted to attempt. Spend a half-hour writing or drawing it out on paper as if you were going to do it.

Wands

The suit of Wands is everything belonging to passion, intention, energy, work, and will. If you are excited, inspired, fired up, and ready and raring to go, it relates to wands.

Ace of Wands: Exciting opportunity. Spark of desire. Eagerness and freshness. Stimulation and motivation. Magic in the air.

   ✦ Set aside a private fifteen-minute chunk of your day. Spend ten minutes reading a piece of erotic literature or watching a snippet of sexy film. Do what you like with the remaining five…

Two of Wands: Planning stages. Exciting pairing. New partnerships.

   ✦ Imagine you could partner up with anyone in the world for your work—perhaps Oprah, Madonna, or Hillary Clinton. Write down why you chose this person, how you would use their resources to help you, and what you'd accomplish together.

Three of Wands: Assessing. Exploring new options. Visions. Creativity. Waiting for your ships to come in.

   ✦ Make a list of your greatest accomplishments. Make a list of what you'd still like to accomplish.

Four of Wands: Stability. Happiness. Celebration. Harmony.

   ✦ Stars and authors have premiere or launch parties when their film or book is ready for release. Plan a launch party for yourself. Write out the venue, the theme, and of course what you are launching…

Five of Wands: Struggle. Agitation. Whipped up in frenzy. Lots and lots of excitement. People getting all worked up. Heat.

   ✦ Time to start moving. Get your favorite music on and dance your ass off for at least fifteen minutes!

Six of Wands: Victory parade. Success. Advancement. Setting an excellent example.

   ✦ Pick a person who inspires you. Spend fifteen minutes writing them an email or letter about how they have inspired you. Be sure to send it.

Seven of Wands: Risking something new. Courage and strength. Igniting the passions of others around you. Having the ability to defend oneself.

   ✦ Pick an activity you have never tried that harnesses the force of gravity: rock climbing, bungee jumping, skiing, or trapeze class. Try it.

Eight of Wands: Safe journey. Swiftness. Working quickly. Speed. Airborne. Energy that is ungrounded.

✦ Deepak Chopra says every wish plants a seed. Send a bunch of wishes energetically into the world. Do you have wind chimes? On a small piece of paper, write eight things you'd like to have happen—quickly. Tape this to your chimes. When you hear them tinkling, it is the energy of your wish moving to fruition.

Nine of Wands: Venturing into the unknown. Nonconformity. Being brave.

✦ Venture into the unknown today. Drive down a new road, walk into a new store, or try a new restaurant. Do so with the intention of venturing into the unknown.

Ten of Wands: Taking on too much. Give yourself a break—relinquish a responsibility or two.

✦ Schedule a massage for yourself, even if it's only for ten minutes, or do some stretches to soothe those aching muscles.

Page of Wands: Playful exuberance. Impulsiveness. Urge to travel. Youthful energy.

✦ Go online and spend fifteen minutes planning a trip anywhere in the world. Choose the destination, hotel, and a loose itinerary. Money is no object.

Knight of Wands: Idealist on a mission. Charging ahead hastily. Not thinking before you speak or act. Extreme passion.

✦ Choose a company that affects you greatly. Write a letter to this company telling them why you either approve or disapprove of their products.

Queen of Wands: A woman who knows what she wants. Strong sexual energy. Fiery, enigmatic, showy, actresslike quality.

✦ Decide who will play you in the movie of your life. Write an imaginary letter to this actress or actor and tell them why you chose them and what they need to know in order to play you.

King of Wands: Implementing and sharing your passions. Inspiring others. Certainty of self. Mastery. Visionary qualities.

✦ There is something you excel at. Find your favorite child and share your passion with them via project, trip, or gift.

Swords

The suit of swords is everything belonging to our mind, our reasoning, our thinking and communicating. If you are speaking or calculating—if you are caught up in your head or lost in thought—it belongs to swords.

Ace of Swords: Fresh idea. Cutting through to the truth. Clear thinking. Seeing something transparently. Trust in a particular action. Bull's-eye. Victory.

  ✦ Think of an idea that no longer serves you. Write it down on a piece of paper and cut it to shreds. Toss the shreds to the air and divine the shapes they make when they fall to the floor.

Two of Swords: Indecision. Mental withdrawal. Ruminating. A moment's pause. Searching inside to find the right action before moving ahead. Checking with your inner self.

  ✦ Refrain from speaking, voluntarily, this evening for six hours: six hours of personal silence.

Three of Swords: Cutting through to the heart of the matter. Confusion. Painful reality. A love triangle. Heartache. Betrayal. Storm clouds will soon pass.

  ✦ Be extra kind to yourself today. Indulge in a relaxing treat, a favorite show, and be early to bed. Take care of yourself the way a kind mother or nurse would tend to a child or patient.

Four of Swords: Stability. Restful night. Relaxing. Knowing all is well. Faith in your decisions. Good choices.

  ✦ Tonight, before bed, place your hands in front of your heart in prayer and breathe. See where your thoughts take you.

Five of Swords: Defeat. Unfairness. Quarrels. Take a moment to consider how your actions affect others. Choose your words and actions with care to avoid hurting others.

  ✦ Sometimes others can be cruel. Make a list of reasons why you are your own best friend.

Six of Swords: Deep movement forward. Understanding. Mental journey. Better times lie ahead. Emotional and intellectual connections to people you love.

  ✦ Plan an outing for yourself and someone you love very much—a bike ride, a walk, or literally a boat ride if possible.

Seven of Swords: Taking what you need from a situation. Mental shortcut. Think things through and don't take the easy way out.

✦ Think about a person you admire. If you could adopt some of their amazing qualities for yourself, what would they be and why?

Eight of Swords: Initiation. Mental bondage. Breakthrough. Indecisiveness. Unfairness from others. The moment when tough choices mean breakthrough.

✦ Write down one major issue that has always haunted, taunted, and bothered you. Put it on a piece of paper, wrap it in twine, and bury it in the ground.

Nine of Swords: Tortured by your thoughts. Imagination overdrive. Sleepless nights. You are stuck in your head. Breathe and relax. Obsessiveness.

✦ Take a walk for fifteen minutes and focus on everything that is outside of yourself.

Ten of Swords: The issue at hand is over. New way of thinking. Out with the old and in with the new. The darkness before a golden dawn. A trick.

✦ Think of a situation you'd like to end. Find an old piece of food in your fridge. Hold it in your hand and say that this food represents the situation. Stick ten toothpicks into it. Toss it in the garbage.

Page of Swords: Young, fresh perspective. X-ray vision. Originality. Smartness and precociousness of youth.

✦ Pull out an old-time board game and challenge someone to beat you, knowing full well they won't.

Knight of Swords: Extreme bravery. Fighting for one's ideals. Moving forward quickly. Jumping to conclusions.

✦ Plan a quick and unexpected outing. Surprise a friend: tell them they are coming with you.

Queen of Swords: Intelligence. Honesty. Strength of mind. A woman deeply connected to intellectual thought, books, and communication.

✦ Do a crossword puzzle—in ink.

King of Swords: Clear expression of thoughts. Precision. Intellectual. Accomplished.

✦ Write down a list of ten reasons why you are super smart.

Pentacles

Pentacles are about the material world, possessions, money, and our bodies. If you can see it, touch it, or feel it, it relates to the world of pentacles.

Ace of Pentacles: A new idea. Having a solid start. Holding something real in your hand.

- ✦ Take a quarter in your hand. Imagine this quarter growing, increasing, and multiplying to a great amount of money.

Two of Pentacles: Balancing your life. A happy choice. A gentle balance, back and forth.

- ✦ Write down two different options you are considering on pieces of paper. Hide them behind your back and have a friend choose left or right. Perform the option they pick.

Three of Pentacles: Collaboration with others. Wonderful creativity. Calling in an expert. Checking in with someone else.

- ✦ Expert information exists on every imaginable subject on the Internet. Think of an area where you need some expert advice and look it up.

Four of Pentacles: Standing on solid financial ground. Planning ahead. Opening your chakras.

- ✦ Stop for a moment and consider all the money you have ever earned in your life. Count it up in your head.

Five of Pentacles: Downturn in the ups and downs of life. Financial problems. There is light if you look hard enough.

- ✦ When you turn on the lights in your home, imagine you are turning on your own inner light.

Six of Pentacles: Charity. Giving. Not judging others.

- ✦ Select an online charity and make a small (or large) donation to it.

Seven of Pentacles: Taking stock of what you have. A pause before finishing a big project. Consideration over further actions.

- ✦ Look around you right now and see the beautiful, solid things you have brought into your life. Write what is your favorite thing and why.

Eight of Pentacles: Happiness in work. Lost in what you are doing. Pleasure in work. Skill. Profitable undertaking.

✦ Think of something you do very well. If you can't think of anything, ask a friend what you do well. Congratulate yourself for doing it.

Nine of Pentacles: Delight in quality alone time. Happy with who you are. Qualities you inherit from your family. Financial windfall.

✦ What is the best quality you've inherited from your family? How can you honor that quality?

Ten of Pentacles: Massive abundance and wealth. Cycle has come to an end. A turn to the more spiritual side of life.

✦ Splurge on an item or indulgence for yourself and a loved one.

Page of Pentacles: The student of the tarot deck. Love of learning. Back to school. Absorption in study.

✦ Select a class you've been meaning to take. Now register for it.

Knight of Pentacles: Slow but steady progress. Planning for the future. Consideration and care.

✦ Literally plant a seed or transplant a flower or vegetable.

Queen of Pentacles: The earth mother, fertility, abundance, providing well for those around her. Fabulous cook. A woman deeply connected to the earth, gardening, and nature.

✦ Cook a special dinner for someone you love.

King of Pentacles: A wealthy man. Protected. Assets. Great abundance.

✦ Make a list of the first ten things you would do with five million dollars.

KITCHEN *Tarot*

Cooking food and reading tarot have much more in common than one might think. They both require use of your intuition and instincts. They require you to trust yourself. It takes a special intuition to see how your card-a-day applies. It takes this same gentle use of your inner voice to know the precise moment your cupcakes are done and remove them from the oven before the bottoms are burned. To pull together an inspired meal, you open yourself up to divine forces so your food will not only taste delicious, it will look beautiful and appealing.

Through cooking, you offer family, guests, and yourself a form of sheer sensory pleasure. Food is a direct line to our senses. Just think: your meals are three opportunities a day to indulge yourself and treat yourself well. A tarot diva knows when there is pleasure to be had. She reaches out and accepts it. She finds delight in a bowl of summer sun–warmed strawberries and in pots of creamy, rich pasta and anything else that tickles her taste buds.

> **Food is an important part of a balanced diet.**
> **Fran Lebowitz**

The Major Arcana provides us with a slew of tarot archetypes. The first ten Major Arcana cards, the Fool through the Hermit, offer us personality archetypes. You can apply these archetypes to your kitchen, cooking, eating, and entertaining style. Doing so, you will get one step closer to understanding what these cards mean. You will discover how you embody them. Find out which major card you identify with—it may be more than one, depending on your mood. Peruse the first ten major cards to figure out which archetype *you* are in the kitchen.

Are You a Fool?

The Fool's Kitchen

Your kitchen is one topsy-turvy hot mess. There is no rhyme or reason in the chaos of what appears to be a stove (or is that a dining table)? Your shelves contain a mishmash of unmatched dishes. Plates and cups pile sky-high in your sink. Ice cream melts across your pantry; crackers, hard as slate, shiver in your freezer. Dozens of paint swatches smear the wall, but you never decided so they never got painted. Green fuzzies grow in the corners of your fridge because someone—YOU—keep forgetting to clean it out. The Fool doesn't have time to clean or organize because he's always onto the next thing…

The Fool's Cooking Style

Completely fearless when attempting a new dish, you cook startling, untried recipes. Cooking is a grand adventure for you, all about spontaneity. Your meals are at times dismal, at times sublime. You don't bother to stress about your meals. You know if a meal goes south you can always order a pizza, so you've got nothing to prove and nothing to lose.

The Fool's Eating Habits

You have never met a food you wouldn't try—even once. Venturing into new, untried restaurants, you order daring, offbeat menu items, easily making friends with the people sitting beside you. You are more than comfortable eating a meal alone in public. You are the first one to get a splash of red sauce across your shirt while diving headfirst into a bowl of spaghetti. Who cares? Just the word *spaghetti* makes you giggle.

When to Invoke Fool Energy

+ Learning a new recipe

+ Dining out while traveling

+ When you get bored cooking

Which came first: the Fool or the egg? You can look at the shape of an egg, hold it in your hand, and be reminded of the Fool's number—zero. Just as the Fool represents pure potential, so do eggs with their infinite varieties of preparation. The egg is considered by many to be a perfect food. Let this idea of perfection remind you that the Fool is safe, no matter what path he follows. Like a newborn, the Fool begins his journey perfect from the offset.

The trick to this French bistro classic is slow-cooking the grilled ham and cheese. A low flame ensures the sandwich is warm and gooey on the inside and crunchy on the outside.

1 tablespoon mayonnaise

1 teaspoon grainy Dijon mustard

1 tablespoon butter

2 slices thick white sandwich bread

½ cup shredded Gruyère cheese

4 thin slices Black Forest ham

1 farm-fresh egg*

Sea salt and freshly ground pepper to taste

Mix the mayonnaise and mustard together.

Melt butter over low flame in a nonstick pan.

As butter melts, assemble sandwich. Spread half the mayo/mustard mixture over one slice of bread. Sprinkle half the cheese over mayo/mustard mix and top with ham. Spread the remaining mayo/mustard over the second slice of bread and sprinkle remaining cheese on top. Press together, cheese sides facing each other, to form sandwich. Place sandwich in pan with foaming butter.

Cook on very low flame, flipping over to ensure even cooking and pressing down with spatula to flatten. When sandwich is golden brown and toasty, after 5 or 10 minutes, remove from pan and place on plate.

Increase heat to medium flame and immediately crack egg into the same pan. Fry the egg, covered, until the whites are set and the yokes are still runny, about 3 minutes. Slide the egg on top of the toasted sandwich and top with a sprinkling of sea salt and freshly ground pepper.

Makes 1 sandwich.

* If salmonella is a cause of concern for you, cook eggs until yolks are set or use pasteurized eggs (in the shell).

Serve the dinner backward, do anything—
but for goodness' sake, do something weird.

Elsa Maxwell

Are You a Magician?

The Magician's Kitchen

The air in your kitchen hums with an invisible yet present, taut energy field. Guests gather at the island in your kitchen to watch you whip up wizardlike meals. Your knife skills are on par with Japanese steak and seafood chefs; your sauce-making skills rival the finest French saucier. Your cupboards are stocked with every imaginable foodstuff. Your kitchen is chock-full of fabulous, shiny appliances. Every item is at your fingertips, ready to be put to use by your expert hands.

The Magician's Cooking Style

You work at a feverish pace, vegetables flying through the air, pots boiling, and flames dancing in a brilliantly orchestrated performance. At the height of summer, crowds gather to watch you flip, smoke, and grill meats and fish. On the coldest winter evenings, you entertain guests with witty jokes and anecdotes while whipping up a hearty, succulent stew. You command the flames that lick the bottom of your copper pots. The Magician, a true Iron Chef, always puts on a show.

The Magician's Eating Habits

Your gift of showmanship means you are always "on," aware of your appearance and actions. For this reason, you are quite careful about what you eat and monitor your caloric intake. Luckily, your high energy level and active lifestyle allow you to indulge in foods you love. Paying attention to what the hot chefs around town are serving, you re-create their dishes at home. You've got a keen eye for fancy food trends and are eager to share them with your family and friends.

When to Invoke Magician Energy

✦ Hosting a party

✦ Demonstrating a recipe

✦ Showing off

> Always serve too much hot fudge sauce on sundaes. It makes people overjoyed and puts them in your debt.
> **Judith Olney**

The Magician's Parmesan Herbed Risotto

Risotto is a labor of love. It requires about twenty minutes of continuous stirring. A Magician uses this time wisely. Write spells, words, and shapes in the risotto as you stir this heavenly Tuscan treat. Act like a proper Magician and you'll know the risotto is finished when it is al dente, like pasta—tender to the tooth. Be sure to use Arborio rice, which is found in any supermarket in the pasta aisle.

5 cups chicken broth

2 tablespoons unsalted butter

1 tablespoon extra virgin olive oil

1 clove garlic, minced

⅓ cup shallots, minced

1½ cups Arborio rice

½ cup dry white wine

1 tablespoon butter

¾ cup grated Parmigiano-Reggiano cheese

1 tablespoon chopped fresh parsley or fresh mixed herbs

Salt and cracked pepper to taste

Bring the broth to a steady simmer in saucepan.

In a heavy 4-quart pan, heat the butter and olive oil over moderate heat. Add the garlic and shallots. Sauté for 1 to 2 minutes until it begins to soften, being careful not to brown it. Add the rice; using a wooden spoon, stir for 1 minute. Be sure all the grains are well coated. Add white wine and stir until completely absorbed. Begin to add the simmering chicken broth, a half a cup at a time, using a soup ladle and stirring frequently. Wait until each addition is almost completely absorbed before adding the next ½ cup, reserving about ¼ cup to add at the end. Stir frequently to prevent sticking.

When the rice is tender but firm, add the reserved broth. Turn off the heat and immediately add the butter, cheese, and herbs. Stir vigorously to combine with rice. Serve immediately; top with more fresh cheese, tons of fresh cracked pepper, and a sprinkling of sea salt.

Once mastering the art of risotto, you can prepare it with an endless number of flavors and additions. Adjust for the season: pumpkin and morel risotto in the fall, hearty beef and mushroom risotto in the winter, sugar snap pea risotto in the spring, risotto primavera for summer.

Note to vegetarians: the chicken stock in above recipe may be replaced with vegetable stock. The white wine may also be omitted.

This recipe makes 4 servings.

Are You a High Priestess?

The High Priestess's Kitchen

Fresh and dried herbs fill your kitchen with heavenly aromas. You have the ability to jump inside of an herb and work magically with their chemical compounds to unleash their healing properties. Loose-leaf teas dance and flitter inside glass jars—peppermint for a sore tummy, mugwort for prophetic dreams, chamomile for peace. Antique cookbooks fill your shelves. They remain dusty, as you never need open them; all your recipes are known by heart. Odd and interesting cooking gadgets from another era dangle from the ceiling.

The High Priestess's Cooking Style

Quiet and refined in your cooking and serving style, you have an innate sense of how flavors mingle with each other. High tea is your specialty; your table is a wooden confessional to the guests who grace it. Friends purge their souls, strangers confess their secrets, traveling salesmen are reduced to tears by the steady gaze you lift to meet them over a cup of tea. You'll carry their information to the grave and beyond, as it's not your style to gab about the stories that grace your ears. You are happy enough simply to act as a mirror to those who would sip your herbal concoctions.

The High Priestess's Eating Habits

Fresh, seasonal food is of utmost importance because you understand the innate value of living in tune with nature's cycles. You eat organically or nothing at all. You are often found gardening amidst the moonlight, nibbling on a carrot to ground yourself, popping sweet peas for pleasure. Listening to your body, you know a craving is the body's way of finding correct nutrients. Beauty lies in simplicity, and you are not one to ever fuss over a meal.

When to Invoke High Priestess Energy

- ✦ Hanging out with your best friend
- ✦ Helping someone mend a broken heart
- ✦ Hosting a tea party

The High Priestess's Cucumber Tea Sandwiches

High tea is a time-honored tradition that encourages one to sit, relax, and indulge. Think of the High Priestess's connection with the moon while spreading the cream cheese and slicing the cucumber in this ultrafeminine and girly delight.

½ seedless cucumber, peeled and thinly sliced (about 32 slices)

½ cup cream cheese, room temperature

½ cup watercress leaves, washed and chopped

16 slices thin white bread

Salt to taste

Place cucumber slices between paper or cloth towels to remove extra moisture.

Combine cream cheese and watercress. Spread mixture on one side of each slice of bread.

Lay cucumber slices onto the cream cheese side of eight slices of bread. Sprinkle with a touch of salt. Top with remaining slices of bread, cream cheese–side down.

Using a sharp knife, cut the crusts from each sandwich. Cut sandwiches in half diagonally, then cut in half again.

If making ahead of time, refrigerate, covered with waxed paper and a damp cloth, until serving time.

Makes about 32 mini sandwiches.

> Did you ever stop to taste a carrot? Not just eat it, but taste it? You can't taste the beauty and energy of the earth in a Twinkie.
>
> **Astrid Alauda**

Are You an Empress?

The Empress's Kitchen

Fresh flowers and crystal chandeliers fill your Provençal kitchen. Extensive vegetable, herb, and flower gardens color the sprawling acres outside your window. Fresh bread wafts from your oven, fruit bowls spill over with citrus, and myriad china patterns grace the length of your walls. Sanding sugar resides in glass jars; stacks of cookies guard iced seven-layer cakes. Eggs, warm from the hen-house, beg to be cracked, poached, and sprinkled with pepper and crunchy sea salt.

The Empress's Cooking Style

As a goddess of gastronomy, you understand one of the most important tenets of cooking: the crafting and presentation of food is equal in importance to how it tastes. You take the time to chill your salad dishes and warm your dinner plates; no touch, no detail, is overlooked. In fact, you view plates and tables as empty canvases. Food is a form of art, and you are a maestro directing your artistic expression both on the plate and on the palate. Hosting holiday meals and grand parties is your specialty, but you don't need a special occasion to grab your finest linen napkins and bone china.

The Empress's Eating Habits

You have no patience for a meal that has had no thought put into it or is, heaven forbid, frozen. Setting the bar high for yourself, you expect others to do the same. You wouldn't be caught dead in a fast-food joint or grimy diner. Sensing a meal is heading south, you quickly rush to aid the faltering cook, rescuing many a disastrous meal. Believing you are what you eat, you consume foods that help you shine and glow with health. You drink plenty of water and eat fresh fruits, nuts, and vegetables.

When to Invoke Empress Energy

- ✦ Hosting a holiday

- ✦ Creating romantic dinners

- ✦ Impressing guests

Empress's Cherry, Goat Cheese, and Walnut Salad

The Empress is as lovely as this creative salad that springs to life with zip and flavor. Make this dressing at home and you'll never reach for bottled again. This salad should not be served in one big bowl. It is best served Empress style and prepared on individual salad plates.

½ cup walnuts, chopped coarse and toasted

1 cup dried cherries

2 medium Granny Smith apples

4 cups mixed field greens, washed and dried

10-ounce log of herbed goat cheese cut into 12 rounds at room temperature

Dressing

2 tablespoons cider vinegar

1 tablespoon Dijon mustard

1 teaspoon shallot, finely minced

¼ teaspoon salt

¼ teaspoon sugar

6 tablespoons extra virgin olive oil

Ground black pepper to taste

The preparation of good food is merely another expression of art, one of the joys of civilized living.

Dione Lucas

Roasting nuts intensifies and brings out their flavor. Place walnuts in a nonstick pan and dry roast until fragrant. Plump cherries in a small bowl with ½ cup hot water for about 10 minutes; drain. Quarter and core apples, and cut into ⅛-inch-thick slices.

Combine vinegar, mustard, shallot, salt, and sugar in a small bowl. Whisking constantly, drizzle in oil; season to taste with pepper. Place greens in large bowl, drizzle vinaigrette over, and toss to coat. Divide greens among individual plates; divide cherries, apples, and walnuts among plates; place two rounds of goat cheese on each salad. Serve immediately. Serves 6.

Are You an Emperor?

The Emperor's Kitchen

Nestled inside your comfy ranch home is a classic 1950s-style kitchen. Your green range top sparkles in the sunlight; your appliances are retro fabulous. Clorox stands at attention by the sink, while the blue formica table is hugged by pink plastic-cushioned chairs. A milkman graces the door in his crisp starched uniform. The morning paper, bacon, eggs, coffee, and toast wait to greet you at your breakfast table.

The Emperor's Cooking Style

Cooking straight from a recipe, you would never, ever dare stray from the instructions. You are "by the book" all the way, in eating *and* lifestyle. You never vacillate in your cooking habits or routines. Shopping by rote, you purchase the same items, loyal to the same brands year after year. Guests at your table are expected to behave with impeccable manners. Anyone who denies their Brussels sprouts can find their dessert elsewhere. Elbows off the table—now!

The Emperor's Eating Habits

Classic American fare is your preferred cuisine, and you never stray from your eating routine. You finish all the food on your plate, not letting a bite go to waste. You eat only in tried and true restaurants and those that have withstood the winds of time. You are a generous tipper when dining out, but fear strikes the chef or waiter who falls short of your high expectations.

When to Invoke Emperor Energy

- ✦ Teaching tableside etiquette
- ✦ Organizing the perfect meal
- ✦ Cleaning the kitchen

I'm trying to eat better. And I do feel wise after drinking tea. After eating vegetables, I just feel hungry.

Carrie Latet

The Emperor represents command- and control-type tendencies. Mull this over while styling yourself this great American classic. The Caesar salad was named after Caesar Cardini, who first prepared the salad at his Caesar's Palace Restaurant. For our purposes, let's channel Rome's great emperor as we prepare it.

2 cloves of garlic, crushed

3 anchovies

¼ cup olive oil

Juice of half a lemon

Worcestershire sauce, a few dashes

Sprinkling of sea salt

Pepper, to taste

1 egg*

1 head romaine lettuce, thoroughly washed and torn into bite-sized pieces

Parmesan cheese, grated

Additional shaved slices of Parmesan

Excellent-quality croutons

In a wooden bowl, using a fork, mash together the garlic and anchovies into a paste. Add to paste olive oil, lemon juice, and Worcestershire sauce, and whisk well. Season to taste with salt and pepper. Boil egg for one minute, crack, separate, and add the yolk to dressing, whisking again to incorporate. Toss with romaine and Parmesan. Top with shaved Parm, croutons, and a turn of a pepper mill.

*If salmonella or slightly raw egg yolks cause you a health concern, omit or resort to a good bottled Caesar dressing and add lots of fresh Parm to zip it up.

Serves 6.

Are You a Hierophant?

The Hierophant's Kitchen

Your cutting board is the heart of your kitchen. This is where you make contact with the gastronomic gods and become lost in the meditative act of chopping, dicing, and slicing. You subscribe religiously to food magazines and gasp with delight when they spill from the mailbox. You have hundreds of cookbooks upon your shelves, read like novels upon your bed pillow. Foodie memoirs line the wall. The kitchen television's always tuned to a cooking show. You are often found honing your skills in cooking classes.

One cannot think well, love well, sleep well, if one has not dined well.

Virginia Woolf

The Hierophant's Cooking Style

You are a strict disciple of Julia Child and James Beard. You have learned from the best and are happy to impart your food knowledge to others. Cooking with you is a joy; friends always walk away having learned something helpful and tasted something delicious. You understand the art and science of cooking. You know the difference between an oven's hot air and the raw flame of an outdoor grill. Old standards like steak and potatoes are born again under your culinary expertise.

The Hierophant's Eating Habits

You possess a divine and cultured palate. Eating a meal, you are already thinking about the next one you will prepare. The act of cooking and consuming food is a spiritual experience for you. Finding it your mission to get to the heart of any given food, you make your ingredients shine in their true purpose. Were you to open a restaurant, the crowds would line up for days to watch as you preach from the pulpit of your stove.

When to Invoke Hierophant Energy

✦ Slowing down and paying attention to your food

✦ Looking for a great recipe

✦ Teaching a child to cook

The Hierophant's Parmesan Wafers

The Hierophant is often seen as a pope figure. With this in mind, the Hierophant's Parmesan wafers are a tip of the hat to communion wafers. Use as salad or salad garnish or have as a light snack with cocktails.

    1 cup Parmigiano-Reggiano cheese, hand grated

    Waxed paper

Preheat oven to 350 degrees.

Line cookie sheets with waxed paper.

Place cheese on cookie sheets in small piles about the size of a quarter.

Bake for 10 minutes or until crispy.

Set aside to cool. Makes 10 wafers.

Note: Parmesan wafers may be created as an edible dish for salads. Make rounds much bigger, bake, then drape over ramekin until cooled.

Are You the Lovers?

The Lovers' Kitchen

Your kitchen awaits, a hidden chamber of delight. A naked chicken lies on the counter. Plucked, skin pulled taut, legs tied back, its dark cavity waits to be filled. Fruit bursts with ripeness while heady aromas tickle the nose. Softly folded linen napkins wait for you to spread them with your fingers and drape them across your lap. Al Green pines away softly in the background. Plush furniture decorates the room.

The Lovers' Cooking Style

An expert on pairing and balancing flavors, you know spicy couples with sweet and smoky entwines with creamy. You layer flavor upon texture upon flavor. You'll use food as a weapon when having your way with a friend or lover. Marketing and shopping is your sensual foreplay to the main act of cooking. You flirt your way to the best cut of meat from the butcher; you entice the cheese monger to offer the finest, ripest hunks of cheese; and the wine merchant has you swimming in the loveliest wines—dry, sweet, and robust. Desserts leave sweet satisfaction on your guests' lips and have them returning for more.

The Lovers' Eating Habits

A slave to your senses, you'll sit and enjoy a meal for hours upon hours. Savoring the complexities and nuances of food brings you a sense of heightened pleasure. The soft fuzz of a peach, the sweet burst of a cherry, and smooth dark chocolate bring you to complete ecstasy. Nothing gets your engines going like the perfect meal. Even alone, you'll treat yourself to beautifully prepared food because you understand that three meals a day offer more than sustenance: they offer escape into the sensual arts.

When to Invoke the Lovers' Energy

✦ Preparing a romantic meal

✦ Shopping for food

✦ Redecorating the kitchen

The Lovers' French Onion Soup

The Lovers card represents desire, choice, and intimacy. Nothing can be more intimate than whispering to that special someone over a crock of this French soup while sharing a bottle of Côtes du Rhône.

2 tablespoons oil

1 tablespoon butter

1½ pounds onions, peeled and thinly sliced (about 5 cups)

1 teaspoon fresh thyme sprigs or ½ teaspoon dried thyme

½ teaspoon salt, or more to taste

5 cups hot chicken stock

¼ teaspoon freshly ground pepper, or more to taste

¼ cup red wine

3 or 4 slices of baguette, about ¼-inch, sliced on diagonal

2 to 2½ ounces Gruyère or Emmentaler cheese, grated (about ¾ cup)

Set a heavy-bottomed 4-quart saucepan over medium-low heat and add the oil and butter. When the butter has melted, add the onions, thyme, and salt, and mix together thoroughly. Cover the pan and cook, stirring occasionally, for about 10 minutes. When the onions are quite tender, uncover and raise heat slightly. Cook another 20 to 25 minutes, stirring frequently, until the onions are dark brown and have caramelized in the pan. (Lower the heat if the onions are in danger of burning.)

Stir in hot stock, scraping any crystallized juices from the bottom of the pan, and bring soup to a boil. Taste and adjust the seasonings, adding the wine and additional salt and black pepper to taste. (The amount of salt will vary depending on the broth.) Cover and simmer for about 10 minutes.

Preheat oven to 400 degrees.

Toast baguettes either in toaster or on cookie sheet in oven (depending on how much soup you are making).

When the soup is ready, arrange individual crocks on a baking sheet. Put the croutons, whole or broken into large pieces, into the bottom of each crock, and sprinkle about 2 tablespoons of cheese on top. Ladle in a cup or more of soup to fill the crock to the inner rim. Heap a large mound of grated cheese all over surface of the soup, using the rest of the cheese for each crock.

Place the baking sheet in the oven and bake for 30 to 40 minutes, until the cheese is dark golden brown and has formed a crust over the soup. Move the hot crocks carefully onto individual plates and serve.

Great food is like great sex. The more you have, the more you want.

Gael Greene

The Lovers

Are You a Chariot?

The Chariot's Kitchen

Two essentials thrive in your kitchen: the microwave and the delivery menu drawer. The microwave gleams with dark, shiny economy, and takeout menus offer myriad food choices. Your fridge is filled with take-home containers of prepared foods. Frozen dinners and frozen pizza line your freezer.

The Chariot's Cooking Style

You lead a busy life and have no time to bother with cooking. You've no patience to shop, prepare, or cook; you've got other things to do. Happy to eat on paper or plastic plates, you'd rather not waste time with messy dishes either. You are happiest when others prepare food for you. When a friend asks, "What are you are making for dinner?" you happily reply, "Reservations."

The Chariot's Eating Habits

Not spending your valuable brainpower on thinking about meals, you're apt to grab whatever is on hand. Road food and drive-throughs are the best inventions ever, as far as you're concerned. You'll often eat while engaging in other activities like reading, working, or driving. You've got your eye on the ball, and food rarely enters the picture as you race through life.

When to Invoke Chariot Energy

+ When you've run out of time

+ Burning the midnight oil

+ For an unexpected guest

I don't even butter my bread;
I consider that cooking.

Katherine Cebrian

A Chariot Dinner

The Chariot implies being in the driver's seat. The clear direction in which you head leaves no time for cooking.

Grab a stack of delivery menus.

Spread menus like a fan of tarot cards.

Randomly select a menu as you would a card.

Dial their number.

Place your order.

Tip the delivery person.

Enjoy.

Are You Strength?

Strength's Kitchen

Your kitchen essentials are the blender, the food processor, and a massive stove. Gleaming knives, wooden spoons, and chopping blocks prevail. Garlic, chilies, and spices hang from every corner. Cake batter, bread dough, and fresh pastas await your firm hand to whip them into something edible. You haven't met a duck you couldn't debone or a fresh chicken you wouldn't pluck.

Strength's Cooking Style

Fearless in your approach to cooking, ingredients tremble in fear at your capable hand. You love using strong, bold flavors in your meals and aren't afraid to whip up dinner for a hungry army of people. You've never met a recipe you couldn't master. Cooking challenges are met with grace and dignity.

Strength's Eating Habits

You know that you nourish your body through the food you feed it. Therefore, you are meticulous in organizing your diet. You make sure to get the right balance of proteins, carbs, and fats. You also have an exceedingly high tolerance for spicy foods.

When to Invoke Strength Energy

+ If you are sick

+ Maintaining health

+ For a wintertime dinner party

I think every woman should
have a blowtorch.

Julia Child

Strength's Warm Garlic, Brie, and Chutney

The Strength card represents a gentle touch over a forceful one, yet power is wielded. In this recipe, strong, pungent garlic is mellowed by slow roasting for an hour. The strength is there, yet it is mellowed and soft. Serve with some olives, a gorgeous red wine, and lots of candlelight. Let everyone help themselves. Heaven!

4 whole bunches of garlic

Olive oil

Salt and pepper

1 large triangle of Brie

1 loaf fresh baguette, sliced

1 jar of chutney, your choice of flavor

Preheat oven to 350 degrees.

Take the whole heads of garlic (keeping garlic and skins intact) and carefully slice off the top pointy side, about ¼ of the head. Drizzle with olive oil and sprinkle with salt and pepper. Place in covered baking dish. Pop in oven and roast 1 hour. Garlic should be soft when ready.

About 10 minutes before garlic is done, wrap Brie in foil and bake alongside garlic.

Place baguette slices on cookie sheet, and throw that in the oven to toast.

Arrange all items on a large cutting board or serving plate with a bowl of chutney.

Scoop out a head of garlic and spread on toast. Top with a smear of gooey Brie and a dollop of chutney.

Serves 4.

Are You a Hermit?

The Hermit's Kitchen

A small dining table is set for one; a lone candle quietly burns. Your kitchen is the picture of simple, pared-down elegance. Wood is your décor of choice. One pan, one pot, and a small set of silverware awaits your use. The pantry and fridge are, for the most part, bare. A tiny bowl filled with sea salt, a pepper mill, and a glistening bottle of extra virgin olive oil wait patiently.

The Hermit's Cooking Style

You rarely cook for others because you keep to yourself. You shop for effortless items, needing little preparation. Simplicity is the name of the game. Should a guest grace your table, you pull out olives and a fresh loaf of bread. Good food need not be complicated.

The Hermit's Eating Habits

Not a big eater, your stomach reminds you to eat long after the dinner hour has past. When you dine, it is on easy foods. You relish eating alone and, often lost in thought, moments of brilliance and deep understanding occur to you over a plate of toast.

When to Invoke Hermit Energy

- ✦ When you are alone
- ✦ When you need a break
- ✦ When the outside world becomes overbearing

Food for the body is not enough.
There must be food for the soul.

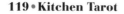
Dorothy Day

The Hermit's One-Pot Pasta

The Hermit represents retreat. When you find yourself alone, offer to feed your soul with this amazing one-pot poached egg, greens, cured meat, and pasta dish.

Handful of pasta

1 farm-fresh egg cracked into a cup

5 slices prosciutto or Spanish ham

¼ pound spinach or arugula greens

¼ cup butter

Sea salt and freshly ground pepper to taste

Bring a pot of water to a rolling boil. Toss in pasta until cooked al dente.

Remove pasta to your serving dish, reserving water.

Reduce water to gentle simmer. Slip egg into simmering water. Let egg poach for 2 minutes and remove with slotted spoon. Place egg on top of pasta.

Toss prosciutto or Spanish ham into water and poach 30 seconds. Remove with slotted spoon and place on top of pasta.

Toss greens in water and poach 30 seconds. Remove with slotted spoon and place on top of pasta.

To brown the butter, melt butter in a saucepan over medium heat. Stir or swirl the pan so the butter does not burn. Remove from heat when butter turns light brown and gives off a nutty aroma. Drizzle on top of pasta.

Mix your pasta dish together, sprinkle with sea salt and freshly ground pepper, and enjoy.

MAJOR *Stylista*

The archetypes of tarot apply to more than just the kitchen. We enter the second half of the Major Arcana, the point where the Wheel card begins to rotate, revolving with the hands of time. We discover the archetypes morph from personality archetypes to experiential archetypes.

What is the one way we viscerally experience ourselves, the world, and other people? Through clothing and personal style. The clothing we drape ourselves in has a tremendous impact on the way we experience day-to-day life. You meet a friend for coffee. Think of the difference you'll feel if you meet her in sweatpants and tousled hair compared to meeting her in your slickest outfit, nails shined, hair coiffed to perfection. You carry yourself differently according to how your clothes make you feel.

A diva is interested in gaining maximum pleasure from her life. Clothing is a gateway to pleasure and personal expression, and it is often a mood enhancer. Whether you embrace or reject fashion, your personal style says something about you. You can use fashion to enhance the quality of life, boost your emotional state, and create loveliness in the world. You can discover more about your personal style by letting it be expressed through the archetype of a tarot card.

A tarot diva may drape herself in luxurious cashmeres or prefer the simplicity of soft, well-worn denim, but she understands that how she dresses sends a message to the world. More importantly, her clothes affect the way she'll feel about herself.

Take a peek below to find out which fashion archetype you are. Borrow some trade secrets from each card for your own personal use…

Are You a Wheel of Fortune?

Wheel of Fortune Style: Timeless Elegance

Classic and ladylike is your signature style. Like the Wheel of Fortune, you know that the wheels of fashion turn, that trends come and go, but quintessential style will always endure. Season to season, you look amazing in a wardrobe that is well thought out and transcends whatever decade you are living in.

It is a good thing the Wheel of Fortune card heralds luck with money because you invest seriously in your wardrobe. You understand spending money on well-constructed garments saves cash in the long run but gives others sticker shock.

You embrace beautiful, well-made clothes. You have an eye for simple cuts and prefer solid colors to prints and foster a fierce appreciation for fine vintage pieces. Whether you enjoy lunch with friends or a night at the opera, you always look flawlessly pulled together.

Wheel of Fortune Wardrobe Staples

- ✦ Little black dress
- ✦ A-line skirt
- ✦ Black pumps
- ✦ Belted coat
- ✦ Ballerina flats
- ✦ Pearl necklace

Wheel of Fortune Style Icons

- ✦ Charlotte (Kristin Davis) from *Sex and the City*
- ✦ Jackie Kennedy
- ✦ Audrey Hepburn
- ✦ Gwyneth Paltrow
- ✦ Grace Kelly

Wheel of Fortune Stores/Designers

- ✦ Carolina Herrera
- ✦ Giorgio Armani
- ✦ Banana Republic
- ✦ Tori Burch
- ✦ Polo

When to Invoke Wheel of Fortune Energy

- ✦ Charity fundraising
- ✦ A night at the theater
- ✦ Formal tea

Wheel of Fortune's Secret Style Weapon

- ✦ The Wheel of Fortune has her clothing tailored to fit every inch of her body. Each garment adorns her like a glove, highlighting her assets and hiding any potential flaw she wants to downplay.

    How You Can Use It: *Find a professional tailor or seamstress in your town or online. Choose a staple item from your wardrobe, one you wear regularly that could be adjusted to fit you better. Look, you've just shaved off five pounds without going on a diet!*

Fashion is not something that exists in dresses only. Fashion is in the sky, in the street; fashion has to do with ideas, the way we live, what is happening.

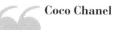 Coco Chanel

Are You Justice?

Justice Style: Power Personality

The Justice card says you reap what you sow. No one works harder than you and your power-house wardrobe. The Justice card exemplifies the quality of work. Mover and shaker that you are, your wardrobe matches your enterprising personality. Persevering at the office and in the board-room in your crisp, professional suits, you show the world you are a force to be reckoned with by the way you dress and act.

Your closet is stocked with power suits that became popular in the '80s but are now adapted to today's trends. Favoring classic designs in muted colors, you carry a smart, understated elegance wherever you go. You may step over the line to preppie, especially when donning casual attire. Your clothing reinforces your power prowess.

Justice Wardrobe Staples

- ✦ Skirts, pants, and blazers
- ✦ Classic trench
- ✦ Briefcase or attaché
- ✦ Pinstripe anything
- ✦ Pumps

Justice Style Icons

- ✦ Margaret Thatcher
- ✦ Condoleezza Rice
- ✦ Diane Sawyer
- ✦ Anna Wintour
- ✦ Miranda (Cynthia Nixon) from *Sex and the City*

Justice Stores/Designers

- ✦ Yves Saint Laurent
- ✦ Elie Tahari
- ✦ Jones New York
- ✦ Ann Taylor
- ✦ Brooks Brothers
- ✦ Theory
- ✦ Chanel

I dress for the image. Not for myself, not for the public, not for fashion, not for men.

Marlene Dietrich

When to Invoke Justice Energy

- ✦ Corporate job interview
- ✦ At the office
- ✦ Power lunch

Justice's Secret Style Weapon

✦ Confident on the inside and out, Justice possesses the sexy secret that women in France have known for years. Her underwear works as hard as she does, each undergarment shaping the body in just the right places. Proper underpinnings support in all the right spots: bras lift and undies tuck.

How You Can Use It: *Find a lingerie shop or good department store with a sales pro who will take your measurements. Have a discussion with the salesperson about vwhat tools are available to lift and tuck your bodacious bod. Be sure your bras fit exquisitely. Look for undergarments that shape and draw you in. Think you're in for granny panties? Think again. Start thinking Spanx.*

Are You a Hanged Man?

Hanged Man Style: Transition Time

The Hanged Man card represents a moment of stillness and seeing the world in a new way. This is because the Hanged Man is quite literally hanging upside down and everything is reversed. We all reach a point when our clothes don't seem to fit right and our style feels stale. We are ready to refresh and revamp but may not be quite sure which direction to move in. We hang suspended like the Hanged Man or a caterpillar chrysalis before hatching into a butterfly.

These style-transition times often come at key moments of life. A young girl finds she's not shopping in the kids' section, but juniors seems overwhelming. You realize you should no longer buy in juniors and move to misses. This also occurs amidst life transitions like moving from college to workplace, working woman to motherhood, or stay-at-home mom returning to the workplace.

You retreat for a moment as your outward style sense catches up with your inward growth. During these moments, you become ambiguous in your fashion sense, and your new clothing is bought for comfort and economy. You wouldn't want to invest in items you aren't sure you will ever wear. This Hanged Man transition may feel uncomfortable, but it is actually exciting. This is the genesis point of moving in a refreshing direction. In the meantime, you'll play it safe in stores.

Hanged Man Wardrobe Staples

XII The Hanged Man

- ✦ Comfy pants
- ✦ Sweatshirts
- ✦ Loose-fitting tops

Hanged Man Style Icons

- ✦ Any film character whose internal change is expressed via her clothing
- ✦ The classic "makeover" movies

Hanged Man Stores/Designers

+ Discount stores

+ Sales racks

When to Invoke Hanged Man Energy

+ Lazy Sunday mornings

+ Working from home

+ Taking a personal day

+ Feeling indecisive

Hanged Man Secret Style Weapon

+ The Hanged Man will never pay retail for her clothes while revamping her style.

  How You Can Use It: *To save money and buy wisely, pay attention to when to shop (see the Hanged Man's shopping calendar below). And remember, a Hanged Man always holds off buying until her item hits rock-bottom price. The Hanged Man has no problem waiting for clothing prices to drop.*

+ July—Fall arrivals, top dollar

+ October—Markdown begins; get to know a sales clerk who will alert you to upcoming sales

+ December—Clearance sales, but coats don't get marked down until January

+ February—Spring arrivals, top dollar

+ April—Markdown begins

+ Memorial Day—Clearance sales

Beauty is how you feel inside, and it reflects in your eyes. It is not something physical.

Sophia Loren

Are You Death?

Death Style: The Dangerous Diva

The Death card comes on strong, unyielding, and so does your fashion sense. The staple of your wardrobe is black, black, and more black. You are smart enough to know this raven color is chic enough for any occasion and is the most flattering of colors.

Your arty side is expressed with chunky statement jewelry. You may have a penchant for the goth look and love to vamp it up. You know your way around a wand of black liquid liner when others tend to shy away, and you are a devoted friend of pleather.

Urban, sexy, and fierce, you mix your black wardrobe with different textures of fabrics to be sure you never look stale. Your makeup is usually on the dramatic side, favoring pale skin and dark eyes and lips.

Death Wardrobe Staples

- ✦ Black leather boots
- ✦ Chunky silver jewelry
- ✦ Black lace
- ✦ Black manicure

Death Style Icons

- ✦ Trinity (Carrie-Anne Moss) in *The Matrix*
- ✦ Helena Bonham Carter
- ✦ Christina Ricci
- ✦ Cher

Death

Death Stores/Designers

- ✦ Alexander McQueen

- ✦ Versace

- ✦ Gucci

When to Invoke Death Energy

- ✦ Art gallery opening

- ✦ Weekend in the city

- ✦ Rock concert

Death's Secret Style Weapon

- ✦ Black liquid eyeliner

  How You Can Use It: *Liquid liner should always be applied over eye shadow and along the top line of the lashes. Have cotton balls or Q-tips ready for slipups. Keep your eyes open as you apply. With a steady hand, begin drawing from the center of your top lash line to the outer part of your eye. Draw as close to the lash line as possible, following your eye's natural curve. For a thicker line, build upon your first line gradually. For a '60s retro fab look, draw liner thin on the inside of the eye and thicker as you reach the outer edge.*

Creativity comes from a conflict of ideas.

Donatella Versace

Are You Temperance?

Temperance Style: The Domestic Goddess

The Temperance card reminds you that life is a great balancing act. You are a Supermom and goddess of the house and home. A jam-packed schedule keeps you on the go. Every day's a play date with your fun, loving personality. You meet the challenging demands of your life without compromising a firm style sense. You look great whether you are attending your child's soccer game or cooking for a crowd.

Flattering jeans and soft, colorful capris make up your daytime wardrobe. You wear comfortable, breathable fabrics that move with your body. Looking pulled together with matching cardigans and camis, you know how to jazz it up for a big night out with a stunning dress.

The key to your style sense rests in the fact you don't have a ton of time to devote to how you'll look. You make sure your wardrobe is stocked full of clothing that mixes and matches well. It offers you comfort and versatility: the ideal embodiment of Temperance.

Temperance Wardrobe Staples

- ✦ Workhorse jeans

- ✦ Comfy pullovers

- ✦ Merrell shoes

Temperance Style Icons

- ✦ Samantha (Elizabeth Montgomery) from *Bewitched*

- ✦ Roseanne Barr

- ✦ Kate Gosselin

Temperance Stores/Designers

- ✦ JCPenney
- ✦ Walmart
- ✦ Target
- ✦ Kohl's

When to Invoke Temperance Energy

- ✦ Carpooling the kids
- ✦ PTA meeting
- ✦ Running errands

Temperance's Secret Style Weapon

- ✦ Perfectly fitting jeans

   How You Can Use It: *Yes, you can find the perfect jeans! Every store and every designer has specific cuts of pants and jeans to suit different body types. Some stores even offer custom-designed jeans. Set aside a day or two. Devote that day to shopping for the perfect jeans. Investigate which cuts and styles look good on you by venturing into stores and trying them all on. This one-time effort will save you hours of frustration in the future. From then on, you'll walk into a store and know exactly what cut and fit complements you. You can purchase in different colors, textures, and fabrics for variety.*

A woman is never sexier than when
she is comfortable in her clothes.

Vera Wang

Are You a Devil?

Devil Style: Fun and Flirty

The Devil card offers the opportunity to become a slave to your desires. You dangerously tempt all who come near you in your come-hither clothes and flirty personality. You are the Seductress, the Bombshell, the Temptress, the Sex Kitten. You make the most of your body and aren't afraid to flaunt your assets.

Your fashion is not for the faint of heart, the shy or easily intimidated. Walking into a room, you always make an entrance. You embrace short shorts with stilettos. You are happy wearing clothing that clings to your sexy body. You don sheer fabrics worn in soft layers and underwear as outerwear.

You are always utterly bewitching, with a hint of danger. Your sweaters cling to your dangerous curves, your skirt hikes up with a peek of garters beneath. Dressing up in fantasy lingerie is a favorite pastime whilst in the boudoir.

Devil Wardrobe Staples

+ Fishnet stockings

+ Push-up bra

+ Stilettos

+ Makeup

Devil Style Icons

+ Samantha (Kim Cattrall) from *Sex and the City*

+ Marilyn Monroe

+ Brigitte Bardot

+ Pamela Anderson

+ Britney Spears

Devil Stores/Designers

✦ Frederick's of Hollywood

✦ Bob Mackie

✦ Gucci

When to Invoke Devil Energy

✦ On the road to seduction

✦ Night out with the girls

✦ Rekindling romance

The Devil's Secret Style Weapon

✦ A signature scent

How You Can Use It: *It seems every sexy celebrity, from Kim Kardashian to JLo, has a signature fragrance on the market. You create your own signature scent by mixing essential oils to fit your taste. Your soft skin and intoxicating oils will have men dropping to their knees in droves.*

> Underwear makes me uncomfortable, and besides—my parts have to breathe.
> **Jean Harlow**

Are You a Tower?

Tower Style: The Risk Taker

The Tower card breaks down barriers in an explosive, surprising way, and so do you with your daring, outrageous style sense. No one knows what you'll be wearing next, and you always court the element of surprise. What's left in the dust? Fashion roadkill.

You mix and match synthetic fibers, embrace color, love a hat, and happily adopt any style of clothing that fits your mood du jour. You wear structurally unexpected silhouettes and hungrily watch haute couture fashion shows. You dye your hair shocking colors, changing the shade to match your current mood.

Your strong personality is perfectly suited for your outlandish fashion taste. You often create looks inspired by characters of films or novels. You have a strong affinity for Japanese futuristic fashion sense and are inspired by Harajuku girls. Mixing punk with a schoolgirl uniform or goth with designer clothes, you fuse your fashion to suit your mood.

Tower Wardrobe Staples

+ Rubber mini skirt

+ Feather accessories

+ Fishnets

+ Sequins, sequins, and more sequins

Tower Style Icons

+ Drag queens

+ Madonna

+ Lady Gaga

+ Gwen Stefani

Tower Stores/Designers

- ✦ Jean Paul Gaultier

- ✦ Alexander McQueen

- ✦ Young avant-garde designers

- ✦ Vivienne Westwood

- ✦ Patricia Field

- ✦ Betsey Johnson

When to Invoke Tower Energy

- ✦ Museum party

- ✦ Opening night

- ✦ Night club

Tower Secret Style Weapon

- ✦ The unexpected

  How You Can Use It: *Shake up your style and add some fun with an unexpected accessory. Buy a feather headband, a handheld Venetian mask, a unique handbag, or outrageous costume jewelry for your next big event and make a fashion splash.*

Above all, remember that the most important thing you can take anywhere is not a Gucci bag or French-cut jeans; it's an open mind.

Gail Rubin Bereny

Are You a Star?

Star Style: Glamour Queen

The Star shines with brilliance, illuminating hope and inspiration to those around her, and so do you. Luxe labels and luxuriousness are the standards you live by. You are a glamour queen and look elegant every moment of the day.

Your feminine flourishes are soft and sexy. You feel better when dressed up rather than dressed down. It doesn't matter the occasion, your diamonds sparkle, slingbacks click, and all eyes are dazzled by you.

The cameras are always rolling as far as you are concerned. You are director and star of a dream-like film called life. Princess that you are, you truly do belong on the red carpet.

Star Wardrobe Staples

+ Cashmere sweaters

+ Evening gowns

+ Diamonds

+ Faux fur

+ Satin clutches

+ Cocktail rings

Star Style Icons

+ Jennifer Lopez

+ Penelope Cruz

+ Salma Hayek

+ Beyoncé

THE STAR

Star Stores/Designers

- ✦ Oscar de la Renta
- ✦ Tom Ford
- ✦ Givenchy
- ✦ Jessica McClintock

When to Invoke Star Energy

- ✦ Elegant dinner parties
- ✦ Weddings
- ✦ The symphony

Star Secret Style Weapon

- ✦ False eyelashes

> Fashion is very important. It is life-enhancing and, like everything that gives pleasure, it is worth doing well.
>
> **Vivienne Westwood**

How You Can Use It: *False lashes are easier to wear than one might expect. They come in every shape and size available. You can apply individual lashes or an entire lash line if you like. Cut false lashes with scissors to fit your lash line. Put a small bit of glue along the edge. Do not apply to lash line right away; let the glue set for sixty seconds before applying. Apply to lash line, holding firmly until glue sets and becomes invisible. After applying your luxe lashes, don super-glam shades and ignore those pesky paparazzi.*

Are You a Moon?

Moon Style: Dreamy Diva

The Moon is a dreamy, evocative card, and you dress in a dreamy, romantic way. Soft and sensual clothes, girly flourishes, lace, soft colors, floral prints, and skirts that fall beneath the knee are your signature. Pastels and sheer fabrics make you happy, happy, happy.

Vintage is an aesthetic you adore, and you rock a serious Victorian look. You'd dress like Kate Winslet in any of her period films, from *Titanic* to *Sense and Sensibility*. Flowing chiffon makes you swoon. Velvet against your skin feels oh so good.

Your mystical attitude translates beautifully into your clothing sensibility; you often look the part of a beguiling gypsy witch, a steampunk princess. You are even handy with a sewing machine and will whip up the garment of your dreams by yourself.

Moon Wardrobe Staples

- ✦ Vintage jewelry and charm necklaces
- ✦ Lace-up boots
- ✦ Flowing dresses
- ✦ Steampunk

Moon Style Icons

- ✦ Any Merchant-Ivory character
- ✦ Andie (Molly Ringwald) in *Pretty in Pink*
- ✦ Olson twins
- ✦ Nicole Richie
- ✦ Stevie Nicks

18 ~ The Moon

Moon Stores/Designers

✦ Vintage stores

✦ Jewelry boutiques

✦ Fabric shops

✦ Anthropology

✦ Free People

✦ Ella Moss

When to Invoke Moon Energy

✦ Romantic summer nights

✦ Shopping at a farmer's market

✦ Casting a spell

The Moon's Secret Style Weapon

✦ Shopping in vintage and thrift stores and walking out with a major find.

How You Can Use It: *Clothing sizes were different in the 1940s and '50s. Yesterday's size 4 is about a size 8 today. Get over the number on the tag and find some vintage that fits. If the clothing smells musty, pass on it. There is usually no return policy in a vintage store, so if you purchase it, make sure you love it!*

> It is about enrapturing
> yourself in clothes.
> **Donna Karan**

Are You a Sun?

Sun Style: Sporty Chic

The Sun card offers the warmth and growth associated with the sun. You are a rosy-cheeked out-doorsy chick and your wardrobe reflects your sporty attitude. You value comfort above all in your active wear and are often found in denim, cute track suits, yoga pants, and workout clothes.

Your outerwear is water resistant, 'cause you aren't afraid to get your hair wet. Your tresses are often found in a short haircut or neat ponytail. You tend to wear minimal makeup. The sweet shine you radiate comes from your best accessories: gorgeous hair, glowing skin and body. Whether dashing to a hatha yoga class or off to run a marathon, you exude health and a sun-kissed glow.

Sun Wardrobe Staples

- ✦ Tank tops with built-in support
- ✦ Sneakers
- ✦ Track suits
- ✦ Yoga pants

Sun Style Icons

- ✦ Cameron Diaz
- ✦ Serena Williams
- ✦ Kate Hudson
- ✦ Jennifer Aniston

Joy is the best makeup.

Anne Lamott

Sun Stores/Designers

✦ Lululemon

✦ Body Glove

✦ Nike

When to Invoke Sun Energy

✦ Skiing the slopes of Aspen

✦ Hiking the Pacific Northwest

✦ Starting a new workout routine

The Sun's Secret Style Weapon

✦ A fierce body

> **How You Can Use It:** *Nothing beats a body that is strong, healthy, and fit. Start a workout regimen at least three times a week for thirty minutes at a clip. This could be walking, running, or a fun exercise class. The trick is to pick something you'll enjoy. Watch your body transform under that tracksuit. Also, be sure to stay hydrated so your skin glows!*

The Sun

Are You Judgement?

Judgement Style: The Trendsetter

The Judgement card is about waking up and experiencing the world in an entirely new way, and you do the same thing with your wardrobe. You wouldn't be caught dead wearing the same outfit twice. You follow all the latest trends and pride yourself by dangling over the cutting edge of fashion.

The ultimate fashionista, you wield your judgment against others sometimes, critical of what people wear. Mostly you keep your critical eye on yourself, ensuring that you look like you've stepped off the pages of French *Vogue*. You love deconstructing an outfit, breaking it down and building it back up to its most fashion-forward self.

You are the first to hop on a trend, and fashion is your true passion.

Judgement Wardrobe Staples

- ✦ The skinny jean
- ✦ Designer shoes
- ✦ Designer bags

Judgement Style Icons

- ✦ Twiggy
- ✦ Kate Moss
- ✦ Sienna Miller
- ✦ Carrie (Sarah Jessica Parker) from *Sex and the City*

Judgement Stores/Designers

- ✦ Saks Fifth Avenue
- ✦ Henri Bendel
- ✦ Bergdorfs
- ✦ Barneys

When to Invoke Judgement Energy

✦ Front row at Fashion Week

✦ Trunk shows

✦ Lunching with the ladies

Judgement's Secret Style Weapon

✦ Fashion blogs

How You Can Use It: *Check fashion blogs and magazines for a list of hot new looks for each season. Buy an affordable version found on the "hot" list. Expensive looks are always reimagined by budget-conscious designers. Next season, you can retire it or donate it to a thrift store without guilt.*

Fashion is architecture;
it is a matter of proportion.
Coco Chanel

Are You a World?

World Style: Worldly Woman

The World card is about success, euphoria, movement, and travel. Your passport is always ready to be stamped; you are a globetrotter. Your love of foreign cultures is reflected in the clothing you wear. A reflection of your travels, your wardrobe is filled with clothing purchased abroad. Each garment, each piece of jewelry, feels like you have brought a little piece of that country home with you.

You adopt Indian and Asian prints and Eastern- and African-inspired clothing into your clothing with flair. Ethnic bracelets clink on your wrist, and dangly earrings adorn your beautiful face.

Your free-flowing clothes offer you the comfort and movement essential for your pilgrimage to India, trek across Thailand, and sail upon the Mediterranean. You throw on a traditional headscarf in Turkey and rock a kimono in Japan. Understanding that the best way to learn about the world is to experience it, your wanderlust and fascination with world cultures is never-ending.

World Wardrobe Staples

- ✦ Indonesian sandals and espadrilles
- ✦ Long belted sweaters
- ✦ Colorful blouses
- ✦ A good suitcase with tissue paper in which to pack your goodies

World Style Icons

- ✦ Meryl Streep
- ✦ Iman
- ✦ Catherine Zeta-Jones
- ✦ Kate Winslet

World Stores/Designers

- ✦ Local artisans
- ✦ Tribal clothing

When to Invoke World Energy

✦ Train trips

✦ Sailing

✦ Jet-setting

The World's Secret Style Weapon

✦ The World woman knows how to shop extremely well. She has limited room to pack her items away in her suitcase, so she knows how to narrow down her decisions.

How You Can Use It: *The following five questions will enhance your shopping:*

1. Do I love it?

2. Do I feel great in it?

3. Does it fit me well?

4. Does it flatter me?

5. Do I have at least two things I can wear with it?

21 ~ The World

It matters more what's in a woman's face than what's on it.
Claudette Colbert

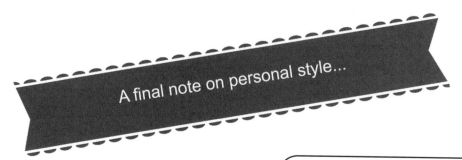

As with all other things in life, it is the attitude with which you wear your clothes that makes your wardrobe, not the clothes themselves. The way you feel on the inside is always projected on the outside. Always shop for things that make you happy, which build you up and support you. Your wardrobe doesn't have to be about keeping up with the latest trends or spending oodles of money. It is your own personal art form and can be cultivated to the extent you wish to take it. Have fun and love your clothes—but more importantly, love yourself!

21 The World 21

Understanding *Court Card Energy*

KNIGHT OF CUPS

The court cards can present a challenge to even the most seasoned tarot reader. At first glance, it can be hard to distinguish between a knight and a king. The quickest way to understand court meanings is to understand that each court card holds a very acute and particular energy. This energy contains individualized personality traits and a specific way of being in the world. Each court card carries a particular energy that is simple to grasp.

Pages represent young energy. The childlike vitality of youth is full of wonder, curiosity, and learning. Think of yourself playing in your room at age five. Your toys held worlds of play, entertainment for hours. Imagine a child you know and how excited they get over presents and how energetic they are.

Knights represent teen energy—explosive hormonal overload and movement. You'll quickly recognize a knight (and differentiate him from a king) because he always appears on a horse. Recall yourself at age sixteen—how pumped up and agitated you'd become over the smallest blip in your day.

Queens represent a mature feminine energy—the nurturing, empathetic, soft yet firm control of a mother figure. The queen is a woman who is grown, able, and sure of herself. Think of yourself as a woman. Think of your own mother or grown women you know.

Kings represent a mature masculine energy—the strong, competent, commanding control of a father figure. The king is a man, fully realized, adult, and capable. Think of your father or other father-figure types.

Masculine versus Feminine Energy

Masculine and feminine energies apply to and exist in all of us, regardless of our sex. Recall that tarot makes use of archetypes. Masculine and feminine cards in tarot represent archetypal qualities of the traditional male and female. It is not the goal of tarot to be sexist. Tarotists do not believe all men are commanding and forceful while all women are soft and subservient. Rather, you can use a general archetype of male versus female to understand subtle differences between masculine and feminine energy. Masculine cards will always carry a certain forcefulness and outward energy, while feminine cards carry a nurturing, intuitive quality.

+ Pages and queens represent feminine energy—the delicious, intuitive, feeling, soft, nurturing, wildly intuitive nature traditionally belonging to the female.

+ Knights and kings represent masculine energy—the commanding, certain, overbearing, strong nature traditionally belonging to the male.

We can also understand the court ranks as members of a nuclear family. Mom and Dad are represented by the queen and king. The knight is the teenage brother, and the page is the baby sister.

A Day in the Life of Your Court Cards

How can each and every court card apply to you? Remember how I stated that the entire tarot deck describes you and all your different qualities? Let's imagine for a moment that you are a perky twenty-four-year-old actress living in New York City. We'll look at a day in your life and see how the court ranks can all apply to you during a twelve-hour period.

9:00 am: Page Energy—Acting Class

You enter your morning acting class, coffee in hand, scene memorized. You listen to your teacher attentively, watch fellow actors perform, explore your character in a group exercise, play, and have fun experimenting in a workshop environment.

It is the nature of the pages to be absorbed completely by what they are doing—to play, explore, and learn.

12:00 pm: Queen Energy—Babysitting

Between acting gigs, you babysit for your six-year-old nephew. He runs to greet you at the door, and you fix him a peanut butter and jelly sandwich for lunch. You laugh while he tells you stories about his friends and makes up fairy tales. Singing a clean-up song together, you pick up toys and tidy up.

It is the nature of the queen to be in charge and in control. Queen energy is nurturing yet firm.

3:00 pm: King Energy—Film Audition

Dressed to the nines and completely prepared, you audition for a movie role. You take command of the room, and all eyes are unable to look away from you. The casting director is putty in your hands. You nail the role. They tell you on the spot that the part is yours.

It is the nature of the kings to be in control. The kings make things happen—they are forceful and certain of themselves and their choices, and they tend to get their own way as they command their domains.

7:00 pm: Knight Energy—Celebration

Enthused and invigorated that you've just won yourself a movie role, you call your friends for an impromptu celebration. Five of you meet at a snazzy lounge for drinks. While handsome boys buy you cocktails, you flirt ferociously and stay out until the wee hours of the morning. A cab delivers you to your door, where, exhausted, you tumble into bed with a smile on your face.

It is the nature of knights to be impulsive, quick, and fun loving.

Understanding Suit Symbolism in Court Cards

Once we understand the ranking of the courts—the difference of energy—we then plug in the qualities of the suits. We'll find ourselves with a very detailed description of a person. It is like a simple math equation:

Rank + Suit = Court card

Teen energy (excitement, movement, certainty) +

Fire (passion, enthusiasm, movement) = Knight of Wands

or

Nurturing energy (mothering, creative) + Earth (grounded, crafty) = Queen of Pentacles

There are suit-symbolism clues everywhere in the court cards if you know where to look. The pentacles are filled with earth symbolism via tilled fields and growing plants. Swords are full of air symbolism via racing clouds, blowing trees, and winged creatures. Wands are filled with fire symbolism via scorching-hot deserts and salamanders. Cups are full of water symbolism via rolling oceans and fish.

In addition to representing aspects of your fabulous personality, court cards often represent other people in your life. Feeling your way through the court cards, we'll have a great deal of fun in the next section. I've described the court cards as people you might have known in high school. We'll take a peek at the pages as your best friends, the knights as the bevy of boys you dated, and the kings and queens as moms and dads.

Page of Pentacles

Page of Cups

The Pages—Your BFFs (Best Friends Forever)

Page of Pentacles—The Princess

The suit of pentacles is about money and the qualities of earth. The Page of Pentacles, often "the princess," always has plenty of "pentacles" in her designer handbags. The Page of Pentacles' idea of heaven is retail therapy and shopping. She spends afternoons at her favorite stores and makeup counters. Looking so great and pulled together, some mistake her for being shallow. Much to their surprise, when they get to know her, the Page of Pentacles is the most grounded of all pages because she is connected to earth. She is an excellent student and an avid reader, often found buried in books and magazines for the sheer pleasure of it.

The Page of Pentacles drags you into stores, throws together outfits for you, and is constantly telling you which are your good colors. She's fascinated with physical transformation and the power of beauty. She'll plop you down and give you the makeover of her dreams. She's Molly Ringwald in *The Breakfast Club*, Alicia Silverstone in *Clueless*, or one of the Plastics in *Mean Girls*.

The Page of Pentacles makes an excellent friend because her advice is always practical. Walking into her bewitchingly beautiful bedroom with a problem to solve, she looks at you lovingly and says, "Let's go shopping."

Classes she excels in: Home ec, English lit, and current events

After-school job: Salesgirl, makeup counter, babysitting

Extracurricular activities: Hanging out at the mall

Page of Cups—The Artsy Girl

The suit of cups is about the emotion and fluidity of the element of water. The Page of Cups type is found haunting the art studios of the local high school. Whether painting a canvas or writing poetic verse, she is always found participating in activities where she can express herself.

The Page of Cups is itchy to get out of her small town, yearning for the culture of a big city. She whispers her future plans to you with wistful excitement in her eyes. She'll introduce you to the world of art via museum trips and takes you to edgy independent films.

The Page of Cups makes a wonderful friend because her advice is always well thought out. She helps you to see your issues in a new way due to her introspective nature. Sleepovers at her house are hair raising, as she is prone to psychic flashes and ghostly activity. The Page of Cups is deeply in touch with her psychic abilities. You go to her for advice and she looks at you from under her dark lashes and says, "You were meant for something better…"

Classes she excels in: Art, English, and creative writing

After-school job: Movie theater, coffee shop barista

Extracurricular activities: Blogging, photography

Page of Wands—The Good-Time Girl

The suit of wands is about passion and the excitable qualities of fire. The Page of Wands is super energetic, the giggliest of all your friends. Full of energy, she is often a cheerleader or amazing athlete. Her adventurous nature makes her campaign for class trips to exotic locales. Her passion and enthusiasm often shows itself in community-service work, collecting clothes and money for people in need. She is very likely to be on the student council and actively changing policies within your school. She's Kirsten Dunst in *Bring It On*.

If she looks like she's always up to something, it's because she is. She's the friend you are most likely to get into trouble with. Looking at you with a maniacal glance, she'll encourage you to sneak out with her at night to steal a parent's car and drive around, because wands are the risk-taking suit. She doesn't think, she just does! She's the most likely of your friends to be found running from the police.

The Page of Wands makes a good friend because she always cheers you up. She reminds you of how much fun life can be. The Page of Wands grins at you from behind a steering wheel and says, "Let's go for it!"

Classes she excels in: Government and world affairs

After-school job: Lifeguard, camp counselor

Extracurricular activities: Working out, dance class, and swim team

Page of Swords—The Smart Girl

The suit of swords is about the mind and the mental qualities of air. The Page of Swords is your typical straight-A student and type-A personality. Holding herself to incredibly high standards, she purposefully puts her schoolwork ahead of all else. She takes her responsibilities seriously. The Page of Swords can be found on the debate team and writes for, if not edits, the school paper. She always gets into her first-choice school when it comes time for college acceptance.

You beg her to come out on a double date with a cute boy, but if she has a paper due, she'll stay home and finish it rather than head out with you. She amazes you with her ability to be so focused when all you want to do is have fun. She's Reese Witherspoon in *Election* and Julia Stiles in *10 Things I Hate About You*.

The Page of Swords makes a good friend because she is articulate and finds the right words for any situation. She uses her x-ray vision to cut straight to the heart of the matter. You may not always follow her advice, especially when it comes to romance, but you respect it. And she never makes you feel bad when she looks at you laughingly and says, "I told you so…"

Classes she excels in: Math, science, and foreign languages

After-school job: Tutor, bookstore clerk

Extracurricular activities: Reading to the blind, math team

THE PRINCESS OF WANDS

Page of Swords

The Knights—Your High-School Dream Team

The Knight of Pentacles—The Dreamy Teen

The suit of pentacles is about the solid, firm quality of earth. The Knight of Pentacles embodies rich, handsome, beefcake dreaminess. The Knight of Pentacles is the stuff teen dream movies are made of. Pentacles represent money, and the Knight of Pentacles is often the rich boy, usually from a family well established in your town. He drives a fast and expensive car, his clothes are designer, and yes, yes…he's popular.

The Knight of Pentacles cares about his body, as pentacles often represent the body. Chances are he works out—a lot. He's an Abercrombie & Fitch billboard model come to life. He usually plays on at least one athletic team. Girls are lined up around the block to be his prom date; he's the ultimate prom king. Because pentacles are so solid and grounded, he dates seriously, sticking with one girl rather than playing the field. His exclusivity just makes girls go that much crazier, pining away to be the one he chooses. We stare at his girlfriend, wondering what she's got that we don't. He's Jake in *Sixteen Candles*.

The Knight of Pentacles is the perfect boy to lose your virginity to because when he's with you, he truly cares about you; you aren't just another notch in his belt. Wrapped in his strong arms, his lips trace your neck; you shiver as he softly whispers, "I want to feel you…"

Classes he excels in: Math

After-school job: Working for his father's business

Extracurricular activities: The gym

The Knight of Cups—The Dreamer

The suit of cups is about the dreaminess and poeticism of the element of water. The Knight of Cups is the artist, the acoustic musician, the poet. He's deep, thoughtful, and creative. The Knight of Cups oozes whatever emotion he's feeling, and it plays across his face. When your eyes are locked in his gaze, you are like a deer in the headlights. You feel like he's looking into the depths of your soul. The Knight of Cups is interested in you and your thoughts and feelings. He's Eric Stolz in *Some Kind of Wonderful* and Leo DiCaprio in *Titanic*.

The Knight of Cups is a slave to his emotions and tends to fall in love with more than one girl at a time. Years later, as an adult, you wouldn't be surprised to hear he has come out as gay or bisexual. Sad to have lost him to the other team, you smile, fondly remembering your times together.

The Knight of Cups sheds tears freely in your arms and laughs maniacally while tickling you. Holding your face in his hands, he decides universal beauty resides on your cheekbones, salvation dwells in your eyes, and perfection is attained with the stroke of your lip with his fingertip. Your eyes grow wide and your heart melts as he whispers, "I want to understand you…"

Classes he excels in: Art and music

After-school job: Intern for a local artist

Extracurricular activities: Alternative music

THE PRINCE OF PENTACLES

Knight of Cups

The Knight of Wands—The Jock

The suit of wands contains the heat and fervor associated with the element of fire. The Knight of Wands exudes these qualities as the ultimate athlete and hot shot. He's often the star quarterback and captain of the baseball or wrestling team. His enthusiasm for life plays over into his partying habits, and he'll be found, surrounded by his buds, at every party, every kegger.

The Knight of Wands plays the field in sports and with girls. He dates dozens but settles for none. He'll bring another girl to a formal but ask you for a slow dance and press his body so close you feel every muscle under his cheap polyester suit. Meanwhile, his date pouts from across the room, pretending not to notice.

He tussles with you in cornfields, sneaks into your sleepover parties, and shows up in unexpected places. He repays your love and devotion by systematically seducing each of your girlfriends in exactly the same way. He's Emilio Estevez in *The Breakfast Club*.

Impossible to resist his scorching sexiness, you dissolve to pieces, falling apart as he whispers into your ear, "You are so hot."

Classes he excels in: Gym class

After-school job: Construction

Extracurricular activities: Drinking with his buddies

The Knight of Swords—The Bad Boy

The suit of swords contains the decisiveness and cunningness associated with the element of air. The Knight of Swords is wickedly devastating because he's so intense about everything. He's always thinking and calculating, and when his thoughts turn to you, you've barely a chance to escape with your clothes intact.

Swords are edgy, sharp, and dangerous by their very nature. The Knight of Swords is the ultimate bad boy and sometimes the kid from the wrong side of the tracks. He rides a motorcycle, the perfect vehicle to represent his speed. The Knight of Swords carries the fastest energy of the entire tarot deck—think Johnny Depp on a motorcycle, Kiefer Sutherland in *The Lost Boys*, or Robert Pattinson in *Twilight*. The Knight of Swords is the ideal vampire bad boy … seductive, wicked, all-consuming.

The Knight of Swords pins you under the stairwell after school and plants hot, wet kisses on your mouth. He takes you into empty classrooms and slides his hand under your green Catholic school uniform while you pray a nun doesn't walk in to discover you both.

He whisks you away and you're in for the ride of your life, so hold on tight. You feel his cool hands slide across your skin; his eyes glimmer intensely as he whispers, "I want to surprise you…"

Classes he excels in: Shop

After-school job: Gas station

Extracurricular activities: Motor biking, skateboarding, getting into trouble

The Queens

The Queen of Pentacles—The Homemaker

Pentacles represent the grounding qualities of earth. The Queen of Pentacles is that mom whose home everyone wants to visit again and again. Her house smells delicious and feels welcoming. Cookies wait for you on the table when arriving home from school. The Queen of Pentacles is always first to the bake sale with goodies. A goddess of the kitchen, she happily prepares meals and offers treats for you and your friends while you hang out.

Holidays roll around and she's the first mom on the block to break out the decorations. An avid crafter, she begins making Valentines for your class weeks in advance. She often teaches knitting or sewing classes. She is often a professional cook, decorator, or gardener. She typically owns a home

business, but her joy is providing a warm and happy home for her family. She's most likely to have a large family. The Queen of Pentacles is the Martha Stewart or June Cleaver type.

Her Greatest Advice: "Nurture yourself and love your body."

When to Invoke Her Energy:

- ✦ Decorating your house
- ✦ Caring for a child
- ✦ All creative endeavors

Queen of Cups—The Therapist

Cups represent the empathy and deep qualities of water. The Queen of Cups is the mom whom everyone turns to when in need of advice. When you are awakened, trembling, from a nightmare, the Queen of Cups soothes you and sings you back to sleep. When you're feverish and drenched in sweat, the Queen of Cups strokes you with cool hands and offers cold ginger ale.

The Queen of Cups' greatest quality is the ability to understand you. She's the mom who doles out the best advice and always reminds you of just how very special you are. The Queen of Cups always has your best interests in mind, and when she focuses her attention on you, you feel important and understood. Her home is dreamy and soft; she's the New Age mom. She's often found in progressive workshops and yoga retreats. Her jobs are typically as the therapist, psychic, tarot reader, guidance counselor, nurse, and humanitarian. She's the Princess Diana, Mother Teresa, Oprah-type personality.

Her Greatest Advice: "Always follow your heart."

When to Invoke Her Energy:

- ✦ Seeking to understand yourself
- ✦ Counseling someone
- ✦ Reading tarot cards

Queen of Wands—The Firecracker

The suit of wands contains the combustible quality of fire. The Queen of Wands is the fun mom and good-time girl. This spark plug often repeats this phrase: "You girls keep me young!" The Queen of Wands thrives on excitement and drama and is always ready to plan a party for you. She's had your sweet sixteen planned since you were two.

This firecracker of a mother may have been divorced and remarried. Regardless of her marital status, she's been around the block a few times. She's the sexy mom who fascinates you with her flashy clothes, beautiful makeup, and sensual boudoir. She often appears younger than her actual age.

She empowers your sexuality from a young age, this mom who encourages you go on the pill. She's the mom whom girls turn to when they've gotten themselves into trouble. Her jobs are typically actress, coach, dancer, or activist. The Queen of Wands type is Heidi Klum, Julia Roberts, Helen Gurley Brown, and Rosa Parks, all of whom carry her personality traits.

Her Greatest Advice: "Follow your passions and have fun."

When to Invoke Her Energy:

+ When you are performing

+ Standing out in a crowd

+ Breaking barriers

Queen of Swords—The Businesswoman

The suit of swords contains the mental qualities of air, and the Queen of Swords is the professional working mom that no one wants to mess with. She's super smart, is there to help with your homework, and challenges you to do your best in school and in life. The Queen of Swords often relies on the help of a nanny while raising you but never slacks in her responsibility as a mother. She always makes time in her busy schedule for you. Her professional life falls away when the two of you are together.

Signing you up for activities and clubs, she keeps your schedule full and challenging. If you get into trouble at school, she'll be there in a flash to defend your case until the administrators see things her way. Her jobs are typically executive, doctor, or teacher. The Queen of Swords is the Hillary Clinton, Madeleine Albright, Margaret Thatcher, and Katharine Hepburn type.

Her Greatest Advice: "Never forget how damn smart you are."

When to Invoke Her Energy:

- ✦ Standing up for yourself in an adverse situation

- ✦ Owning your personal power

- ✦ Gaining strength

The Kings

King of Pentacles—The CEO

The suit of pentacles contains the security and safety of earth. The King of the Pentacles is the dad who is happiest when providing for his family. His ego is completely tied to the amount of money he makes. The King of Pentacles is the ultimate provider. Because he understands that money buys a certain amount of freedom and security, he's had investments and a college fund going since the day you were born. He's happiest spoiling his little girl and has a hard time saying no to you, springing for a new car when you turn sixteen.

You run for his hugs, and he looks devastatingly handsome in his tailored suits, ties, and trench coats. He'll treat you to a fancy lunch when you visit him in the office. You always feel safe with his large arms wrapped around you and know he'll protect and cherish you forever.

The King of Pentacles is the classic CEO, businessman, real estate investor, and banker. Donald Trump, Warren Buffett, Rupert Murdoch, Ted Turner, and Richard Branson all carry his personality traits.

His Greatest Advice: "Always protect yourself."

When to Invoke His Energy:

✦ Investing money

✦ Choosing insurance plans

✦ Protecting your family

King of Cups—The Composer

The King of Cups is the artsy, dreamy dad. The King of Cups dad opens your world in a new way because he constantly shows you new ways to understand it. A true visionary, he takes you on trips around the world, supports your artistic dreams, and writes poems to you. He's the father most likely to dissolve into hysterics with you and enjoys taking you to movies, concerts, and museums.

A consummate philosopher, the two of you stay up until all hours of the night talking about the wonders, intricacies, and nature of the universe. He'll introduce you to the world of art and explain why artist expression is the most vital and essential part of life. You are the apple of his eye, bringing him joy, and he'll often use you for inspiration in his creative projects.

The King of Cups is typically a composer, film director, or artist. Steven Spielberg, James Cameron, D. H. Lawrence, T. S. Eliot, Sting, and Matisse all carry King of Cups qualities.

His Greatest Advice: "Create something beautiful."

When to Invoke His Energy:

+ Selling your creative work

+ Making your dreams a reality

+ Owning the strength of your creativity

King of Wands—The Rock Star

Wands contain the impulsive qualities of fire. The King of Wands is the "rock star" dad: dominating, strong-minded, and full of adventure and impulsiveness. The King of Wands works really hard, and if he's concerned with a project, it may be hard to get his attention. When he does turn his mind to you, you consume him. He wants to ignite imaginations, stir things up around him. He follows his own rules and bends to no one's will.

He's the sort of dad who is fun to be around because he brings an element of excitement to all around him. The King of Wands runs a serious risk of embarrassing you in public with his enthusiasm, however, standing up to clap or yell before your performance in the school play is even over. Regardless of being mortified by his public behavior, you know he would never hurt you on purpose. He's your greatest champion and can barely contain himself when he's proud of you.

The King of Wands is a rock star, an actor, a politician, and a salesman. Sean Penn, Bono, Tom Cruise, Martin Luther King, and Malcolm X all carry King of Wands personality traits.

His Greatest Advice: "Do it!"

When to Invoke His Energy:

◆ Getting your point across

◆ Getting others enthused

◆ Exercising

King of Swords—The Intellectual

The King of Swords is the super-smart, intellectual father. He has taught you to utilize the power of your divine intellect since you were tiny. Interested in your opinion, he always empowers you by challenging you to do your best.

The King of Swords is a stickler for the rules he creates. You would not want to cross him; after all, those swords are dangerous. He's the dad who insists everyone eat together at dinnertime. He turns off the phones and computers and wants good conversation. Happy to debate you, he adores intellectual sparring. He often enlists you for help when trying to figure something out; above all, he values what you think. He tends to be the strictest of the court dads, and only your most clever arguments can sway him once he's made up his mind to ground you. He values books and your excellence in schoolwork.

The King of Swords is the scientist, the physicist, the intellectual, the professor, the lawyer, the mentor. Stephen Hawking and Albert Einstein carry King of Swords qualities.

His Greatest Advice: "Figure it out."

When to Invoke His Energy:

✦ Finding the right words to express yourself

✦ Figuring out the answer to a problem

✦ Defending yourself and demanding truth

Super-Fun Exercise: Family Portrait

Create a childhood family portrait out of the court cards. In your tarot journal, re-create your family, person by person. Start with a family portrait when you were sixteen. You can move on to other ages or deconstruct your current family later. Choose one court card for each family member; you may want to use two court cards. You can use reversed cards to explore negative, repressed, or blocked qualities of the person. It is okay to repeat cards.

Write each person's name, the card(s) you chose, and exactly why you chose each card to represent them.

Example:

Portrait of Myself at Age Sixteen: Page of Cups and reversed Knight of Wands

> I was a Page of Cups because I was very emotional and loved music, art, and books. You could find me writing poetry and constantly weaving fantasies in my head.

> I was also a reversed Knight of Wands because I had so much energy but didn't know how to channel it. I used this energy to wind myself up and make some messed-up choices—like a knight out of control. But I did have that fire, and if I wanted to make something happen, I could. I also loved racing through the night—only in cars, not on a horse. I thirsted for freedom.

By writing out exactly why you selected each court card to represent yourself, your sister, mother, or grandfather, you will foster intimate personal connections to the court cards. These intimate openings to the cards are the golden strands of tarot. They link you, fusing you with your deck. Your readings will spring to life.

You could potentially discover a new quality about your family members. Upon this realization, you may open a fresh path of understanding them and even heal yourself in the process.

Ace of Pentacles

The pentacle on the Ace of Pentacles represents a seed. The five-pointed star on the pentacle represents the four elements and your higher self. The lush garden represents the fertileness where you will plant your pentacle, and the garden gate offers a new direction in which to move.

An ace is a beginning, the first card of the suit. Aces always represent a fresh start, a birth, a gift. An ace is where everything is established. Imagine a self-made millionaire. Their fortune began with the first bit of money deposited in the bank. Those coins, money earned, and that first bank slip is an ace. The culmination of their millions resting in an account and their financial goals fulfilled are representative of a ten in tarot.

Many aces in tarot show a mysterious hand emerging from a cloud. This hand offers a gift. Will you accept? The gift of the Ace of Pentacles is money, your body and health, food, your clothes, your objects—everything the physical world contains and your ability to experience it.

The Ace of Pentacles heralds the beginning of something real, an actual sum of money. It could relate to your body—you look at your body, realizing you can make it stronger through regular exercise. You look at the food you eat, realizing you can make healthier choices. You decide to re-decorate your house or purchase a new property.

Gratitude Exercise

The easiest way to usher in Ace of Pentacles energy is through this gratitude exercise.

Do This Exercise When You Are:

◆ Improving your finances

◆ Reevaluating your wardrobe

◆ Becoming healthier

◆ Wanting to feel better physically

◆ Deciding to redecorate

Expressions of gratitude take the attention off yourself and place it firmly on the world and gifts around you. You'll feel full of abundance, enjoy the things you have, realize the building blocks you possess, and accomplish wonderful things with your money. You'll see the abundance in your life.

To invite Ace of Pentacles energy, place the Ace of Pentacles where you can see it. Fill in the blanks below, writing your answers on a separate piece of paper or journal.

I'm so lucky for _____, and I am grateful because _____.

I love my body because _____, and I am grateful because _____.

I feel good about making money because _____, and I am grateful because _____.

The thing I love about my house is _____, and I am grateful because _____.

The outfit that makes me feel the greatest is _____, and I am grateful because _____.

I love the skin I'm in because _____, and I am grateful because _____.

My favorite food is _____, and I am grateful because _____.

My favorite animal is _____, and I am grateful because _____.

My family makes me happy when _____, and I am grateful because _____.

Two of Pentacles

Should/Should Not Do Spread

The Two of Pentacles is about the weighing of choices. Twos in tarot imply duality, opposites, and pairing. See the juggler managing two pentacles set within a lemniscate? A lemniscate is an ancient symbol representing infinity and flow. The background of the card suggests an interesting change is afloat. What will you do?

The Two of Pentacles represents choice and making a decision. Tarot is your best buddy when feeling indecisive.

If you find yourself stuck with a decision, you can pull a card for each option and see what the tarot has to say. You might also try your hand at this helpful three-card spread created by tarot diva Zoe Matoff.

It is our choices that show what we truly are, far more than our abilities.

J. K. Rowling

Choose three cards:

1

2   3

Card 1: Your situation as it stands.

Card 2: What you should not do.

Card 3: What you should do.

Three of Pentacles

Facial Mask and Hair Rinse Activity

The Three of Pentacles is about creation in the material world. The Three of Pentacles represents craftsmanship, artistry, and apprenticeship. Threes represent creativity in tarot. Pentacles often represent the body; think of the pentacles as our tiny cells. Pentacles remind us it is important to take care of ourselves. Your best accessory, other than your personality and point of view, is glowing skin and healthy hair. Here you'll find a creative and affordable trick to glowing health and beauty.

Money is always an issue in pentacles. The Rider-Waite image depicts consultation and calling in an expert for help with a project. But experts often come with a hefty price tag. You could spend tons of cash consulting beauty experts and visiting salons or you can get creative and give yourself a spa treatment for practically free! Save your pentacles for a special indulgence and offer yourself the following low-cost treats once a week.

I think your whole life shows in your face, and you should be proud of that.

Lauren Bacall

Three of Pentacles

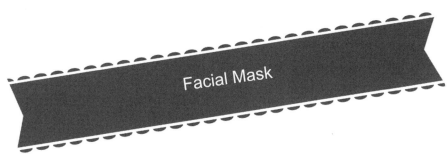

Facial Mask

2 egg whites, separated from the yolk and placed in a bowl

(save your egg yolks for hair rinse, below)

2 tablespoons plain yogurt (not flavored)

Combine the egg whites and yogurt. Whisk them up and apply to your face. Lie back and relax for a few minutes. Indulge in a daydream as you rest. Rinse face in warm water, followed by a warm washcloth.

Hair Rinse

2 egg yolks

2 tablespoons olive oil or baby oil

1 cup lukewarm water

Whisk yolks briskly. Add olive oil and whisk again until well mixed. Mix in the lukewarm water, making sure it is not hot enough to cook the egg. You don't want a mass of scrambled eggs in your hair!

Wash and rinse your hair normally. Pour half of egg mixture on top of your head, avoiding face. Work remaining rinse into the bottom half of your hair. Let it set for five minutes before rinsing. While it sets, engage in part two of said daydream.

Four of Pentacles

Pay Yourself First Exercise

The Four of Pentacles is often understood as the miser card, of holding tightly to the money you have made. Conversely, you can understand this card via the stability that fours in tarot imply. Rather than grasping his money, the fellow is manifesting it magically around his body. Pentacles represent money, an issue many of us struggle with. A recent poll indicates that half of all Americans could not come up with an emergency $2,000 without pulling out their credit cards. Every diva should stand on solid financial ground.

Take out the Four of Pentacles and look at the financial stability of the four. Notice the lush city behind our miser. The towers imply abundance and wealth. The Four of Pentacles shows the first solid financial foundation in the suit of pentacles. You can create the same stability. Money alone will not bring us happiness, but it does offer freedom and the sustainability to take care of ourselves and others. You owe it to yourself to take this exercise very seriously.

David Bach, author of *Smart Women Finish Rich*, offers a suggestion we can apply to the Four of Pentacles. Simple enough for anyone to do, it completely changes our financial future and manifests the stability fours imply: pay yourself first. We pay the rent or mortgage, utility bills, and car payments like clockwork every month (or at least we should). We spend money on a variety of things on a daily basis. But do you pay yourself? Invest in yourself?

Make a commitment, right now, to pay yourself first.

Select an amount of money you will put into savings before you pay your monthly bills. The amount is entirely up to you. It can be as small as $5 monthly if that is what your budget affords. It can be $50, $100, $500 per month—whatever amount you can allow while keeping up with your other bills is what you should be investing in yourself.

No dollar amount is too small. The act of paying yourself first creates a fabulous financial habit. Good habits are worth their weight in gold. You can increase your investment as opportunity allows. You will also notice the law of attraction working as your bank account grows faster than you might expect.

Writing out your check or heading to the bank to make your deposit, pull out the Four of Pentacles card and recite the following mantra:

> Four of disks, four of four
> Build my money more and more.
> Pay myself first, I'm at the top of my list
> No matter what others insist.

Four of Pentacles

FOUR OF PENTACLES

Five of Pentacles

Money Journal

The Five of Pentacles depicts a couple trudging through a cold, snowy, black night, reminiscent of the famous opera scene in *La Bohème*. Hardship is implied as the woman grasps for warmth inside her shawl, the man behind her limps on his crutches, and they have lost their shoes.

The brighter side of the Five of Pentacles, whose struggle is the common theme in the fives of tarot, is that this card reminds us of the ups and downs of any long-term relationship. We can understand the couple as married or in a relationship. It is by sticking together, facing challenges through thick and thin, overcoming defeat, that these two ultimately receive the salvation offered from within the glowing church window. This bright light calmly reminds us that there is hope even on the darkest of nights.

The Five of Pentacles can herald a moment of financial hardship. If you find yourself struggling to make ends meet or want to put more dough in the bank and feel downtrodden about your financial state, do yourself a solid favor and go on a money diet.

Remove the Five of Pentacles card and focus on its imagery.

Know there is light at the end of the tunnel.

Repeat the following mantra:

> Cold, snowy night, dreary card
> I persevere when things get hard.
> Don't think you'll give me a fright
> I'll pull through, make it all right.
> Power in actions, happens quick
> My money journal does the trick.

Make a commitment to write down every day for at least two weeks every single thing you spend money on. You may use a little notebook, the back of a calendar, or an app for your phone or iPad. To be sure to record your expenditures, have it with you at all times.

It may be challenging; you may find resistance in yourself. Like any other habit, though, you'll settle into the routine within a few days. You may be shocked to discover where your money is going. Your daily pilgrimage to the coffee shop adds up to a good sum of money at the end of the month. Recording your money helps you to reevaluate how you spend. It offers a fresh point of view, a dose of reality, and a helping of empowerment that will put you back in the driver's seat so you may persevere through the darkest of nights.

Six of Pentacles

Charitable Giving Exercise

The Six of Pentacles is understood as the charity card, and for good reason. The Rider-Waite deck depicts a gentleman doling out coins to beggars kneeling below him, reminiscent of the Hierophant card. Meanwhile, he balances scales in his left hand as if to measure what is the fair amount, reminiscent of the Justice card.

Engaging a spiritual practice, be it tarot or otherwise, empowers us with an invaluable tool. We learn to step out of our own way. We reach clarity about ourselves, our problems, our sticky issues. Walking a path of enlightenment, we become available to the world around us. We can help make the world a better place. This is why charity is a major tenet of all major religions.

Have you ever wanted to do something that makes a difference, but you haven't found the right outlet? Does it make you feel helpless to see national disasters play across your television screen while you sit, helpless, on your couch? You don't have to pick up and fly halfway around the world in the midst of crisis to make a difference. There is someone in your back yard who needs your help right now. Will you answer their call?

This exercise should get you started on the road that will lead to enjoyable generosity, a habit of making the world a better place. Be sure your charitable work is done with the intention of truly helping others and not performed to make yourself feel superior. Either intention leads to helping others, but the latter form of charity stems from a narcissistic point of view that belittles. And a tarot diva always empowers.

It's easy to look at a diva like Angelina Jolie and say to yourself, "I could never do what she does. I'd never be able to parent six children and embark on a journey through Africa while starring in blockbuster films and snagging America's sexiest man." Hate to be a naysayer, but chances are you probably won't—nor should you. Your life is your path, not someone else's. Allow yourself to be inspired by the Angelinas and Oprahs, but then create your own distinct form of giving. Before you know it, you'll be inspiring those around you to give back as well.

Invoke the energy of the Six of Pentacles, examine the card, and answer the following questions:

How you would like to give to the world?

✦ Will you donate your time?

✦ Will you donate money?

✦ Will you donate both?

Donating Time: Donating your time is a wonderful and effective way of making a difference. One-on-one community service, spending an afternoon assisting in a classroom, becoming a big brother or big sister, etc. It costs nothing more than a few precious hours. Research your charitable opportunities before you start. There is no end to the ways people are utilized for volunteering. Large time commitments are sometimes required for different levels of volunteer work. Be sure you are able to make the required commitment and find work that suits you and your personality.

Donating Money: Monetary donations are a great way to give back, especially if you are super busy and don't have loads of extra time. They are also super easy. Many investors donate a specific portion of their yearly income to charity. You can arrange for financial contributions to be deducted from your account on a regular basis. You may give to a different charity or nonprofit organization each month. You can support institutions that offer gifts back to the givers. Local museums, zoos, and cultural institutions often offer member subscriptions that include appealing benefits. You may support National Public Radio or PBS or any company that holds pledge drives or fundraisers. There are loads of tax benefits to be gained by financial gift giving.

You Don't Have to Save the World

A little help on your part can make a large impact on someone's life. Help out a single mom, pick up groceries for an elderly neighbor, lend a helping hand to a soup kitchen once a month. Small gestures can make a tremendous difference in a person's life. Never doubt the effects you can have.

Don't Underestimate Your Valuable Services

You don't have to physically be there to help someone in need. Your office skills may be put to use in many nonprofit organizations, and your professional skills may be of use as well. You may have donatable items in your closet.

Host a screening of a documentary that speaks to an issue you care about. Choose a plaguing issue that concerns you, be it human slavery, childhood prostitution, genocide, or rainforest destruction. Chances are you'll find a documentary created about the subject. Rent the documentary and invite all your friends to watch it with you. Ask your friends for a donation, say $10 each, for attending your screening. Donate the collected money to an organization who supports solutions for your particular cause. You will have made a financial contribution and spread awareness to your friends about the issue.

Seven of Pentacles

Managing Your Abundance Magic

The figure on the Seven of Pentacles leans on his rake, thoughtfully reassessing the harvest he has reaped. The fruits of his labor burst abundantly in his garden, the tendrils suggesting further growth, and he appears to be thinking about what comes next. The Seven of Pentacles suggests an accumulation of material things, projects, and items.

We want so much from life, don't we? We want more, more, more. Credit cards make it all too simple to indulge in the immediate gratification of shopping now and considering the consequences at a later (fuzzy) date when the bill arrives. This can lead us into a closet jammed with clothes never worn, bathrooms filled with useless products, and kitchens bursting with gadgets hardly used. Even if you don't harbor shopaholic tendencies, it seems that if you have empty space, it will eventually become filled.

Abundance and money are wonderful things to have in your life. Before you start asking the world to shower you with more stuff, take a moment to step back and look at the massive amount of things you already have.

Look at the abundance in your life. Consider your healthy body. The people you love and who love you back. The animals you love. The food in your fridge. The clothes on your back. The electronic gadgets that make tasks simpler. The clean water cascading from your faucet and hot water available for a restorative shower. Music that lifts your spirits. Glance out your window or walk outside to welcome the abundance of life offered by blue skies, puffy clouds, brisk wind, warm sun, and lush grass. Do you realize how much you already have at your fingertips? Ponder the following:

Do I take care of the pentacles I already have?

Consider your relationships, finances, home, and body. Consider how you treat the abundance you already have been graced with. You may consider the archetype of a spoiled child who hungers for more and more toys while not appreciating what she's already got. Ask yourself:

Do I have items I can let go of?

We can pave the way for abundance and work attraction magic by appreciating what we already possess and clearing our clutter. This act creates space for new things to come to us.

Pick one area of your home where you desire abundance and perform the following exercise. As you clean, organize, and expel, imagine you are paving the way for new and wonderful things to come your way. Cement it with a physical action as suggested in the following activities.

The following activities are inspired by the Seven of Pentacles. Each activity also concludes with an extra tarot card whose energy may be invoked.

✦ Clothing and Fabulous Wardrobe Attraction

What would Lucy, the child from the *Chronicles of Narnia*, discover if she ventured into your wardrobe? Loads of unused clothes? Time to organize. If you haven't worn an item in a year, get rid of it. Clothing in need of repair or dry cleaning should be attended to. Look in a fashion magazine, find pictures of items you desire, and tape them to the inside of your closet. (The World)

✦ Finances and Money Attraction

If Suze Orman paid you a visit, what would she discover in your financial organization? Go through your financial filing systems and rid yourself of old papers and receipts you no longer need. Look at your budget, see where you are spending your money, and find an area you can save on. End by writing a financial goal and placing it where you can see it. (The Emperor)

✦ Kitchen and Nurturing Magic

If Julia Child were to manifest her spirit in your kitchen (and perhaps she has already, if you cook her famous recipes), what would she discover? The kitchen is where we nurture others and ourselves. Clean out that junk drawer; polish your pots so they sparkle like you (denture cleanser is an excellent secret weapon to polish up stainless steel). Time to clean the oven? No time like the present. Clear out your fridge and get rid of old condiments. Fill up your fridge with the superfoods suggested in the Nine of Pentacles exercise. (The Sun)

✦ Bathroom and Beauty Magic

If Cindy Crawford magically projected her five-foot-nine-inch frame into your bathroom, what would she find, rummaging in your medicine cabinet? Throw out old, used-up mascaras and products you don't use. Organize your hair products and soak your brushes and combs in the sink with a half cup baking soda and warm water for fifteen minutes. Clean and scrub away any dirt or grime in the tub. Pull a fresh look out of a beauty magazine and tape it on your mirror to inspire you the next time you get ready to leave the house looking fierce! (The Empress)

✦ Attic and Spiritual Magic

If the Dalai Lama chose to meditate in your attic, what would he find? If you have an attic, you can look at the upper recesses of your house as being a spiritual place—literally the highest level. While cleaning out those old boxes and cobwebs, attempt to connect with your higher wisdom, spirit guides, and astral friends. (The Hierophant)

✦ Basement and Subconscious Magic

If Oprah were to pull up a stool in your basement and interview you on the complexities of your childhood, would she be confronted with musty boxes, damp mattresses, and piles of old crafting supplies? We can understand basements and lower sections of the home as representing our unconscious. As you clean and organize, consider your unconscious inner pool. Visit thoughts, ideas, and dreams you rarely allow to rise to the surface. Consider how these basement feelings affect life on a regular level. (The Moon)

✦ Laundry Room and Cleansing Magic

If Martha Stewart were to pop over and throw in a load of laundry, would you be mortified? The simple act of washing laundry can be elevated to a magical level as you focus on the cleansing aspect of a washing machine. (The Star)

7 of Pentacles

Eight of Pentacles

A Spell for Work You Love

The figure on the Eight of Pentacles diligently hammers away. He is thoroughly engaged in his process. Examples of his craftsmanship hang for all to see and also form a ladder leading both upward toward spiritual manifestation and downward toward material expression. The Eight of Pentacles card is about taking pleasure in the work you do—seeing its fruitfulness, whether the work itself is displayed physically or it brings you money.

Do you work in a profession you adore? Do you find your work meaningful and satisfying? Is your work challenging enough to keep you satisfied? Does time cease and the world stop as you do your job?

There are plenty of people out there telling you that your work should feel like play and to do what you love, regardless of money. Well, yes! Duh! Wonderful in theory. What if you carry a tremendous financial burden? What if you don't know what your work should be? What if you are unsure of the direction you should head in? Does it ever feel like everyone but you has it figured out? What if you just plain don't know what you love to do?

Take a cue from the figure hammering away on the Eight of Pentacles. You may use the number eight as a magical reminder that eights contain the double stability of a four.

Create your sacred space, light a candle, and center yourself. Draw the Eight of Pentacles card.

List eight things you absolutely love to do. This can be as passive as watching television or as active as rock climbing. Do not worry about financial rewards; focus instead on things that bring you joy and capture your marvelous imagination. Then continue with these prompts:

+ List eight qualities you wish to enjoy in your life.

+ List eight subjects or books you studied in school and fell in love with.

+ List eight people whose work you admire and who inspire you.

+ List eight different professions you have at one point considered doing.

+ List eight pleasurable rewards from jobs you have already held or have.

+ List eight qualities people compliment you on.

+ List eight sleeping dreams you can recall.

+ List eight places you'd like to live.

Finish off by reciting the following:

Eight of Pentacles, work I love
I find that which fits me like a glove.
The work is me, my soul, my fire
Through work I gain my heart's desire.

An extra power boost for manifesting a professional direction to go in is to keep this card with you as you go about your day. Ask yourself diligently, each and every day: "What work should I be doing? What is the perfect job for me?" If you focus on this question and let your unconscious seek, you will receive the answer. I'd bet diva dollars on it.

Nine of Pentacles

Superfoods and a Million-Dollar Body Activity

The Nine of Pentacles depicts a gorgeous diva, sublimely blissful with herself and surroundings. The castle in the background implies familial inheritance akin to European vineyards that remain within families for generations. The falcon resting on her glove denotes loyalty. Secure and safe within her lush vineyard, this is a woman comfortable in her own solitude and delighted in her skin.

The Nine of Pentacles reminds us that while pentacles represent money, they often apply to issues surrounding our body image. Scientists over the years have attempted to calculate exactly how much money it would cost to construct a human body from scratch: to create our cells, eyeballs, nervous system, muscles, skin. Guess how much our bodies are worth? An estimated hundreds of millions would be spent, and to date, no one has been able to accomplish such a task. You are walking around in a multimillion-dollar body! If you owned a multimillion-dollar mansion, island, or jet, wouldn't you want to take care of it? More inspiring, your body provides temporary shelter for your soul. Priceless.

There is any number of ways to treat your body well. The easy way to nourish your body is through food. Every time you nibble on a snack or enjoy a meal is an opportunity to delight your taste buds and simultaneously take care of the million-dollar eyes you are using to read this book.

Take the Nine of Pentacles shopping with you—pop her in your bag and stock up on the nine superfoods listed below. Make sure to purchase and consume these divine superfoods in moderation and in accordance with any doctor's orders. Each time you bring one of these magical foods to your lips, remind yourself you are cherishing, cultivating, and healing yourself.

Apples: Apple skins are packed with antioxidants, the flesh is loaded with fiber, and an averaged-sized apple contains only 47 calories. Eat one a day to keep that doctor away. Use an apple's beauty power to bring him close if you desire. Magically, apples enhance beauty and health.

Avocado: Packed with fiber and healthy monounsaturated fats, an avocado is an outstanding superfood. Slice onto sandwiches, mash into dips, or eat raw with a sprinkling of sea salt. Place avocado paste on your skin for a refreshing mask. Avocados are great for fertility spells and encouraging lustful encounters.

Beans: Beans are a lowfat source of protein and fiber and can be incorporated into every diet. Add to soups, purée for dips, or use in cold salads. Beans, beans, the magic fruit…can be planted in the back yard with a magical wish.

Blueberries: Blueberries brimming with antioxidants are a sweet treat that may be consumed daily. Eat alone, mixed into yogurt, or baked into muffins. Magically, blueberries are marvelous for protection spells.

Broccoli: Broccoli is one of the most nutrient-dense foods available. Nibble it raw, sauté with a bit of garlic, or steam and drizzle with lemon. Use broccoli's vibrant green color to aid you in money manifestation spells.

Dark Chocolate: Dark chocolate lowers high blood pressure. Eat in small quantities to give yourself a healthy and indulgent treat. Use dark chocolate in love and lust attraction spells.

Nuts: Nuts are a great source of protein, fiber, and antioxidants. Eat small handfuls for snacks and replace for your highly saturated fats. Magically, use nuts for grounding energy.

Tomatoes: Tomatoes are full of lycopene, potassium, and fiber. Eat them raw and in sauces, pastas, and salads—they are the most versatile of foods. Magically, you may crush a tomato to squelch a bad habit.

Lowfat Yogurt: Yogurt is high in protein and calcium, and excellent for digestion. Enjoy for breakfast, a snack, or dessert. Use magically for moon spells and beauty enhancement.

✦ *All medical information was retrieved from superfoodsrx.com.*

Ten of Pentacles

Financial Windfall Spell

The Ten of Pentacles is packed to the brim with abundance. Money and people color the card. The Ten of Pentacles represents success, culmination, and financial stability. Interestingly, the Ten of Pentacles is the only card in the deck that shows a gateway, a doorway into a city. Tarot imagery is full of towers and villages, but only in the Ten of Pentacles do we find an entrance. We can look at this arch as the magical space between desire for money and its physical manifestation. The Rider-Waite deck depicts an older man, a grandfather perhaps, approaching the city. Ten pentacles follow him as if attached to his back by invisible strings. Before him are a couple and child, implying a generational theme.

Tens always suggest completion, curtains closing after the third act, applause at the end of the show. A ten of any suit implies the issue at hand is over. But like the World card, with an ending, the cycle begins anew with the Fool. So with a ten follows an ace. We can access this magical gate and utilize its energy to aid in bringing financial abundance to our lives.

Every now and again you need a financial boost. I'm talking cold, hard cash in your hands—money in the bank. This is a wonderful spell to perform when you need to attract some green. The locution of this spell is built upon the names of the ten Sephiroth on the Qabalistic Tree of Life (pictured on the opposite page). Sephiroth are the way "the Infinite" is revealed. It adds a delicious magical boost to your desired manifestation. For more Tree of Life tarot connections, visit Wald and Ruth Ann Amberstone's Tarot School online or in person.

Contemplate the Ten of Pentacles and feel the abundance packed into this picture, then gather the following:

✦ 10 dimes (dimes, worth ten pennies, again represent 10)

✦ Peppermint tea

✦ Green candle

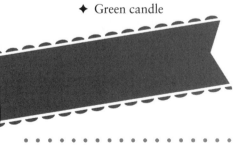

Prepare your tea so it is ready to sip while performing the spell. Let the peppermint remind you that the money is coming toward you in an exciting, energetic way.

Light your green candle and call to the four corners and your higher self.

Seriously, with feeling, begin placing dimes on top of your Ten of Pentacles card, beginning with the pentacle at the top. As you place each dime over a pentacle on the card, recite the following phrases:

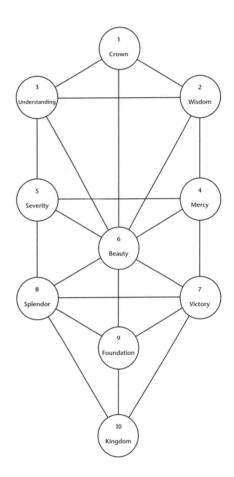

Crown: "This coin represents the crowning achievements that attract money."

Wisdom: "This coin represents the wisdom of my financial choices."

Understanding: "This coin represents the understanding of my financial responsibility."

Mercy: "This coin represents the compassion and mercy with which I use my money."

Severity: "This coin represents overcoming financial hardships."

Beauty: "This coin represents the beauty I spread as a result of attracting money."

Victory: "This coin represents my victorious attitude toward money."

Splendor: "This coin represents the splendor of my abundance."

Foundation: "This coin represents my solid financial foundation."

Kingdom: "This coin represents the kingdom, the life I create with my riches."

Recite the following chant:

> Money, money, comes to me
> You find me so easily.
> Abundance packed, I feel the wealth
> Coins increase as does my health.
> My family is flush with cash
> I can feel my money stash.
> Our bank account does grow
> It piles up like pounds of snow!

Do any other meditation or work you'd like before closing your magical space.

SUIT OF *Cups*

Ace of Cups

Aces always represent a fresh start, a new beginning, and a gift. An ace is the first card of the suit. Imagine a clothing designer staging a fashion show in Paris. The designer begins with a basic theme or inspiration and builds upon it. The fashion show commences; the clothing becoming more dramatic and intense as the show unfolds. The same thing happens in each of the four suits of tarot in the run between ace and ten. Consider the ace a little black dress and the ten a wedding gown.

Many aces in tarot contain a mysterious hand emerging from a cloud. Is it a coincidence? I think not. The hand offers a gift. The gift offered in the Ace of Cups is love, emotion, feelings, art, compassion, empathy, and your ability to experience all of it.

The Ace of Cups can signify the start of a new relationship (you meet a new friend you have an immediate liking for), a new love (you realize you harbor a crush for someone you know), or a new emotional understanding (perhaps you cry freely as you finish reading an amazing novel). You feel free, clear, and emotionally open.

The overflowing cup on the Ace of Cups suggests emotion that flows freely and unbounded. Think of an actress's reaction upon receiving an Academy Award, your open emotional state while watching a great film, or the happy feeling you get when goofing around with little kids.

Gratitude Exercise

The easiest way to access Ace of Cups energy is through this gratitude exercise.

Do This Exercise When You Are:

- ✦ Feeling emotionally blocked

- ✦ Feeling sad

- ✦ In need of love

- ✦ Beginning your day with joy

Experiencing gratitude takes the attention off yourself and firmly places it on the world and the gifts around you. You'll feel lighter, better, happier, and ready to experience the delight your day has in store for you.

To invite Ace of Cups energy, place the card where you can see it. Fill in the blanks below, writing your answers on a separate piece of paper or journal.

I'm thankful for my friends for _____, and I am grateful because _____.

I'm so happy about _____, and I am grateful because _____.

I'm lucky _____, and I am grateful because _____.

It makes me feel good when I _____, and I am grateful because _____.

I am so in love with _____, and I am grateful because _____.

When I open myself up to joy, _____, and I am grateful because _____.

My favorite music is _____, and I am grateful because _____.

Someone who always inspires me is _____, and I am grateful because _____.

Two of Cups

Spell to Attract a Soul Mate

The Two of Cups represents meeting your heart's desire. Remember, cups represent feelings, love, and emotion. Twos in tarot represent duality, choice, and opposites. The imagery on the card shows a wedding ceremony. When the Two of Cups appears in a reading, it represents finding the companion who suits you and the joy of your heart found in another. This other could be a person, soul mate, child, or spouse. It can represent anything that fits you like a glove or the Cinderella shoe.

We all want to meet our heart's desire with open arms. If you are looking for a special someone, use the Two of Cups to help you attract it. A tarot diva knows she can attract just the thing she needs with her deck of cards, so what are you waiting for? Bring on the love!

This spell has been created especially for you to attract your soul mate. It is the seriousness of your intention that gives magic its power. You are releasing your intention to the universe and manifesting your desire.

> Take your time.
>
> Read the instructions carefully.
>
> Try to forget about the spell once you have cast it. Let your magic work for you.
>
> Perform this spell on a Friday.

Ingredients

> Bath salts
>
> Body scrub
>
> Two of Cups card
>
> Pink candle
>
> Lighter (do not use matches to light the candle)
>
> New pen (pink ink if possible)
>
> Fresh piece of paper
>
> Piece of your favorite dark chocolate or small piece of chocolate cake

Two of Cups

Cups

2

Create a Magical Cleansing Bath

You will begin with a magical bath. The purpose of this bath is to calm, center, and bring your awareness to the spell you are about to perform.

Clean your bathtub and fill with hot water. Add a cup of bath salts for protection.

Hold your hands over the water and state three times: "This spell attracts my soul mate."

Enter tub.

As you soak in the tub, imagine you are surrounded by shining silver light. Breathe deeply and imagine the light circulating around you.

When you breathe in, take cleansing breaths.

When you exhale, feel negativity and stress releasing. The silver light around you becomes brighter and cleaner.

Before you exit the tub, use the body scrub to exfoliate your skin. This process clears away the old and makes way for a fresh start.

Exit bath and get ready to cast your spell!

Cast Your Spell

You will call to the energies of the four suits of tarot for aid in your spell.

Face east and say: "I call to the powers of the cups to aid me in my spell."

Face south and say: "I call to the powers of the wands to aid me in my spell."

Face west and say: "I call to the powers of the pentacles to aid me in my spell."

Face north and say: "I call to the powers of the swords to aid me in my spell."

Center yourself and say: "I call to my higher powers to aid me in my spell."

Light your pink candle with the lighter.

Place the Two of Cups tarot card where you can see it. The Two of Cups contains love attraction energy.

Sit down with your new pen and new paper and begin to write the following:

> I am (your name).
> I am unique and wonderful.
> I am worthy of a romance full of
> love, security, and joy.
> I respect myself as I respect others.
> I participate in healthy relationships.

I accept only positive energy and
people into my personal space.
When I love, I love fully and completely,
and I receive nothing but the same.
Assist me in drawing my soul mate to me.
My partner will be (fill in a trait).
My partner will be (fill in another trait).
My partner will be (fill in another trait).
My partner will be (fill in another trait).
My partner will be (fill in another trait).

Recite your written words three times. Recite with as much feeling as you can muster.
Now, recite the following statement (you don't need to write this):

Sun, earth, moon, stars
I see my soul mate where they are.
Earth, moon, stars, sun
Now my spell has just begun.
Moon, stars, sun, earth
To this relationship I give birth.
Stars, sun, earth, moon
Draw him to me very soon.

If there is anything else you would like to do in your magical space, do it now. Take as long as
you like.

When you are finished, thank your higher powers and the four corners/directions/suits for aiding
you in your work, and recite the following:

With love and peace and harm to none
I now declare this spell is done!

Eat your chocolate treat and think about how sweet your life is.
You may leave your candle burning as long as you like, extinguishing it when you are ready.

• • • • • • • • • • • • • • • • • •

Three of Cups

Form a Secret Society

The Three of Cups shows three maidens, their cups raised for a toast. (A modern version would likely show the *Sex and the City* girls saluting with their Cosmo cocktails.) The maidens are free, in an open field, and removed from the constraints of a town. Vegetation growing on the ground indicates something marvelous has manifested.

I'm about to let you in on a little secret—a secret that changed my life! It is something you can and should do. This secret is strongly implied within the Three of Cups. This card is about friendship and championing one another. The Three of Cups is about supporting your group and having each other's back. A girl is nothing without her gal pals, her posse. My advice to you, diva? Start a secret society. Why should the Skull and Bones, the Freemasons, and the Golden Dawn have all the fun? Some girlfriends of mine had recently suggested getting together to do goal setting. We took it one step further…

Business professionals often pair up with what are called success partners, support systems with whom they set business goals. They check in weekly to be sure each member is taking appropriate steps. In a group like Alcoholics Anonymous, you are assigned an accountability partner. By the way, AA has the greatest success rate of any group like it. Why? *Accountability*.

Why not combine a covert society with goals, magic, accountability, and some good old-fashioned fun? This is a marvelous excuse not only to spend time with friends but to champion, aid, and celebrate each other on a weekly basis. Just think: once a week, you can focus on objectives, support, and friendship. You'll be surprised how helpful a secret society can be on a number of levels. Here's how to do it:

Select Your Members

Simplicity is key when forming your group. Three is an ideal number of members to begin with. In tarot, three is the number of creativity. Three offers a group feeling and also emulates the Three of Cups. If one member is unavailable, the other two can always meet. Plus, three is not too overwhelming to coordinate or organize.

Write Your Mission Statement

What is the goal, the aim, of your clandestine society? Do you offer each other emotional support? Inspiration? Accountability? Friendship? Philanthropy? Look at the Seven of Cups. The figure on the card gazes at swirling possibilities. Your society can be anything you choose it to be. Select your goals with care.

The goals of our society are based on the advancement of our members. We help each other live the most complete, happy, and fulfilling life possible. We help each other stay on track; we offer kind ears and helpful suggestions for moving forward. In one year of secret society meetings, one sister paid off her considerable credit card debt, another sister found the apartment of her dreams, and I watched my business boom!

Plan Your Meetings on a Calendar

Any society worth its salt has regular meetings. Create a meet-up schedule and stick to it. Regular meetings will ensure your success. This helps to integrate meetings into a regular, dependable habit.

Pick Your Meeting Spot

Will you meet at an undisclosed location? At each other's homes? At a coffee shop? We move our location around based on our schedules. We meet at our apartments, over picnics in Central Park, and even in a tony restaurant. Imagine our delight reciting our opening ritual in the midst of a crowded hot spot with no one the wiser!

Create an Opening Ritual

An opening ritual can be as simple as each member lighting a candle and dedicating themselves to the group for the duration of the meeting: "I, _____ , dedicate myself to _____ and _____ to listen, support, and inspire us on our journey." It can be as intricate as memorized phrases, hand signals, and secret languages.

Do not bypass the opening ritual at each meeting. It sets the stage and marks the space as sacred and special. This means cell phones off, outside world at bay. It is in the sacred space of your society that you get meaningful work done.

Create a Closing Ritual

Just as the opening ritual marks your space as sacred, it is important to close the space when you are finished. Once again, this could be a simple or intricate process. You may just reverse your opening ritual, thank the members, and extinguish your candles.

Create an Initiation Ceremony

Secret societies throughout the ages have used intricate initiation ceremonies. The point of initiation is to dedicate yourself to the group and be reborn into your group's ideals. You can see initiation in the Eight of Swords card. Notice the figure is hoodwinked, blindfolded, and bound. When she is released, she will view the world through a new set of eyes.

Decide on the Order of Business

How will your group go about doing its work? Will you each set aside half an hour for each member to talk about what is going on in their lives? Will you make a list of weekly goals? Will other members help you be accountable for them?

Plan Time for Reassessment

Like a marriage, a secret society needs room to grow. Your society will grow and change according to the needs of its members. Plan time to reevaluate; make sure members are meeting their needs, and reassess as needed. Don't be afraid to amend your mission statement.

Recordkeeping Devices

It's fun to have matching notebooks to record your notes. This also marks your growth within the society. I bet you'll be surprised after a year of secret society meetings to see how much you've blossomed as a group. You can put secret symbols on the cover, inside, and all around your notebook.

Select a Name

Maybe your title is "The Society for Fierce Chicks of the World" or "The International Association of Tarot Divas" or "The Love and Light Society"? It doesn't matter if your title is lighthearted or serious. What matters is that it resonates with your members and reflects how fabulous you are.

Make Sure Your Secret Society Is Fun

Plans weekend getaways, spa trips, and yearly retreats. If it ain't fun, you won't do it. Make it fabulous and fun; pamper yourselves while moving ahead in your covert operations!

Four of Cups

Tarot Spread with Music

The Four of Cups card depicts a fellow looking glum. He seemingly ignores an offering while seated beneath a tree. Does he notice his gift? Is he about to discover it? Is he so wrapped in his own thoughts he misses the opportunity in front of him? That hand looks surprisingly like an ace hand and cloud, doesn't it?

Fours in tarot always imply stability. The truth is, we all have our emotional ups and downs or we wouldn't be human. The trick is, if we are having a down day or indulging in a moment of melancholia, we should not don blinders. A tarot diva understands that even when she's not feeling one hundred percent, she can still look for the good surrounding her.

Music is a wonderful way of arousing the subconscious and altering our mood. Why not combine music with tarot cards? Set your iPod to a random shuffle so you don't know what song will play. Play music that carries an emotional attachment. I often used a Sting playlist. Sting works beautifully; his lyrics always contain stories and parables, which is very compatible with tarot cards. And if you have access to the lyrics, all the better. By combining the music and the cards, you'll receive a powerful reading.

Select your playlist, set on random shuffle (but don't turn it on yet), and thoughtfully shuffle your tarot cards. Place four cards in front of you, face-down. Now, hit play on your iPod. Listen to what song comes on and turn over the first tarot card.

Use the following questions for each card:

Tarot Card 1: Why am I feeling this way?

Tarot Card 2: How can I get out of my own way?

Tarot Card 3: What opportunity is right in front of me that I do not see?

Tarot Card 4: Knowing this, what can I do now?

Find the answer to your first question in the music. For the duration of the song, listen and gaze at your card. How does the song affect the message from your tarot card? Do your random song's lyrics match the card's meaning or contradict it? Spend the duration of the song absorbed in your card and let your mind go where it needs to.

As the second song comes on, flip tarot card number 2, and so on…

You will want to record your reading in a notebook. Music adds a deeper dimension to the reading. It is uncanny the way each card's meaning is supported by the song that plays with it. It is a rich and visceral experience, and you might even feel a bit better.

Five of Cups

Spell to Break an Addiction

Fives in tarot are the roughest numbers to wrestle with, as fives present a challenge. I view the Five of Cups as the addiction card. The gentleman in the black cloak on the Five of Cups looks so dejected, so sad.

The Five of Cups representing addiction is easily viewed in the context of the image placed on the card. We understand the three spilled cups as the addiction, be it drugs, cigarettes, sex, negative thought patterns, booze, gambling, food: take your pick. We understand the two cups behind the caped figure as more of the same vile fluid. This card represents the point at which you make a decision…choice time.

If the fellow (you) turns back to drink what is left in the two full cups, the addiction has won. If he chooses to walk away and cross the distant bridge, you prevail over the addiction. You can understand the castle in the distance as all of the comforts and happiness you can imagine—the life you wish for, long for, hope for…

My sister runs a rehabilitation center in California. The first thing she will tell you about any issue or addiction is that the root is emotion. Cups in tarot are filled with emotion. She'll tell you emotions can't hurt you by themselves—they're just feelings. Feel them.

Take out this card and perform this spell when you want to break a nasty habit. The habit could be a substance, thought pattern, or person.

This spell has been created especially for you to rid yourself of addiction. It is the seriousness of your intention that gives magic its power. You are releasing your intention to the universe in order to manifest your desire.

Take your time.

Read the instructions carefully.

Try to forget about the spell once you have cast it. Let your magic work for you.

If possible, perform this spell during the waning moon.

Ingredients

> Five of Cups card
>
> The Sun card
>
> 2 pieces of paper
>
> Pen
>
> Small black candle
>
> A sharp object to carve your candle with, such as a nail
>
> Lighter
>
> Ashtray or flameproof plate/bowl

Cast Your Spell

Your candle is indicative of the man in the black cloak on the card. It will absorb the negative energy.

Inscribe your addiction onto your candle with a sharp object.

Light the candle.

You will call to the energies of the suits of tarot for aid in your spell.

Hold the candle in your hands as you recite the following:

> Face east and say: "I call to the powers of the cups to aid me in my spell."
>
> Face south and say: "I call to the powers of the wands to aid me in my spell."
>
> Face west and say: "I call to the powers of the pentacles to aid me in my spell."
>
> Face north and say: "I call to the powers of the swords to aid me in my spell."
>
> Center yourself and say: "I call to my higher powers to aid me in my spell."

Gaze at the Five of Cups and ponder your issue. When ready, write your addiction on a slip of paper.

On the second piece of paper, write the following:

I am (your name).

I am strong and powerful.

(Your addiction) no longer holds

any power over me.

I believe it is possible to stop this behavior.

I am ready to deal with the issues

that have caused it.

I have new coping tools to aid me.

I will maintain my new life until it becomes

normal and ceases to be any work.

I love myself.

I love my healthy body.

I love my healthy mind.

Now recite this out loud three times.

Recite the following statement (you don't need to write this):

Water flows

My addiction goes.

The cups that spill

They do my will.

Cups that stand

Offer a helping hand.

Thunder crash and lightning strike

I am now free to be as I like.

Take the slip of paper with your former addiction written on it and burn it in the ashtray.

Take a long gaze at the Sun card.

Feel the warmth of the sun around you and a powerful yellow energy surrounding you. It energizes and fills you with health.

Enter the bathroom and draw a healing bath or shower. Play music you adore. As the water drains, remain in the tub. Imagine your addictive behavior diminishing as the water flows down the pipes, carrying your addictive habits with it.

Once out of the bathroom, recite the following:

> With love and peace and harm to none
> I now declare this spell is done!

Let the black candle burn down until it has absorbed all negative energy caused by your addiction. Keep the Sun card in a visible place to remind you of what you have accomplished.

Six of Cups

"Take the Good, Release the Bad" Spell

The Six of Cups is often understood as the card of childhood friends, happy memories, and general well-being. We see an older child generously handing a younger child the gift of a cup filled with flowers. They are enclosed in a town, which offers protection and symbolizes home. Yet, in the background of the Rider-Waite deck, we see a figure moving away.

I've always understood this card as something deeper than just happy memories. To me, the Six of Cups symbolizes the emotional makeup we inherit from our family—those who have gone before us and influenced us.

Every family has its issues, right? Take your pick. Perhaps your family is wildly funny, with a streak of addiction running through it? Maybe your family is emotionally stoic and serious, yet genius at business? Maybe your family is a hot mess?

Six of Cups

As children, we can't pick our family. We deal with the cards we are dealt. As adults, we have the choice of what familial behavior we will embrace and what we will cleverly discard. This is how we grow and evolve into our unique selves. This is also how we change family patterns.

For instance, my family is wickedly creative and fun, yet issues of self-esteem and emotional coldness thrive. Throw in a history of depression, alcoholism, and generations of money mismanagement, and we have quite a potent family brew. I want all the creativity and thirst for life, but I want to control my finances, I don't need to battle addictions, and goodness knows I want to stay emotionally open, both for my own sake and for the sake of others around me.

A tarot diva knows she can engage the good and disregard the bad to lead the most fulfilling life possible. A tarot diva knows that she is in charge of her life and that what happened in the past occurred to make her the unique and fabulous individual she is today.

Here is a powerful spell and exercises in which you will embrace all that is wonderful in your family—and reject what you do not need or want.

Write Your Family Story

Sit down like a novelist and sketch out your family story. Who are the main players? What are the stories your family always told about you? What is the theme that connects your family? What is the storyline here? What does your family's story say about you?

Write Your Future Role

What role do you play in your family? How would you like to play this role in the future? Tarot divas understand that the future is fluid. How will you change your family's future by your actions?

Pick Your Favorite Family Member

We all have family members we adore and family members we could do without. Perhaps you had a divine grandmother but a creepy, molesting uncle. Who are the most notorious characters? Who are the people you idolize and wish to emulate? Pick one person, dead or living, who above all others carries the qualities you cherish.

Select a Family Recipe

Pick a dish to cook or simmer on the stove. Most of us have certain meals that remind us of home. For me, it's a slow-roasted chicken and mashed potatoes. Pick a family meal you can easily prepare. If you can't think of any, use a roasted chicken (or a vegetarian equivalent if you're a vegetarian).

Prepare Your Kitchen

Place the Six of Cups tarot card where you can see it while cooking (don't get any grease on it!). Charm your kitchen with the following incantation:

Earth, air, fire, water
I cook today, my family's daughter.
I nurture the good and expel the bad
Happiness and love is to be had.
I keep what's needed, toss what's not
A bright, shiny future I cook inside this pot.

Cook the Family Recipe

Proceed to cook your meal.

As you slice, cut away, or boil off something—anything you expel—imagine you are discarding the bad behavior and negative habits.

As you roast, simmer, and bring out the flavor of the food, imagine you are nurturing and bringing to the surface all of the good qualities you want to embrace and emulate.

Set a Place for Your Guest of Honor

Your guest of honor is the family member you have chosen as your favorite. You may invite them to dinner. If they are unavailable or have passed on, set a place in honor of their remembrance. They will be there in spirit.

As you eat your meal, think about how far you've come. Think about the roads you've traveled and how you experience the world each day. Remember that with every move you make, you are creating history. You will wake up in the morning feeling lighter yet more powerful than ever, having expelled the bad and invited the good.

Seven of Cups

Lookbook Activity

The Seven of Cups shows a fellow looking at myriad marvelous possibilities. He hasn't chosen yet but stands dazzled as potential plays before him like flickering images on a movie screen. Like a wall of dreams, the floating cups are all connected to Major Arcana cards. (Look to see if you can figure out what Major Arcana card each cup is connected to. After guessing, find the answers on the next page.)

Diva, there comes a point in time when you must choose. We can find ourselves being caught up in the role of people pleasing, putting others ahead of ourselves and letting others dictate what we like or don't like. You must develop your own distinctive point of view. Your point of view can be about anything—your clothing style, your home decoration, your environmental views, your lifestyle, etc. This comes easier to some of us than to others. If there is an area in which you are not sure about how you feel, here is a simple and fun exercise. Are you stuck in a Hanged Man fashion moment as described on page 126? Create a lookbook. By creating a lookbook, you embody the Seven of Cups, then move a step further to develop your point of view.

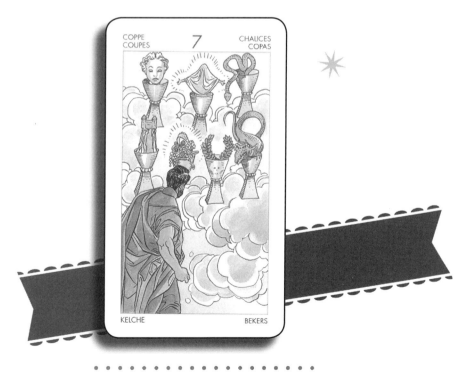

Lookbooks are often used by models and fashion designers to showcase their work. You can think of a lookbook as a portfolio. A lookbook is different from a vision board, which is created and displayed as a reminder of what you want to manifest. A lookbook is a process by which you discover and uncover themes you are attracted to and bring them all together. You can then bring these themes, these points of view, into your life.

Thumb through magazines, search the Internet, and take stock of what you like and don't like. Sit back like the CEO of a large company and ask the magazines to impress you. Leafing through the magazines, pull out any page containing something appealing to you. Perhaps it is a color, a texture, a lifestyle, or a room. Cut out images, textures, clothes, and all applicable items you are drawn to. Do not judge. Do not edit.

When you have successfully gone through all your mags, sort by color, theme, style. Paste it all together in a notebook according to color and style—blues on one page, greens on the next. Do you see a theme emerging?

Major Arcana connections, clockwise from the top left cup: the beautiful face is connected to the Empress, the veiled figure is the High Priestess, the snake is the belt from the Magician, the fire-breathing dragon corresponds to the Sun, the laurel wreath is connected the World card, the jewels are connected to the Wheel of Fortune, and the towers literally correspond to the Tower.

Eight of Cups

Writing Exercise

The Eight of Cups marks a unique moment in time. The Eight of Cups is the moment you move away from behavior, attitudes, and feelings that no longer aid you in any way. The Eight of Cups signifies great change, yet it is not as obvious as the change signified in the Death card or the Tower. The Eight of Cups marks a true moment of emotional growth. It is the moment you move into your future.

The Eight of Cups shows a figure moving onward and upward. He is indicative of the Hermit, yet he leaves something behind. What remains in the cups he has abandoned? The moon passes over the sun in a solar eclipse. Have you ever witnessed a solar eclipse? It is a unique astral event that happens once every few years. Solar eclipses cast a strange light as the nocturnal moon passes before the daytime sun.

What do you make of this card, my tarot diva?

What are the moments that defined you
in your emotional life?

How old were you when you realized your parents
had a life of their own?

How old were you when you left home,
and where did you move to?

When and how have you succeeded,
even if no one believed in you?

What was the moment you grew up?

When did you willingly walk away from
a relationship that no longer served you?

What relationships have you said no to?

What are you willing to leave behind
in order to move forward?

Nine of Cups

Can't Fail Spread

The Nine of Cups is the card that happily states your wish *will* come true. Notice the grinning genie on the face of the card? He is smiling, arms crossed, because he is ready to grant your wish. The nine cups behind him are filled with all the things that satisfy you.

So here's my question to you, tarot diva: *what would make you happy?* Better yet, I'd like to pose one of my favorite questions to you: *what would you do if you knew you couldn't fail?*

Yes, what if the failure option didn't exist? What if fear didn't stop you? You'd glide through life. You'd have exactly what you want. The marvelous thing about human nature is that, once you master something, you are already onto the next. This spread gives you an opportunity to take a good, hard look at what you desire and provides a roadmap on how to accomplish it. Because, let's face it—when you put your heart and soul behind a desire, there's no way you can't make it happen!

What Would You Do If You Knew You Couldn't Fail?

Pick one thing you would do if you knew you couldn't fail at it. Take your time. Do not choose haphazardly. This is an important question. Write your answer on a piece of paper.

The cards are placed in a stairway-spread configuration, created by my brilliant tarot teacher Ruth Ann Amberstone. The card formation literally is the steps to take for your desired outcome.

Select three cards:

+ Card one is your suggested first step. It could be a small step—a phone call or conversation. Decide as you look at the card what your first step is, then write it down and take it!

+ Card two is a suggestion of what to do next.

+ Card three suggests you've got that ball rolling and what you should do to keep up the momentum.

Repeat this spread as often as you need to, and keep climbing those stairs!

Ten of Cups

Self-Love Spell

We see the nuclear family rejoicing under a rainbow in the Ten of Cups. The card of contentment and culmination, the Ten of Cups is the "happily ever after" card. Our fairy tales lead us astray when we discover there is much more to be lived and learned after our supposed happy ending.

We long to fulfill our dreams. Our happy ending may be professional ("I'll be happy when I get that promotion"), personal ("I just want to get married already"), cries for fame ("If I'm famous, then I'll really be loved"), or cries for fortune ("I'd be happy if only I were rich"). It is a stinging slap on the cheek when we pursue a goal, achieve it, and then don't feel any different. Satisfaction in our lives does not depend on outward circumstances or supposed happy endings. Happy endings lie inside yourself and do not hinge on outward circumstance.

The key to living out the Ten of Cups is connected with your own feeling of self-love and worth. We all come equipped with our own happiness barometer—the place where we hover in terms of emotional satisfaction. Outward circumstances, say winning the lottery, do not make for long-term happiness if the person winning is not already a generally happy person. Conversely, a person with a high happiness barometer, even after suffering the loss of a limb via freak accident, will generally retain the same level of satisfaction after their misfortune. A year or two after a life-changing event, people tend to resume their same happiness level. Where does your happiness barometer hover?

Let's take the Ten of Cups card. Return to the first page of your story. Start with yourself.

Perform this spell, if possible, during the daytime and in natural light. Remember, the Ten of Cups is a happy daytime card. Plus, a daytime bath is the ultimate in luxury…like a trip to a spa.

Purchase children's body paint for the bath, found in any drugstore.

Draw a bath and fill with cleansing salts and yummy flavors. Slice up a lemon and toss into your bath water. Strip naked and look at yourself in the mirror. Examine every inch of your body. Talk to your body. Tell every inch that you love it.

Take your body paint and write *I love me, I love my elbow, I love my boobs, I love my thighs* over said body parts. Get creative and write whatever feels good to you. Draw arrows to what you really love. Point the way. You may even want to photograph yourself in the mirror to remember this loving feeling.

Now, step into your bath, all written up like a novel. Use an exfoliating scrub on yourself. Scrub under your arms, between your legs, between your toes; work over every inch of your body. Imagine as the rough skin flakes off that you are born again. The words are scrubbed off and you are set free. Feel free to shave and perform any body primping that makes you feel gorgeous and light.

Let the water run out of the tub while you remain in the bath. As you feel the water ebbing, feel your body being born again. Let your skin air-dry. Like a queen or a princess, primp and enjoy your happy ending.

I don't understand why people talk of art as a luxury when it's a mind-altering possibility.

Jeanette Winterson

SUIT OF *Swords*

Ace of Swords

Aces in tarot always represent a fresh start, a new beginning, a gift. An ace is the beginning, the first card of the suit. An ace is where everything is established. Think of a novelist. Every book begins with one thing: an idea. The writer takes this clever concept and diligently writes about it. In tarot, the novelist's idea can be seen as an ace, while the finished manuscript is a ten.

Many aces in tarot depict a hand emerging from a cloud, and this hand offers a gift. The Ace of Swords offers clarity, thinking, communication, ideas, and your ability to experience all of it. The Ace of Swords can signify a stellar idea (you've found inspiration for a project), a new way of understanding a situation (you need a vacation), a solution to a problem (you can afford a cleaning person), and cutting through to the heart of the matter (you need to let go of negative people in order to move forward).

The sword pictured on the card (your mind) pierces through a crown (your genius idea). Think of a moment when a good idea hit you and you knew you were onto something.

Gratitude Exercise

The easiest way to usher in Ace of Swords energy is through this gratitude exercise.

Do This Exercise When You Are:

✦ In need of inspiration

✦ Wanting to communicate better with others

✦ Trapped in negative thought patterns

✦ Seeking clarity of thought

✦ Writing

Experiencing gratitude takes the attention off yourself and places it on the world and gifts around you. You'll feel lighter, better, happier, and ready to experience the smart ideas, calm mind, and excellent communication of which you are capable.

To invite Ace of Swords energy, place the card where you can see it. Fill in the blanks below, writing your answers on a separate piece of paper or in a journal.

I'm a great thinker because I _____, and I am grateful because _____.

I make excellent decisions because I _____, and I am grateful because _____.

I feel clever when I _____, and I am grateful because _____.

My mind feels calm when I _____, and I am grateful because _____.

I get it right when I _____, and I am grateful because _____.

Fresh ideas come to me when I _____, and I am grateful because _____.

I sleep well when I _____, and I am grateful because _____.

I communicate well when I _____, and I am grateful because _____.

Opening my mind to new ideas _____, and I am grateful because _____.

Your own words are the bricks and
mortar of the dreams you want to realize.
Behind every word flows energy.

Sonia Choquette

Two of Swords

Forgiveness Milk Moon Bath

The Two of Swords speaks of venturing deep into one's inner self for meditation and contemplation, closing one's eyes to the outside world via the blindfold and protecting oneself via two swords. The water in the background evokes the High Priestess. When the Two of Swords appears in a reading, it means there is a deeper issue at play. One must figure out what it is.

A diva wants the freedom to be herself. The entire suit of swords illustrates the way our mind, our thoughts, can hold us captive. Do you harbor anger over past issues? Are you smoldering over events that occurred long ago? Past issues sometimes clench us in their grasp and we don't even realize it. The seriousness within the Two of Swords requests we venture deeper to find out if we are holding tight to an issue. We may be reacting to events without realizing it.

The milk moon bath is not a complete recipe for forgiveness; rather, it's a first step. This exercise may yield surprising results. You may discover suppressed issues that shockingly rise to the surface. Know that this is the first step to living a life free of the bonds of the past. You can forgive a person without inviting him or her back into your life. You may find forgiveness for people who are dead and long gone. Finding peace with others and with yourself, you set yourself free.

Draw this moon bath on an evening when you will not be disturbed. Prepare to do serious thinking. The moon pictured on the Two of Swords reminds us of our connection to our deepest self, the self connected to the High Priestess.

Embody a water nymph and draw on the mysterious female power of the moon to aid you. Have you ever bathed, danced, or made love in moonlight? It is a magical experience. You needn't have a pool in the back yard or tub next to a window, but if you do, all the better. The milk in this bath mix creates ivory water and fills you with the luminosity and brilliance of the moon. The mix will offer enough for four bath soaks.

Prepare this mix:

> 2 cups dry milk
>
> 1 tablespoon cornstarch
>
> 2 teaspoons each dried lavender and thyme

Mix ingredients in blender and place a half cup in your bath. Unclothe yourself and enter the white waters of your tub.

- ◆ As you soak, think about your parents. Are you still holding anger about what they did or didn't do for you as a child?

- ◆ Consider the relationship you hold with your lover. Are you holding grudges over past arguments and issues?

- ◆ Consider your children. Are you angry or disappointed with them in any way?

- ◆ Consider your friends. Are you upset by the way they treat you?

- ◆ Consider your relatives. Are you still angry over the way they act toward you?

- ◆ Consider the world in general. Are you angry over something a politician has done or angry at the universe for your current situation?

- ◆ Consider yourself. Are you angry at choices made and actions taken?

When you have gone through your mental list of relationships and grudges, see if you have it within yourself to forgive these things.

If so, unplug the bath. Let the waters flow down the drain and feel anger slipping away, down the pipes. As the water flows away from your body and your skin feels the air, feel yourself being reborn.

Exit the bathroom. You might choose to wear a white nightgown like the figure pictured on the Two of Swords. Open your tarot journal.

Write down the thoughts that occurred to you in the tub. Were you surprised by your findings? If you detected old anger floating around, how do you think you might alleviate it? How do you think you might begin forgiving them? See what comes up. Choose a path of forgiveness. You may choose a mantra, a daily meditation, and dedicate your physical exercise practice to it. However you choose to bring forgiveness to your life, know that forgiving has little to do with the other person and everything to do with yourself.

> Nobody can make you feel inferior
> without your permission.
> **Eleanor Roosevelt**

Three of Swords

Julia Cameron's Morning Pages Exercise

The Three of Swords typically describes heartache, distress, and pain. A quick glance at three swords penetrating a heart is simple enough to interpret. At times, the Three of Swords represents a love triangle, causing emotional distress. Look beyond textbook meanings of the cards and recall how swords relate to issues of the mind—*your* mind. How often do we hold ourselves captive with our mental thoughts and anguish?

Artist, author, and teacher Julia Cameron offers an amazing series of exercises in her book *The Artist's Way* to set you free of mental constraints and blocks. The cornerstone of her book, the most important of her exercises, are morning pages. Morning pages work like magic to alleviate any swords—ideas or issues—stuck in your heart or head.

Julia, a darling teacher and fierce diva whom I've had the pleasure to study with, recommends you wake up first thing in the morning and record three pages of freehand, free-thought writing. These pages need not make sense, need not be grammatically correct, and need not be anything other than your stream of conscious. An example would be, "Im so sleepy just want to go back to bed dont feel like facing the world and I really like the song playing right now why does my back hurt I need a massage…"

By performing this exercise on a daily basis, you literally remove any swords that are piercing your heart and mind. You have a chance to vent your anguish, thoughts, and fears before you've even had your coffee. On the opposite end of the spectrum, you may be recording euphoric, exciting, and thoughtful entries. Regardless of the context, you enter your day lighter and freer by having already expressed yourself. I can't think of a better way to combat the pain pictured on the Three of Swords.

Everything begins with language.
Language begins with listening.

Jeanette Winterson

What You Need:

    A notebook specifically for morning pages

    Pen

    20 minutes of alone time as soon as you wake up

Each morning, as you rise, write three pages in freeform thought. You may have to set your alarm twenty minutes earlier, but it is well worth it. You may do this activity to clear your mind before selecting your card of the day. Send those swords flying away and embody the peaceful state of mind found in the Four of Swords card.

Write your morning pages every day, not only when feeling Three of Swords energy. The marvelous quality of this exercise is that it helps you work through whatever emotional state you wake up with, helping to exercise it and free your mind.

THREE OF SWORDS

Four of Swords

Inner Peace Meditation

The suit of swords mostly depicts scenes of strife and confusion. The Four of Swords offers peace, respite, and the stability implied by the number four. The stability available in this card is the stability of the mind—a pause in thoughts, and rest. You see the figure resting inside a church, a building that implies safety and protection. Light shines through the illuminated stained glass window, denoting qualities that are bright on the outside when you've found peace on the inside.

The hands of the figure resting are in the sign of Christian prayer or the Hindu gesture of namaste, an expression of reverence in cultures spanning the globe. When the Four of Swords appears in a reading, it implies you can rest easy. We can use this card to encourage peace and calmness by engaging upon a simple meditation. You will embody the figure depicted in The Four of Swords. Lie down in a comfortable spot. Place your hands beside you, although you may assume the prayer position as the figure on the card does. You may also place a pillow beneath your feet to increase comfort and blood flow to the heart.

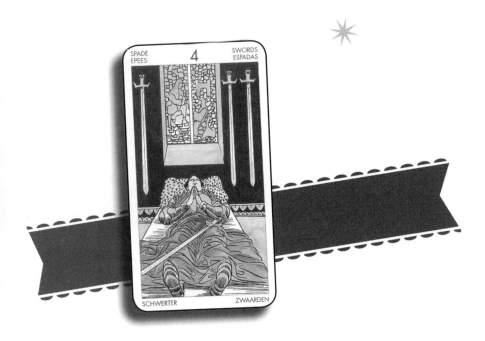

Close your eyes. Feel your way through your body, beginning with the top of your head, and find relaxation. Tense or move parts of your body and release to usher in relaxation and release. Working down the inches of your spine, find complete release.

When you are thoroughly relaxed, imagine that you are surrounded by the expanse of a great cathedral. You hear the quiet echoes of a grand expanse of space. You smell candles burning and the trace of warm incense lingering in the air. You feel the peace reverberating in a space that has been used for prayer and meditation for eons. You are completely protected from the outside world.

You venture deeply into the recesses of your mind. Repeat to yourself:

My decisions are good, and I am protected.
I find peace. I find love.

You may repeat this mantra as often as you like. You may let your mind wander to explore other things that pop up. If you become distracted, know this is normal and human and return to your mantra. If you should fall asleep, surrender to it and enjoy the gift of restorative slumber.

Return to the world gently and in your own time. When you are ready to rise, sit up with your hands in prayer. Bow gently, hands to your heart, and offer thanks to the Four of Swords.

Now, don't you feel better?

Five of Swords

Meditation on How You Treat Others

The Five of Swords suggests humiliation and defeat—a fight that has ended badly. Fives are notoriously challenging cards in the tarot, and the Five of Swords is no different. When the Five of Swords appears in a reading, it is helpful to determine which figure you identify with on the card. Are you the victor grasping your swords? Are you the mediator, looking to console the humbled figure in the background? Are you hanging your head in defeat and dejection? Pick, right now, which figure you identify with at this moment.

The Five of Swords offers a powerful reminder about how we affect others with our words and actions. We can all identify moments in our lives where the hurtful words of another stuck to us like glue. We sometimes hear these words reverberating in our ears years after they were uttered. Can you still hear the words uttered by a nasty, insensitive teacher? Can you still feel your emotional reaction to a person who looked at you in disgust? By the same token, good and helpful encouragement can, and hopefully does, stick with us, empowering us.

The Five of Swords offers an important reminder of how we affect others in the world. A diva wants to make the world in which she walks a better place. She knows that by empowering others, she empowers herself. We've all wounded others, even if it was unintentional. You will offer an apology to someone in this meditation. You may decide beforehand who this person is or, venturing into the card, let it come to you as a surprise.

Take the Five of Swords and place it before you. Sit comfortably in a chair with your feet firmly on the floor and your hands resting comfortably by your side. Slowly work your way through your body to find relaxation from your head to your toes. Gaze softly at the image on the card.

Imagine you are the figure in the foreground collecting the swords. The swords are heavy and sharp. You feel the cold steel in your hands and the chilly air blowing through your hair and across your face. Make a conscious decision to release the swords and toss them aside.

You look at the tiny figures in the background and walk over to them. An ocean spans behind them. They are sad and distraught over something you have said or an action you have taken. Walk toward them and tell them you are sorry. Embrace them. Smell their skin and their hair. Let them know you are not angry. While holding them in your arms, remember how powerful you are. Know you have the power to brighten someone's day. Know that the power to heal and help is more powerful than destruction and negativity. Feel the person you are holding forgive you.

Now, look at the third person in the card. Walk over to this person and tell them something positive to brighten their day. Make sure what you say is grounded in reality and truthful. Watch them smile as you say the words. Notice the effect you have by being positive to someone else. Wave farewell to these people. Walk to the ocean, which has now become placid. Bend down and look at your reflection in the still water. Say something kind to yourself. Slowly make your way out of the card and back to the room you are sitting in. Notice how light your body and spirit feel. Make a commitment to walk with compassion through the rest of your day.

Six of Swords

Magical Travel Spell

The Six of Swords depicts an image of what appears to be a mother and child being ferried across a river. The water behind their boat is choppy but the water ahead is smooth, implying they leave trouble behind them. This card is often understood as "better times lie ahead." The water of the river can represent the deep emotional connection between mother and child, and the rower evokes the Greek ferryman Charon, who chartered dead souls across the river to the land of the dead. There is silence and irrevocable beauty in this card.

Did you know you could use any trip you are about to embark on as a magical act? It doesn't matter if you are headed to the grocery store on foot, driving to your friend's house, on a train to visit the in-laws, taking a ferry to the beach, or hopping on an airplane. When you travel, you can charm yourself and use your own body as an instrument of magic. A body in motion is powerful, especially when other forces are pulling it. It is a powerful metaphor and a magical act.

What You Need:

> 6 of Swords card
>
> An upcoming journey

Decide what your goal is in this spell. What is your metaphor?

> ✦ To evoke more glamorous trips to new places?
>
> ✦ To evoke movement forward in a good relationship?
>
> ✦ To evoke the fact you are leaving something negative behind?
>
> ✦ To evoke your career taking off (airplane only)?
>
> ✦ To seek consciousness of a higher level (airplane only)?
>
> ✦ To bring about hot sex (trains through tunnels only)?

Place the Six of Swords card before you.

Before you depart for your trip, be it to Kinko's or to the Caribbean, take a moment to mentally walk yourself through your anticipated trip with your mind's eye. Throw in any lovely travel elements you'd like to include, such as rapid check-in at the airport, a super-duper sale at the grocery store, extra leg room while flying, or an empty seat to stretch out in.

Take a moment to visualize how this trip is a great metaphor for you. Envision yourself doing whatever action you hope to accomplish with this spell.

Visualization done, pull the Six of Swords toward you. Wave your hand over it and recite the following charm:

> Six of Swords, you traveling card
> This spell is simple and not hard.
> Plane, train, bus, car
> This works no matter where you are.
> My body goes and off I set
> My goals are reached and happily met.
> I free myself and my soul
> As my body travels, so does my goal.

Seven of Swords

Take What You Need Exercise

The Seven of Swords is another tricky card with a vast number of ways in which to be interpreted. On its surface, it suggests that a person is getting away with something. It can be a reminder to be thorough and not look for the easy way out—in other words, dot your i's and cross your t's. Be thorough. We remember swords are a challenging suit. The Seven of Swords is not just getting away with something, as the figure who appears to be sneaking away suggests. It is also a reminder to take what you need from a hairy situation. Let me explain…

There are cards in tarot that suggest tough situations. Certainly, we never want a bad card to predict hardship or disaster. Remember the entire deck of tarot describes a person, a life, and a journey, and no journey is without its pitfalls. It is often in hard times we discover what we are made of; we surprise ourselves and learn our great lessons. These lessons save us from future pain and ensure we don't repeat actions or patterns that hurt us. With this in mind, we can look at the Seven of Swords as a card that represents the lessons we've learned from sticky situations. We can understand the figure on the card as literally taking what is needed from a bad situation.

Think of your own life, the cards you have been dealt. Think of times of crisis. It may have been a situation you experienced as a small child, or it could be a time you were unfairly fired or in a relationship that went horribly wrong. I'm willing to bet you learned and grew tremendously as a result.

Become the figure on the Seven of Swords. Note he carries five swords with him as he exits the scene. Grab a notebook and write down three specific moments in your life when you were challenged beyond belief, when your world crumbled around you. When it all felt terribly unfair, we can be reminded of the background figure in the Five of Swords.

Under the three challenges, write down five things you learned while dealing with your adversity. After listing them, take a moment to consider how these lessons shaped you as the person you are now, reading the words of this book.

Congratulate yourself for your growth, and look back at the Seven of Swords. Remember: you can deal with anything the universe throws at you, and what doesn't kill you makes you stronger.

History, despite its wrenching pain,
cannot be unlived, but if faced with
courage, need not be lived again.

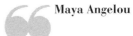
Maya Angelou

SEVEN OF SWORDS

I want to feel my life while I'm in it.

Meryl Streep

Eight of Swords

Cultivating Your Taste

The Eight of Swords shows a woman bound and floating above water as eight sharp swords form a fencelike structure behind her. The castle in the distance fades as time marches forward, and a sense of darkness and bondage prevails in this card. We can understand this card as the card of mental imprisonment. The inability to move forward—frozen, bound, and unable to move. Release is implied by the fact that the bonds are loose, and she could break free if she really wanted to. This card, like many of the swords, is a strong reminder that we are held captive by our thoughts and inability of self-expression.

The world is full of pleasure; there are delights to be had, emotions to be experienced, and joys to be pursued, but you can't access this when you are wrapped up and blinded by your own thoughts.

Everything your body does is potentially enjoyable. The cultivation of taste is an essential component to experiencing pleasure. When you consider cultivated taste, do you think of snobs—wine snobs, food snobs, or culture snobs? True, it can be obnoxious to listen to a holier-than-thou expert going on and on about something you don't necessarily understand. But we must not allow the fact that something is new, unexplored, or over our heads get in our way of deriving pleasure. In fact, you should never let newness get in your way of experiencing it. If we fear new experiences, new avenues of experiencing pleasure, than we are in fact bound up like the figure on the Eight of Swords, helpless to reach out and claim the joy that is rightfully ours.

Let's use the eight swords planted in the ground behind our damsel in distress as eight specific things we can do to escape our mind and seek pleasure in the world around us.

Sword One: Purchase tickets to a performance in a medium you have never experienced. This may include a modern dance piece, stand-up comedy routine, art exhibit, walk through a sculpture park, ballet, or opera. If you live in a rural area with few cultural offerings, rent a foreign film.

+ Example: Purchase tickets to a modern dance performance at the local college.

Sword Two: Plan a day trip to a place you have never ventured to.

✦ Example: Go to the nearest train or bus station. Randomly select a destination (within an hour or two of travel time) you have never been to before. *Side note:* This exercise results in surprising finds, once resulting in my discovery of a robber baron's mansion nestled in the Hudson River Valley.

Sword Three: Dine on cuisine you have never tasted. This could be an ethnic restaurant. If you have little eating selection in your town, find a recipe and ingredients online for an outrageous culinary adventure.

✦ Example: Go to your favorite restaurant but order the oddest item on the menu.

Sword Four: Pick a food you adore. Eat one version of it in its most simple, natural form. Then, try the same food in a complicated preparation.

✦ Example: Eat a garden-fresh tomato straight off the vine. Take another tomato and slice it in half; slow roast in the oven; sprinkle goat cheese, olive oil, thyme, sea salt, and fresh ground pepper on it; and pair with a side of caramelized onions.

Sword Five: Find a CD or album representative of a genre of music you don't normally listen to; this could be country, experimental jazz, rap, or heavy metal. Be sure the album is considered a classic. Listen and figure out why it is a classic.

✦ Example: Take this exercise one step further. Purchase tickets or find a free live performance of a music show. Choose a different genre than what you are used to hearing. Treat a friend and rock out.

Sword Six: Visit an art museum and pick a painting or photograph to ponder for twenty minutes. If you do not live close to a museum and can't get to one, visit a library or bookstore with a good selection of art books. Select an image within the book and consider it for twenty minutes. This exercise is better performed in public.

✦ Example: Find the nearest Rembrandt and enter his world by considering his painting for twenty minutes. You'll discover it is much like entering a tarot card as you induce a meditative state.

Sword Seven: Explore sex and the sensual art of touch. Your skin is an organ that covers your entire body and is one-way ticket to pleasure and arousal. Create a basket or bag full of items that can be used for enhanced sensual pleasure. Indulge with said items alone or with a partner.

✦ Example: feathers, leather straps, pieces of silk, reeds collected in a bundle, ice cubes (grabbed at last minute)—run items all over your lover or your own body before engaging in the main course.

Sword Eight: Attempt an exercise or outdoor sport that you have never tried before. Many classes offer a free trial.

✦ Example: Sign up for a class on karate, rock climbing, circus arts, or the trapeze.

Nine of Swords

Can't Sleep Exercise

The figure on the Nine of Swords has woken from her sleep and grips her face in anguish. The colorful, cheerful quilt, covered in beautiful symbols and astrological signs, is a reminder that things aren't so bad. The quilt was most likely a gift made with love, and it warms her. On a physical level, things are stable, but the nightmares her mind evokes leave her no peace. In a reading, the Nine of Swords represents mental distress over an issue. The swords on the wall form a ladder she could use for escape.

We've all been there: sleepless nights when we'd do anything for peace—peace from the thoughts banging around in our mind, obsessing over seemingly small problems that just won't disappear. Our feet sweat, we toss and turn, bumps and odd noises sound like vampires clawing their way into our bedroom. The Nine of Swords perfectly illustrates how our minds can hold us physically captive.

The secret to the Nine of Swords lies in her posture. Were she to sit up straight, cross her legs, and assume the peaceful lotus position, she could relax. I know; easier said than done.

If you find yourself wide awake one sleepless night, don't reach for a sleeping pill or the remote control. There is a simple way to set your mind at ease. You can remove the Nine of Cups card if you happen to have it near your bed, but the card itself is so memorable, you probably don't need a pictorial reminder.

Do this exercise when you can't sleep:

◆ *Be present in your discomfort.*

Being present sounds harder than it is. A painful tug of war happens in your mind when you are awake and stressing out. Thoughts repeat themselves over and over again in a vicious cycle. Your mind races and, the more you try to escape it, the more these thoughts come rushing back, crashing into your mind, which should be slumbering.

You can control this by being present and not trying to fight these thoughts, whatever they contain. Focus on your breath, focus on your mind; focus on your breath, focus on your mind. Take control over the situation by being present. Bring your attention to your physical body. Feel yourself in your uncomfortableness. People often talk about being present in your waking life with the people around you and in your activities. Try to be present in your body if you experience nighttime wakefulness.

When you give up the fight, you give up the ghost. When you are haunted no more, the resistance to whatever is happening up in that brain of yours disappears. Focusing on your body, feeling your thoughts, reminding yourself to be present, you'll fall into a state of sleepiness.

9 of Swords

Ten of Swords

Release Meditation and Exercise

The suit of swords gets scarier and more hard-core as we travel from the ace to the ten. We see ten swords in full effect nailing a gentleman to the ground. The ten in tarot cards always implies that a troubling situation has reached its conclusion; it is over and done. But just because the problem is resolved, will we let the situation hold us back in other respects? How did we go from the clarity of the Ace of Swords to the darkness of the Ten of Swords? By mistrusting, doubting, and distorting ourselves. By not paying attention to our intuition. By letting others rain on our parade or letting old habits get in our way.

A beautiful sunrise is about to bust forth in the background of the Ten of Swords. Will you let yourself experience it? It is a golden dawn. The sunrise speaks of waking up and seeing the world in a completely new way, evocative of the Judgement card. When an issue is resolved, do you let it hold you captive or do you brush yourself off to greet the new day?

The trick to the Ten of Swords is letting our mental bondage, our spent issues, disappear so we are free to be ourselves—no constraints. Use this exercise to free yourself from swords.

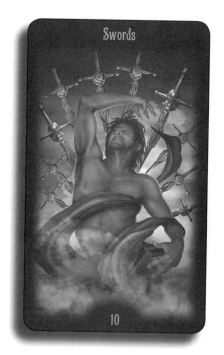

You may also do this meditation to release yourself from the hurtful things, true or untrue, that people have said and that you believed at one point.

Write down ten hurtful things people have ever said that hurt you:

+ Did someone tell you you were fat?

+ Did someone call you a slut?

+ Did someone tell you "Nice girls don't do that"?

+ Did someone call you ugly?

+ Did someone tell you you couldn't follow your dream?

- ✦ Did someone say you were stupid?

- ✦ Did someone ignore you?

- ✦ Did someone say you were perverted?

- ✦ Did someone tell you you were weird?

- ✦ Did someone say you were no good?

Now, look at your list of ten accusations and write the opposite affirmation. If you wrote: "Susie told me I was stupid," your affirmation will be: "I am brilliant!" Do not reiterate a negative in your affirmation. If you wrote: "Dad told me I was ugly," your affirmation should sound something like: "I am gorgeous on the inside and out."

Take your list of ten affirmations and your Ten of Swords card. Place the card and your list in front of you on the table. Take a comfortable seat in your chair. Visualize yourself inside the card, an observer seeing a body on the beach at night with ten piercing swords. Walk over to the body and recite your first affirmation out loud. Yell it if you want! After you have done so, imagine you lift one sword from the body. Turn behind you and throw it into the dark abyss, watching it dissolve into black nothingness.

Go to your next affirmation and say or yell it. Then remove a second sword and throw it into the dark abyss. Do so until all the swords have been removed and you have stated all your affirmations. The body disintegrates into the sand. You take its place and watch the sun rise slowly over the peaceful water and distant mountains. As the yellow and orange sun warms your face, smile to yourself as you greet a new day. Free. Open. You. In all your glory!

I am a woman in process … I try to take every conflict, every experience, and learn from it.

Oprah Winfrey

Ace of Wands

Aces in tarot represent a fresh start, a new beginning, a gift. An ace is the beginning, the first card of the suit. An ace is where everything is established. Think of the start of a play: the curtain goes up, an actor appears on stage—the appearance of something new like an ace. At intermission, things are challenged, whipped up, like in the fives. The curtain falls at the end of the show and all is resolved, just like the tens. But you can't start anything dramatic without an ace.

Many aces in tarot show a mysterious hand emerging from a cloud, and this hand offers a gift. The gift of the Ace of Wands is passion, desire, sparks, spirituality, force, business, motivation, intention, and your ability to experience all of it.

The Ace of Wands signifies being passionate and fired up—you get really excited with an idea. You decide to move your business in a new direction. You reconnect with someone inspiring or see a performance that fills you with exhilaration. You discover you have the capability to create something amazing. After all, aren't magic wands full of power? The Ace of Wands gives you a tool to direct your power.

The wand on the card represents your burning passion; it's also a symbol of the male phallus. The leaves sprouting off the top are the fruits of your labor, the result of your passionate action.

Gratitude Exercise

The easiest way to usher in Ace of Wands energy is through this gratitude exercise.

Do This Exercise When You Are:

+ Needing to get pumped up

+ Needing to get your creative juices flowing

+ Wanting to whip up something out of thin air

+ Moving a project along

+ Needing an extra push

Experiencing gratitude takes the attention off yourself, placing it on the world and the gifts around you. You'll feel energized, alive, and eager to experience the passion, excitement, and amazing gifts your day brings.

To invite Ace of Wands energy, place the card where you can see it. Fill in the blanks below, writing your answers on a separate piece of paper or in a journal.

My greatest passion is _____, and I am grateful because _____.

I get really excited when I _____, and I am grateful because _____.

My blood gets pumping the second I _____, and I am grateful because _____.

The most passionate person I know is _____, and I am grateful because _____.

The person who gets my blood racing is _____, and I am grateful because _____.

My greatest spiritual understanding is _____, and I am grateful because _____.

The successful person I look up to is _____, and I am grateful because _____.

I feel great when I _____, and I am grateful because _____.

I lose myself in the moment when I am _____, and I am grateful because _____.

I feel magic when I _____, and I am grateful because _____.

+ Ladies, if the thought of the male penis as the symbol of forceful creativity and spark bothers you as sexist, just recall the circular wreath on the World card. This may be understood as a woman's birth canal—literally giving birth to the world. Like it or not, male and female energy is taken very literally in tarot. Feel free to select a more feminist deck if that is to your liking.

Two of Wands

Goal-Setting Spell

The Two of Wands is about creativity and doing something amazing with your passion and talents. The figure on the card holds a small world in his hands. The world he holds recalls the World card. Is it a snapshot of you looking out the window, dreams in hand? The Two of Wands is really about seeing the big picture of your life. The Two of Wands suggests planing and plotting how to get exactly what you want. Never forget the fire, passion, and activity associated with wands. The Two of Wands suggests the work that is to come in making your goals a reality.

It is a proven fact that people who set realistic goals for themselves will reach them, find satisfaction, and create new goals. What do you have working to your advantage while goal setting, diva? Why, the tarot, of course! These cards can aid you in setting goals.

Take the Two of Wands and place it where you can see it. Remind yourself that the figure on the card is you and that you hold the world in your hands. You are the weaver of your own destiny.

> Bath water with 2 sliced lemons
>
> 2 red candles
>
> Two of Wands card
>
> 3 pieces of paper
>
> Pen
>
> Tarot deck

Prepare a bath with two thinly sliced lemons floating in the water. Lemon is magically used for longevity and refreshment. Its bright, sunny color is a reminder of your certain success, and it softens the skin. Bathe and reflect on the variety of things you want to do with your life, your time, your effort, and your energy. Think about the quality of your time and how you would like to be spending it. See if you can imagine where you'd like to be five years from now. What is your lifestyle? What are you doing? How do you look? Who surrounds you? How do you feel?

Exit your tub and come to your table. Open your space. Light your candles. One candle represents your passion; the second candle represents your intention.

Examine the Two of Wands as it reflects you. Know that you hold the world in your hands.

Begin writing out your goals. On one piece of paper, write six-month goals; on the next paper, write one-year goals; and on the last, write five-year goals. Put time, effort, and thought into each one. Reach for the stars, yet be realistic. It is also important to list goals you know you can reach. Fulfilling realistic goals fosters good feelings about yourself.

When you have written down all your goals and feel satisfied with your lists, pull a random tarot card for each goal. The cards will give you hints with their advice. They may suggest which goals are easily attained, highlight challenges to overcome, or give you a fresh idea on how to proceed. This is the meat and bones of *Tarot Diva*, because it is your intuition that provides you with the valuable advice you need in order to make your goals come true. And your goals will be reached if you put work behind them.

To finish your spell, take the two candles, merging the flames together into one, reciting:

> Passion fills me
> Intention runs free.
> The power of my goals is set
> I look forward, no regret.
> With love and light and harm to none
> I do declare this spell is done.

Three of Wands

Manifesting Spell

The Three of Wands shows a fellow similar to his friend on the Two of Wands, yet an action has been set forth. Rather than thinking about what he wants, the figure is literally waiting for his ship to come in. The most exciting part of working with tarot and magic is watching the results come back to us, often in the most surprising of ways. A surprise is indicated in his body language, his back to us, indicating there is a gift yet to be revealed.

Presumably, you've performed the goal-setting spell suggested by the Two of Wands. Now select one particular goal you wish to manifest quickly. This could be to bring an opportunity to you, such as a new job; manifest a wish; or grant a desire. Select your desire with great care. As the old saying goes: "Be careful what you wish for, 'cause you just might get it." In the case of this spell, assume you will. This spell is inspired by the Asian ritual of setting candles afloat in bodies of water. You will use this ritual to set your manifestation free. Collect your twig, leaf, and bark from the ground.

Mint or peppermint candy

Red candle

Paper and pen

Large leaf, twig, and piece of bark

String (optional)

Body of water (stream, lake, river, pool)

White votive candle

Fireproof container/matches

Three of Wands card

If you always do what interests you, at least one person is pleased.

Katharine Hepburn

Perform on a waxing moon. Place the mint in your mouth. As you feel the spice slip over your tongue, feel energy spread through you. Light your red candle, feeling passion grow as you do. Write your desire upon a piece of paper.

Fashion a small boat. The leaf is a sail, the twig is a mast, the bark is a boat. Place your written desire, folded, upon the boat. Bring to a pool of water and light the white votive candle, placing it on top of your desire. Set the boat, candle, and wish free to the waters. Contemplate your desire as you watch it sail away. Extinguish the candle if there is any chance whatsoever of igniting real fire via dry brush or arid conditions. Attach a string and pull the boat back to extinguish if need be.

Life begets life. Energy creates energy. It is by
spending oneself that one becomes rich.

Sarah Bernhardt

Four of Wands

Creative Project Spell

The Four of Wands suggests stability of work, passion, and excitement. A wedding or May Day celebration is pictured in the card, and the four wands remind us of the stability implied. When the Four of Wands shows up in a reading, it ensures successful completion and reason to celebrate.

No matter our work, we all have projects we'd like to get off the ground and complete to the best of our abilities. Perhaps you'd like to write a book, paint a painting, remodel your living room, reorganize your finances, or plan your wedding. Anything you pull together may be considered a creative project, even if it doesn't utilize traditionally creative elements.

In order to ensure success for your given project, cast this spell. Watch the world bend to aid you in surprising ways.

You Will Need:

> Red candle
>
> Pen and paper
>
> Four of Wands card
>
> The Star card
>
> The Magician card
>
> The Wheel card
>
> The Empress card

Write out an outline of your project—what you want to create.

Take the Four of Wands and place it in the center of your space. Then recite the following:

> The Four of Wands is my project.
> It is stable and strong.
> Getting this off the ground won't take long.

Now, arrange each of the following cards at the four corners of the Four of Wands, starting in the upper right-hand corner with the Star and placing the remaining cards—the Magician, the Wheel, and the Empress—in a clockwise fashion.

Say the following for each card:

The Star:

> The Star offers inspiration, hope, and light
> Its magic surrounds me through the night.

The Magician:

> The Magician is my conduit to the Divine
> Completion, satisfaction will be mine.

The Wheel of Fortune:

> Forces and fate around me spin
> They all line up to help me win.

The Empress:

> The Empress shines with creative light
> She works through me with all her might.

Focus on the Four of Wands in the center of this spread, and say:

> Four of Wands, stable and true
> Good work is what I shall do.
> With love and light and harm to none
> I do declare this spell is done.

Five of Wands

Jackson Pollock Exercise

The Five of Wands shows us five youths in the midst of a skirmish. They may be fighting angrily or they may be fooling around playfully. Whatever the intention of their scramble, one thing is certain: there is an intense amount of energy raised, flying around; anything could potentially happen.

There is a sense of chaos within the Five of Wands. We often feel confused when chaotic energy rears up in our lives. We should remember that it will all add up to something even if we are not sure of the outcome.

Jackson Pollock, famous modern artist of the mid-1900s, set the art world on fire with his seemingly random paint swatches and streaks thrown upon his canvas. These streaks of paint created an ordered chaos, incredible to look at. The great news is that Pollock is one of the easiest painters to emulate, in terms of style. In this Five of Wands Jackson Pollock exercise, you will capture the energy suggested by the Five of Wands.

Love the moment, and the energy of the moment will spread beyond all boundaries.

 **Corita Kent**

You Will Need:

> Five of Wands card
>
> A canvas of any desired size
>
> 3 colors acrylic paint
>
> Paint cups
>
> Paint brushes or sticks
>
> Newspaper and protective floor covering

Purchase a canvas of any desired size and at least three colors of acrylic paint. Mix your three colors to create any other colors, if desired. Five colors are great to choose, as it reminds you of the five wands on the card. Set newspaper and protective floor covering beneath your canvas.

Focus on the energy represented in the Five of Wands card. Voilà! When you are ready, start flinging paint at your canvas. Have fun. Keep in mind this is a metaphor for the unexpected in your life.

You may do this exercise alone or invite friends and family members to join you. I have a series of "Pollock" canvases that my family created, and we all love seeing them hang on the wall.

Hang your painting up. You may use your canvas as a mandala, a focal point of meditation at a future point, finding peace amidst the chaos of your life.

I am my own experiment.
I am my own work of art.

Madonna

Six of Wands

Victory Is Yours Spell

The Six of Wands is a card depicting a victory parade and celebration. Wouldn't you love to be sitting on that horse, crowds whistling and yelling for you, showering you with flowers? While the Six of Wands shows a personal victory, it also reminds us of how we inspire others with our actions. After all, the crowds are out cheering you on. When you do your best, the world can't help but look up and take notice. They become inspired by you.

This victory spell is inspired by the bay leaf wreath, which signifies victory.

> 4 candles
>
> Victory bath with sea salt and bay leaves
>
> Tarot deck

To ensure victory, in any given circumstance, choose a card to signify the outcome you desire and relating to what you want. (Refer to charm examples on page 53.)

Take a victory bath: add cleansing sea salt and bay leaves in tub. Soak in bath and call upon the High Priestess to connect you to the deck.

When the bath empties, imagine negativity floating down the drain.

Put on a gorgeous, yummy nightgown or pajamas.

SIX OF WANDS

Go to a large open space on a rug or on the floor.

Light four candles for each direction, each suit. Place one candle in each direction and, when doing so, ask each direction to aid you in your work.

Beginning with the east, start to place your tarot cards in a circular fashion around you, making a victory circle. Place until the cards completely encircle you. You may overlap them and even reverse some cards if you would like to lessen their energies in your life.

Take the card you are calling on for victory. Place it in front of you.

Magic tarot circle flows
The magic in me grows and grows.
I call upon the _____ card
Victory here will not be hard.
Tarot fills me with life and love
Success fits me just like a glove.

Read aloud any other things you would like to state.

When you are finished, recite:

With love and light and harm to none
I do declare this spell is done.

Collect your cards, blow out your candles, and relax.

Seven of Wands

Inspiration Party

The Seven of Wands depicts a man standing high on a rock. He holds a wand in his hand, and it appears he is fighting off the aggressors below. This card is often understood as taking a stand and defending yourself. But what if we look at the card and imagine he is igniting flames rather than fighting? What if he is inspiring each figure as he touches them? The Seven of Wands then takes on a wonderful meaning.

Using the Seven of Wands in a positive way, why not inspire a crowd of people with an inspiration party and embody the Seven of Wands?

An inspiration party is a fabulous way to spend an evening, have fun, get inspired, and meet new people. It is a gathering in which people come together and each member shares an idea of something they would like to do, accomplish, or cre-

ate. After stating the desired idea, project, or dream, guests offer useful suggestions and comments of how you can best achieve your idea. For example, say you are a full-time working mother with little time on your hands, and your dream is to write a novel. Suggestions from the group might include a local writer's group, a playgroup for children where moms switch child-care responsibilities at no cost, a contact for the person running a fiction writing group, an excellent writing fiction website, Julia Cameron's book *The Artist's Way*, and so on.

The genius of an inspiration party is that everyone gets excited about everyone else's ideas and you walk out the door full of inspiration and potential contacts.

How to Host an Inspiration Party

Invitations: Invite a large variety of people and ask them each to bring along a friend, preferably someone from outside your circle of friends, to foster diversity of ideas. Each person is required to bring an idea with them—an idea they would take action on if they knew they couldn't fail.

Food and Drinks: Ask each guest to bring a dish à la a potluck. This may be simplified by having a dessert idea party where everyone brings something sweet, or a cheese and wine idea party where everyone brings a lovely vino, cheese, or fruit. It is important for the hostess not to be working too hard so she may enjoy the party.

Ground Rules:

+ Pull seats into a circle.

+ Select a timekeeper. Each person stating their idea is allotted a specific time, say five minutes per guest (adjust to fit the size of your group). This will ensure everyone receives equal floor time.

+ Select a recordkeeper. The recordkeeper records and writes each suggestion on a piece of paper so that the person stating ideas can focus, without distraction, on ideas offered.

+ Rule of stating your idea: Each guest takes turns sharing an idea they would accomplish if they knew there was no way they would fail—what they would do if success were guaranteed (this is very important). After you have stated your idea, wish, or desire, you must listen to suggestions from the group with an open mind. Even if you are offered an idea you have heard before, you must listen as if it is brand-new to you. Keep an open mind!

+ Rule of suggesting ideas: You must offer positive, helpful ideas to help the person reach their goal. In the same way that you would always be supportive and uplifting in a tarot reading, each guest must state ideas in a positive manner or be asked to leave. You can also offer personal contacts that may aid the person stating their idea.

+ Take a fifteen-minute break every hour to keep everyone alert.

+ Most important, have fun.

Eight of Wands

Fantastic Trip Spell

The Eight of Wands shows eight wands flying through the air at a super high speed. The wands haven't landed yet, but when they become grounded, something marvelous is sure to ensue. This card often suggests a safe journey and an airline flight. Traveling and divaness go hand in hand. In fact, we often see our famous divas hiding behind sunglasses and dashing from paparazzi through the airport.

By now you understand the world is your playground. I'm willing to bet there is a dream trip you have always wanted to take. It may be a glamorous week in Paris, traveling across India by train and staying at an ashram, helping the needy in Nepal, or maybe you want to plant yourself seaside in a lush tropical resort. Well, nothing wrong with planning that trip right now and giving yourself a magical boost to make sure it happens.

Begin by plotting and planning where you'd like to go. Look through magazines and cut out pictures of the places you'd like to visit, what you'll be wearing, and how you'll travel. Look online at how much it costs to reach your destination, what you need to save, how much time you'll need. Pick up a travel guide for the country you shall visit.

Once you have your trip in mind, perform this spell. Watch the world bend to greet your desire to become a jet setter!

Eight of Wands tarot card

Paper and pen

Red candle

Fruit and cheese plate (prepared and waiting)

Light your candle and reach for your pen and paper. Write your name in a circle. Draw a larger circle around your name and fill in the name of where you would like to go. Draw a larger circle around where you are going, and inside this circle write the places you will see on your trip and the qualities it will contain.

Focus on the Eight of Wands tarot card and say aloud:

Eight wands fly through the air
Work your magic, bring me there.
I fly with safety and speed
I'll receive everything I need.

Now fold your paper into a paper airplane and throw it out the window, saying:

> With love and light and harm to none
> I do declare this spell is done.

Now, enjoy your plate of fruit and cheese as if it has just been served to you by a handsome waiter.

When you are done eating, go outside to retrieve your paper airplane. Fold it again and place in an envelope. In one week, mail it to yourself. When your paper airplane arrives by mail, you will have manifested at least one thing that brings you closer to your trip.

Nine of Wands

Breaking Your Barriers Spell

The Nine of Wands shows a bandaged fellow; it appears he's been through the wringer, beaten and worn, yet he forges ahead. The wands form a fence behind him, and we can understand this card as a final breakthrough. He is literally walking through a gate, venturing where others fear to tread.

If we understand the suit of wands as energy, passion, and work, then we understand that when we complete a project, we have broken down a wall. The combustible energy behind the suit of wands can consume anything in its way.

The walls we create are not easily destroyed. Like a normal wall, we built them for protection, to remain in a space we feel comfortable in. When the wall breaks, we feel uncomfortable, uneasy, edgy. This is only because when a wall is broken away, we feel exposed to the new. This is also why sometimes, even when we are getting the very thing we want, we can feel uncomfortable and strange.

Use this spell when you feel ready for a final breakthrough or you are just simply ready to move past the barriers you have created for yourself. You will literally build yourself a wall of cards and then break it down.

Select:

> Nine of Wands card
>
> 9 randomly drawn cards

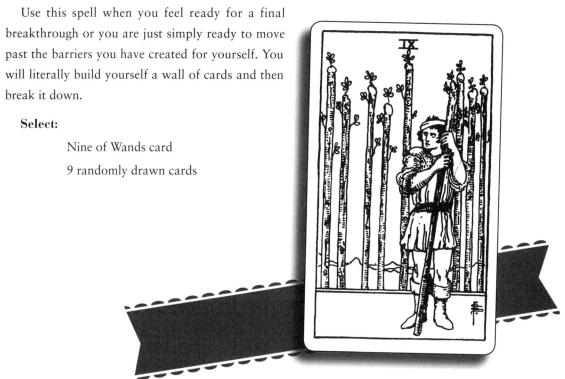

Contemplate the Nine of Wands card, and close your eyes. Imagine your life and a self-imposed wall that stands before you. What is it made of? On the other side of the wall is the life you want—the way you would like to live. Who is there? What are you doing? What are you engaged in? How do you feel? Decide you are going to break down this wall; use any imaginary instrument to do so.

Now, take your nine tarot cards and place three before you as if you were going to build a house of cards: place one card horizontally, with two cards leaning on the sides until they are freestanding. Repeat using the next three cards, and repeat again with final three.

You are constructing a wall. What do you do when you encounter a wall you don't want? You bust it down. Again imagine the life you want on the other side of this wall. Decide that right now is the moment of breakthrough, and say:

> Nine of Wands, I'm almost there
> Break this wall so I can care.
> For life, for love, the world awaits
> I knock you down and break your gates!

With one swipe, destroy your wall of cards!

Look down and examine and interpret the cards as they lie haphazardly. Cards facing down represent energy you leave behind. Cards facing up are suggestions of things to come.

Pat yourself on the back for your breakthrough!

Ten of Wands

Spell for Letting Go

The Ten of Wands depicts a man who carries ten heavy wands. His load is cumbersome; he looks tired. It looks like he needs to let it all go and book himself a massage, huh?

Tens represent the end of a cycle. The reason the end of the cycle of wands seems so tiresome, so burdensome, is the energy and passion that it took to get to this point. Often, even when we are finished with a project, a person, or a path, if we've put a world of time and energy into it, we do not want to let it go. We have become attached to it.

It is worth noting that we must release ourselves from the old so we can begin afresh at the ace. In this way, we ensure that we move forward and do not stay mired in the past. Better yet, we are free to move lightly.

Pick something you want to let go of. This could be a project, a person, an idea, a habit, a way of being, or way of thinking. Even if it once brought you joy, if you feel the need to let it go, follow your instincts and do this spell.

Take the Ten of Wands from your deck.

On ten separate slips of paper, write down ten reasons why this particular thing was important to you.

Light a fireplace or fire pit or get a fireproof receptacle like an ashtray.

Insert each of the ten pieces of paper, one by one, into the fire, and doing so, say:

I release my attachment to _____.

Congratulate yourself on completing a cycle and learning lessons.

Let your fire burn out. The next day, walk to the fireplace, pit, or ashtray. Light a white candle to usher in new fire energy. Bring on that ace!

You play. You win. You play. You lose. You play.
Jeanette Winterson

FUNTASTIC *Divinations & Readings*

Assuming you have diligently followed directions and fostered a sacred space where you read the cards, here comes the fun part—actually reading and interpreting them. If you are just beginning to work with the cards, you will find interpretations and patterns become stronger, easier to see, the more you practice. The very same way a great novel leaps to life before your eyes and within your imagination, the same will happen with a deck of tarot.

How to Shuffle

There are no right or wrong ways to shuffle a deck. The only important things are that the cards are mixed and you have given your issues the appropriate thought while shuffling.

How to Casino Shuffle

What do you get for waking up in Vegas? A mixed deck. Do like old-school professional dealers do with a classic casino shuffle. Cut the deck into two piles. Hold a pile in each hand. Position cards on table, at a slight angle and close together, nearly touching, with the backs of the cards facing upwards. Lift the inside of both piles with your thumbs while pushing on the opposite ends down with your fingers. Move your thumbs slowly to release each card one at a time. Combine back into one pile and repeat a number of times.

How to Cut Shuffle

Hold the deck vertically in one hand. Slip top cards into other hand, a few at a time. Keep going until the entire deck has been transferred into the other hand.

How to Make Card Soup

Spread all the cards, face-down, in front of you upon the table. Stir them up like soup until they are good and mixed.

Focus While Shuffling

As you shuffle, think about the question and the situation you will examine in your reading. Put as much energy and focus as you can into the cards. This will ensure they will be succinct in answering your question. When you feel the cards are shuffled and ready to be read, you may begin your reading.

Who Should Shuffle?

When you are reading for another person, you may ask them to shuffle the deck to work their energy into the cards. However, some readers prefer to have only themselves touch the deck, thereby protecting the deck's energy from another person. It is entirely up to you who shall shuffle.

Flipping Your Cards Over

Even if you don't utilize reversed card meanings now, chances are you will read reversals at a future point. You will want to know if a card appears reversed or not, thus not doubting your interpretation. For this reason, you must make a habit of placing the deck in front of you and turning the cards over from left to right, the same way you'd flip pages in a book. Draw from the top of the deck. This way, you will be certain if the card is upright or reversed. Get in the habit so when you move on to reversals, you will not be confused by which way the card appears. You'll find more about reading reversals later in this section.

Spread 'Em!

One-Card Spread

A one-card spread is a great way to focus on a single subject. Along with the card-a-day practice, this is a wonderful way to focus and learn about the cards. Using fewer cards when you begin reading tarot is helpful. You won't become distracted and confused by a multitude of possible meanings.

Helpful questions for a one-card spread include:

◆ What do I need to know right now?

◆ How does my particular situation stand?

◆ What should I focus on?

◆ What do I need to know to help me at this particular moment?

◆ If I do _____, what will be the outcome?

◆ What issue is holding me back?

Three-Card Spread

1. Past   2. Present   3. Future

Place three cards upon the table. The first card represents the past energy of the situation—the issues that have contributed to the question at hand. The second card represents the present situation, or things as they stand at the moment—where you are presently. The third card is the future outcome, the energy of the present situation unfolding in its natural way.

Stairway Spread

             3. Two Weeks

        2. Next Week

    1. Today

I love the stairway spread. Created by intuitive diva Ruth Ann Amberstone, my tarot teacher, the stairway spread appears like steps up to a secret room containing your future behind a locked wooden door. Will you place the rusty key in the keyhole, turn, and peek? This spread reveals how the energy of your current situation will play out. Feel free to exchange weeks for days or months.

It is helpful not to project too far into the future, unless you are focusing on long-term goals. Also note the way this spread depicts your energy moving upward in a positive, growing expression of energy/attitude. Let the upward staircase spread remind you that things are looking up.

Deconstructing the Classic Celtic Cross

The Celtic Cross spread is found in nearly every little tarot book sandwiched alongside a new pack of tarot cards. The Celtic Cross is the workhorse spread of the tarot world because it contains so much information. You can literally use it like a surgical tool for examining a life; it covers every little angle. Different books contain assorted interpretations of what the card positions mean; don't let this confuse you. There is no hard and fast, right or wrong way to do the Celtic Cross. In fact, you can alter position meanings to suit yourself. Remember, *you* are in charge of the cards. Tarot is in your hands; it is your practice, and tarot shall leap to life before your fingertips.

If this is your first attempt at reading the Celtic Cross spread, I offer you a very simple system for understanding and interpreting it. It is easier to understand and interpret the Celtic Cross by breaking it up into small individual readings, mini spreads, and one- or two-card readings. After examining each question and position individually, you place the cards together to read the Celtic Cross as a whole at the end.

An extra added benefit is that you won't be distracted or overwhelmed by the amount of cards on your table. Each position, given careful consideration and attention, will then be brought together at the end, akin to combining all the individual instruments of an orchestra together for a grand finale. This is where you look for card patterns and extra information. I've made this easier by breaking up the deck specifically for each position. Also note that each section offers questions to ask yourself about each position. This will make it easier to understand what the card position means. Every tarot reading should invoke a number of questions, which, answered by you, will bring clarity to any situation you encounter. People often state it is quite challenging to read their own cards because they are so close to the situation. If you ask yourself the answer to questions the positions bring up, you should easily find clarity for yourself and for others. This is a wonderful exercise to perform in a tarot classroom setting.

Separate your tarot deck into three piles of cards: court cards, Major Arcana, and Minor Arcana. Shuffle each set thoroughly and state the issue or question you would like to examine.

Cards 1 and 2—Your Personality and What Is Crossing You

Select the pile of court cards and pull card one, upright, and card two, to cross it. Study them. Card 1 represents you at this very moment: how you are feeling, the energy of your current state, where your head is at, and the general actions you are taking.

◆ What am I most concerned about?

◆ What energy am I projecting?

◆ How do I feel right now?

◆ What is my energy level?

Card 2 represents the direction you are being pulled, what is influencing you, where you feel you ought to be going, what you feel impelled to create, and why your question or situation is occurring to begin with.

◆ What energy do I need to embody?

◆ Where do I feel impelled to go?

◆ How am I moving forward?

◆ What is challenging me?

Court cards have been chosen because they represent your personality traits. Court cards make up the complexities of your personality and offer a concise picture of your inward and outward state. Please refer to the court card section for more information on how to interpret the kings, queens, knights, and pages.

Set these cards aside, face-up, and pull card 3.

Card 3—Higher Self/Soul Card

Pick up your Major Arcana pile and select one card. This card represents what is happening for you on a soul level and represents your higher self. This card is the great lesson you are to learn, the quality you are meant to embody.

◆ What does my intuition want me to bring forth?

◆ What is my higher self asking me to do?

◆ What is the greater lesson for me?

◆ What am I meant to learn?

Set this card aside and select cards 4, 5, and 6.

Cards 4, 5, and 6—Your Past, Present, and Future

From the Minor Arcana, select three cards representing past, present, and future. These positions are meant to shed light on the energy of the situations you are moving through. Past and future events are relegated to a fairly short amount of time, no more than a few weeks in either direction. The minors were chosen for these positions because this is an examination of the nature of your daily life. I pose no questions for these cards, as past, present, and future are quite simple and straightforward to interpret.

Set these cards aside and proceed to question/card 7. Take all remaining piles of cards—courts, majors, and minors—and shuffle them together thoroughly in one pile. Choose from the remaining cards for the following card positions.

Card 7—Your Attitude

Card 7 refers to your current attitude. Here is where you discover the decisions you have made, what you feel capable of, and what you are expecting from yourself and from others. This position refers to how you have made up your mind, what you believe in, and how you are filtering the world around you. It is important to note that we hold opinions and ideas that often change.

✦ Can I make an adjustment about how I view the world?

✦ What assumptions have I made about other people?

✦ What assumptions have I made about myself?

✦ What cycle am I caught up in?

Set this card aside and pull card 8.

Card 8—The People Surrounding and Influencing You

At any given time, there are people who influence our general life. This card offers information as to who is having the most impact on your thoughts, as well as how the energy surrounding your family and friends is affecting you.

✦ How does this person/situation make me feel?

✦ Am I surrounded by people who build me up?

- ✦ Am I surrounded by people who break me down?

- ✦ Who is influencing me most?

Card 9—Challenge Card

Card 9 is offering up what is your greatest challenge, your fears and desires, and what stands in the way of you getting what you want.

- ✦ What will it mean to manifest my desire in reality?

- ✦ What must I confront within myself?

- ✦ What is my greatest challenge?

- ✦ Am I afraid to realize my dreams?

- ✦ What is my heartfelt desire?

- ✦ What cycles do I repeat?

Card 10—Outcome

Card 10 is the zinger, the weighty meat of the spread, the holding-your-breath-till-you-turn-it-over card, because it represents the ultimate outcome. This card represents what is to come if you continue on your current path without taking any further action. What will happen if you don't adjust anything you have learned as a result of this reading? If the card pleases you, by all means enjoy its predictive energy. If you dislike the ultimate outcome card, look at the information you have been given from prior cards to see how you can temper and adjust your actions to encourage the situation you would like to create for yourself.

- ✦ What would it mean to me if this actually happens?

- ✦ What can I do to embrace/reject this card?

- ✦ Does this represent a major change?

- ✦ Do I dislike this outcome?

- ✦ Do I like this outcome?

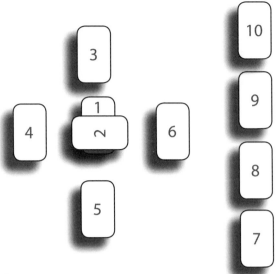

Celtic Cross Position Reference

Position 1: Where you are at.

Position 2: What is crossing/influencing you.

Position 3: Best possible outcome and highest self/soul card.

Position 4: Recent past around the situation.

Position 5: What is the root, what led up to this, the deep unconscious elements you might not be aware of.

Position 6: Near-future events and energy coming in.

Position 7: Your attitude.

Position 8: How those closest to you feel about the situation (friends/family).

Position 9: Block or hurdle to overcome hopes and fears.

Position 10: General outcome.

✦ *Side note:* Should you use this Celtic Cross exercise for a tarot class, don't tell your students you are creating the Celtic Cross. Rather, state that you are performing individual readings. Be sure they hold on to the cards as they read and then surprise them at the end by placing them all together in the cross format.

Graphic Novel Spread

The graphic novel spread is an advanced yet super-fun exercise in reading the tarot just as you would a comic strip or graphic novel. Lay out the cards in the same form you would see in a graphic novel:

1, 2, 3, 4 (past)

5, 6, 7, 8 (present)

9, 10, 11, 12 (future)

Read the cards purely as a story that is playing out. Look for repeated patterns, numbers, and suits. Be sure all the cards are touching, as they would in a comic strip.

Wow, What a Spread!

Creating your very own spreads is a creative, fun thing to do. You can create them with unique questions that apply to any situation you can imagine. The reading will really resonate because it has been created by you. The sky's the limit. Create a spread based on a chocolate chip cookie, a holiday, or just the way you are feeling at the moment.

Tips and Tricks When Reading for Yourself

Reading tarot for yourself can be tricky, especially when you are emotionally bound to the issues. You are so close to the questions. You are drawing your own interpretation. Your mind races to find the answer, but is it too close? Can you pull back far enough to see the big picture? Will you become overwhelmed as you draw answers? Can you stay on track?

There are two simple things you can do to keep your focus on personal readings:

Write Down Your Question

By writing down your question, you will stay focused. Your mind may be tempted to leap to other issues as you draw cards. If the question is looking at you from a written page, allow it to draw you like a magnet back to the specific question at hand. Stay focused. Stay disciplined.

Write Down the Answers and Wisdom Received from the Cards

Writing down your answers gives a moment's pause to the rapid-fire thoughts in your mind. Writing your answer offers a chance to be concise and direct in the answer/advice you find.

Reading for Others

The gifts of tarot are many. Reading for others provides insight, solutions, confirmations, excitement, and clarity. As a reader, you have a marvelous opportunity to empower people. With power comes responsibility, and I implore you to use your powers wisely.

Tarot usually provokes one of three reactions in people. One: their eyes light up, they get excited, and they want a reading right away. They find the idea of tarot intriguing and are excited to see what the cards say. Read for these types as much as you like. Two: they are offended, believe in old-fashioned and antiquated ideas of what the tarot is, and think the cards are an affront to their religion. They laugh or sneer and want nothing to do with it. Never force tarot or your spiritual beliefs on others. You may calmly explain what the cards mean to you and how you use them, but at the end of the day, it is not for them; it really is their loss. Three: they get frightened. People who are afraid of tarot and scared about what you may see are not ever worth reading for. A reading should never come from a place of fear. If it is not helpful, don't bother doing it.

A tarot diva knows she uses her cards to heal and create love and light for the people around her. In an effort to be a true tarot diva and create goodness in the world, it is helpful to adhere to a couple of rules when reading for others. The power of suggestion is strong. Be aware that what you say to another person has a powerful effect, especially when the cards are involved. Never say anything that is hurtful or destructive to a person.

If it ain't helpful, don't say it. Never use your knowledge of tarot or something you see in the cards if it is not going to help a person. Most people who work with cards are sensitive enough to know the difference between hurtful or helpful. Make sure your observations are firmly in the latter camp. You want the person to walk away satisfied and empowered—not terrified, not judged.

Never force a reading. You should never, ever force a tarot reading on someone who is frightened of the cards. You may gently explain how you use the cards for guidance, empowerment, and inspiration, but don't force it down someone's throat.

If you want to take a trip, book a flight: don't take a power trip with the person you are reading for. Oftentimes, when a person sits in front of a psychic or reader, they are completely in awe of the reader because they believe the reader has incredible powers—that the reader can see everything in their life. Even if you possess super-psychic, amazing abilities, never *ever* use this ability to go on a power trip with the person. Never tell them the future is set in stone. Never use the cards to convince them that you know what is best for the person sitting in front of you.

Offer useful suggestions. Give your querent something useful to walk away with—something they can do to help ease whatever situation they are facing. Let them know the future is fluid and very much in their control.

> Faith is not belief.
> Belief is passive; faith is active.
> **Edith Hamilton**

Tell them why they are special. Tarot reading offers a unique opportunity to allow a person to really be seen. Think for a moment about a time you may have seen a reader or even read your own horoscope. You wanted to find out what is special about you. Do the same thing for the person you are reading for. Use the time as an opportunity to point out their strengths and unique qualities. Use your reading as a chance to really empower the person in front of you.

Approach the reading from a place of love. The number-one most important thing you bring to a tarot reading is your attitude. If you come from a place of love—if you offer yourself as a gift to the other person—the reading will be wonderful. With love in your heart, you cannot fail.

Beware of your own preconceived notions of romance, especially when discussing issues of love with a client. Just because a man is sitting in front you, don't automatically assume the object of their love is a woman, or vice versa. Human sexuality is a complicated, evolving form of personal expression. Don't assume that just because you and your circle of friends might be married with kids that everyone else follows that form of lifestyle. Keep an open mind when reading.

Reading Reversals

Reading card reversals—cards that appear in a reading upside down—is a practice that will add immense depth to your readings. There are many ways in which you can read a reversed card.

Typically, when first learning tarot, there is a tendency to understand reversed cards as the opposite of the traditional meaning. So, if the Nine of Cups means your wish will come true, a reversed Nine of Cups means your wish *won't* come true—seems pretty cut and dried, huh? Well, that's all fine and good if you believe there are "good" cards and "bad" cards. Simple, if you wish to memorize simple definitions and offer simple readings. But a true tarot diva knows that each tarot card offers an endless depth of meaning and that the world is not a simple cut-and-dried place. A tarot diva reads between the lines, and it is in these fuzzy, muddy places that the truth is often found. Learning to read reversed cards is a skill that will offer richness.

Reading reversals calls a reader once again to use their intuition as to what exactly the card is saying. Just as each card has a multitude of meanings, reversals have many ways in which to be read.

Ways to Interpret Reversals

+ The energy of the card is blocked, and you can look for ways to unblock the card.

+ The reversed card is calling out for extra attention, saying "Look at me!"

+ The reversed card is talking about a very deep, internal-level issue.

+ The reversed card is giving you a new way with which to look at the symbols on the card.

Yes or No Questions Using Reversals

You may use reversals to answer yes or no questions. If you are asking a simple yes or no question, shuffle the deck and flip a card. If the card is upright, the answer is yes. If the card is reversed, the answer is no. Look to the card for more information regarding the subject.

High-Level Readings with Patterns, Numbers, Suits, and Courts

Look for card patterns to appear in spreads, as this offers extra information. This is especially helpful if you read with three or more cards.

A tarot diva is very interested in abundance of all forms because she wants everything she can in life. She wants lots of fun, tons of pleasure, endless laughing, and abundance of beauty. They say if you look hard enough, you are sure to find it. Look for abundance in your readings as a clue to what's going on.

Look for patterns in the cards. All of the patterns below are connected to the meanings of the cards. Aces represent beginnings, so many aces in a reading suggests lots of starter energy. Major cards represent major life-altering moments. An abundance of majors signals important issues.

An abundance of aces suggests the beginning of something new.

An abundance of twos suggests duality and partnerships.

An abundance of threes suggests tons of creativity.

An abundance of fours suggests stability.

An abundance of fives suggests struggle.

An abundance of sixes suggests renewal.

An abundance of sevens suggests victory.

An abundance of eights suggests working hard.

An abundance of nines suggests luck.

An abundance of tens suggests a cycle has ended.

An abundance of majors suggests a life-altering issue.

An abundance of minors suggests everyday issues.

An abundance of court cards suggests there are many people involved in the situation.

An abundance of cups suggests emotional issues.

An abundance of pentacles suggests money/body issues.

An abundance of wands suggests high energy and passion.

An abundance of swords suggests thinking and communication.

> Luck is a matter of preparation meeting opportunity.
> **Oprah Winfrey**

Happy Endings

You may end your reading with another nugget of information. Be a clever tarot diva by finding your finishing card as a final say to a reading. Look at your pile of unused cards and turn the deck over. The card on the bottom of the deck is your final note.

Dreamy Divinations

Did you know your intuition is at work long after you fall asleep, the same way facial moisturizer works overnight? Our unconscious mind continues to wander, figure things out, and work long after we put our active mind to sleep. We can use our sleeping mind to garner extra information on any subject long after we've fallen asleep and in the shadows of our sleeping mind. Intending to access your unconscious yields powerful results.

Brew yourself a cup of psychic tea. Sip it slowly and open up your sacred reading space. Pull out the High Priestess card. The High Priestess is the guardian and keeper of all inner knowledge, and her wisdom resides in the dark places, the silent quarters and deepest valleys of your soul. Ask her for guidance, answers, and assistance in dreamland while you sleep. Request an answer to your question when you wake up. Restate your question and select a tarot card. Take this card and slip it beneath your pillow. Focus on the card and the energy of the High Priestess as you fall asleep.

Sleeping Charms

The same way you can charm a tarot card for your day, you can access the power of a tarot card to fill you with power while you are sleeping. Say you have a really important interview in the morning. Perhaps you are moving in the morning and want to keep on top of all the little details. Select the card with its appropriate powers. Open up your visualization and enter the card. Journey through the card and decide the energy of that card will enter your body and fill you up while you are sleeping. In fact, imagine the energy of the card is energizing you, filling you to the brim with its power while you snooze the night away. Try to look at the card right before you close your eyes to sleep and then slip it under your pillow. Look at the card first thing in the morning.

Pentacles, wands, cups, and swords, burn bright
Let your magic fill my night.
(Name of card), illuminate me with your powers
Work this enchantment during my sleeping hours.

Stage Cards and the Way You Appear to the World

There is a marvelous hidden detail within the original Rider-Waite cards. This mysterious fact, often overlooked, can add fabulous dimensions to your readings. Let's unravel this mystery together and then look at how you can use it in your readings.

Rider-Waite artist Pamela Colman Smith drew stage cards that appear throughout the Minor Arcana. What is a stage card, you ask? A stage card is a card from the Rider-Waite deck, drawn as if the action on the card were taking place upon a stage. The characters stand upon flat and smooth boards—as if on the floor of a stage. The backdrop of the card appears flat, like a scrim. A scrim is a painted screen used for theatrical backdrops. A double horizontal line represents the spot where the scrim meets the stage.

The divine Ms. Smith was to suffer the fate of many a great artist and die penniless, without knowledge that her work would go on to influence millions of people. She was by trade a theatrical backdrop designer. She painted, constructed, and created sets that appeared on London stages. Her theater background and knack for dramatic expression is probably why the Rider-Waite deck is a classic. Her pictures clearly express characters playing out a story. We viewers immediately see the drama unfolding before us in the cards.

What is surprising and quite curious is there are only thirteen stage cards. Thirteen is a number of mysteries, even a superstitiously dangerous number. Many buildings do not include a thirteenth floor; elevators skip from floor twelve to floor fourteen. Thirteen is a number known to cause discomfort and superstition. It's no accident that the Death card is numbered at thirteen; it's no wonder that the average Joe doesn't want to disembark onto an unlucky floor. Why did Ms. Smith create stage cards? Why not make them all stage cards? Why thirteen? How do we apply this notion of theatricism to our readings?

Take a look through your deck. See if you can pick out the stage cards for yourself before looking at the list below.

Stage Cards:

✦ Two of Swords

✦ Five of Swords

✦ Seven of Swords

✦ Four of Wands

- ✦ Nine of Wands

- ✦ Ten of Wands

- ✦ Two of Cups

- ✦ Ten of Cups

- ✦ Page of Cups

- ✦ Two of Pentacles

- ✦ Four of Pentacles

- ✦ Six of Pentacles

- ✦ Eight of Pentacles

Why didn't Ms. Smith design all her cards upon a stage? Why did she choose only thirteen cards with this specific setup? We will probably never know the answer. Still, there are no accidents in this deck; each object contains a specific meaning, a reference to a hidden system of divination. It is important we look at what the artist has given and make our readings soar.

How to Interpret a Stage Card

Let us first examine what the word *stage* means. Then we'll use this implication to inform our readings and questions. Stage, by its very definition, contains levels of meaning. A stage is something you move through. You chat with a friend about moving away from home: "At that stage in my life, I needed to break away from my family and experience life on my own."

A stage can refer to a horse-drawn carriage, the popular mode of transport used up until the motorcar was invented. Understood this way, this connects the stage cards to the Chariot, indicating a moment when wheels are in motion and you are moving forward in a powerful, profound way.

The universal and most typical usage of the word *stage* is in reference to that platform on which a form of entertainment takes place for a seated audience: a play, musical, dance performance, concert, opera, award ceremony, speech, or presentation.

There are three ways in which we participate in staged events:

- ✦ Audience member

- ✦ Performer

- ✦ Creator

Of the three components of stage performance, it produces questions we can use when a stage card appears in a tarot reading.

One: Audience member, with tickets and Raisinettes in hand, waiting, watching for the entertainment to unfold, transporting us. Lucid group hypnosis as we, the audience, watch heightened reality dance before us.

- ✦ Am I waiting and watching, expecting the issue to unfold for me?

- ✦ Am I entertained and amused by the way this issue plays out in my life?

- ✦ Is all this drama worth the price of admission?

- ✦ Can I get up and walk away from this drama?

- ✦ What do I learn as this unfolds?

- ✦ Do I need Twizzlers to get me through the second act?

Two: We are the actual performers upon the stage. We are actors, singers, teachers, and dancers baring our souls to the audience, hoping to leave an emotional impact on the people watching from the hushed crowd below. We walk onto the stage feeling the living, breathing entity that is an audience. The audience sits in the dark, a lion in wait. Will the audience approve, enjoy, and engage in the story we are about to tell?

- ✦ Am I engaged with this issue to grab the attention of others?

- ✦ Is there an emotionally addictive catharsis that I experience with this issue?

- ✦ Do I care too much about my appearance and what others think?

- ✦ Does this issue allow me to freely express myself?

- ✦ Am I too busy trying to please everyone?

Three: We are the writers, directors, stagehands, and constructors of the event that is to play before the hushed masses. We toil on a mode of expression that comes from somewhere deep inside. It must be played before an audience. In this case, we, like the great Wizard of Oz, tinker behind the scenes, dazzling the audience with special effects and tricks.

- ✦ How am I purposefully manipulating events to get my point across?

- ✦ How do I construct this issue in a physical way around me?

- ✦ What is the subtext, the story I project?

- ✦ Do I care about what reviewers—or other people—think about me?

- ✦ What stories do I weave about myself?

No matter how we choose to participate in a staged event, regardless of whether we are spectator, player, or creator, we are engaged in a game of heightened reality—an illusion, an act of magical transference and group hypnosis. This is what marks the stage cards as remarkably different than the rest of the cards in the deck.

Historical Note

The Rider-Waite cards were born at a sliver in time where theater was the mass form of entertainment. There was no television, Internet, video, or films. Did Ms. Smith somehow foresee entertainment would eventually be projected onto screens for the masses? This idea is expressed in the Seven

of Cups card. We see the silhouette of a man who appears to be looking at a projected screen of choices and imagined realities playing out before him. If you wish, you may use the Seven of Cups as a modern stage and screen card.

In examining a stage card or the idea of a filmic life, it is worth a minute to think about how we view ourselves, the star of our own personal drama. We tend to understand the world in the context of how it affects us. The world, our lives, can be understood as a "movie" playing out before us—a movie in which we take an active part. Our family and friends, the recurring characters; people on the streets, the extras or bit players. It is perfectly normal to view our lives this way. Our point of view extends from inside ourselves; our eyes, the lens of the camera. We point, shoot, and focus on what we choose at will.

A disconnect happens when our cameras roll if we begin to take everything that happens to us personally. The bank teller is grumpy at you while making a deposit. We wonder: "Why doesn't she like me? Why did she say that to me? Why'd she look at me that way?" A speed demon cuts you off in traffic, honking at you. It riles you up: "Why is that guy being such a jerk? I'm just driving here. Why did he do that to me?" Arriving home from work, your significant other ignores your cue for a hug: "He doesn't love me. He doesn't see me. I never get what I want!" Your child throws a tantrum, and you think: "I'm a lousy parent. I can't handle this. Why is she doing this to me?" We assign personal meaning to every little thing that happens to us.

Stop for a moment: freeze that frame. The bank teller was sad about her son and angry to be at work, and that informed her exchange with you. The speed demon was rushing to his hospitalized mother. Your significant other was wrapped up in their own thoughts, not seeing you at the precise moment you needed. Your child acted out because she was overtired and that's what children do at age three when they hit bottom. None of these things had anything whatsoever to do with you—yet you assigned personal meaning to them.

The lesson of starring in your own film? Don't take it all so personally. It ain't all about you, sister—no matter how much you wish it were. You'll live a life less full of angst when you stop taking it all so personally. Sit back, enjoy the view, and allow others to be themselves. After all, they are living out their own personal dramas, and guess what? To them, you are but a bit player, a recurring guest star.

The Ten of Cups takes place upon a smooth stage, but the double horizontal line between scrim and stage does not appear. Rather, it stands as a thick black line, as if to indicate that the finale of action has been reached and the backdrop has unraveled and dropped behind the performers, a happy ending in this happily ever after card.

A Little Black *Book of Shadows*

Each and every tarot card offers secret symbols not normally available to the average viewer. You've come this far, diva, so I'd like to let you in on a few trade secrets. Use your wisdom wisely, and let these secrets add deeper dimensions to your readings.

The imagery examined below comes from the images on the classic Rider-Waite deck.

The Secret Symbols in the Cards

0, The Fool: The ground the Fool is about to step off of is not actually a cliff. The land regenerates before the Fool's footsteps like magic. The dog with the Fool is there to represent the animal side of our nature.

I, The Magician: The wand the Magician is holding is actually a magic wand. This wand may be used for spiritual advancement or material gain. How shall you use it? Peek at the World card to discover that she holds two of the same wands in completion and balance.

II, The High Priestess: The High Priestess and her two pillars are actually a pictorial metaphor for the three pillars on the Tree of Life. The High Priestess herself is the middle pillar. Look carefully to discover this same symbolism upon Justice, the Moon, and the Hierophant cards.

III, The Empress: The twelve stars upon the Empress's crown are the twelve signs of the zodiac.

IV, The Emperor: The Emperor wears carefully concealed armor under his red robes. This armor is a reminder that he is protected and a great warrior. Note the armor also appearing on the Chariot, Death, the King of Pentacles, and the four knights.

V, The Hierophant: See the three-level crown on his head and the three-level cross in his hand? They represent the three levels, or degrees, of Freemasonry: Entered Apprentice (first level), Fellow Craft (second level), and Master Mason (third level).

VI, The Lovers: Notice the giant mountain peak in between the man and the woman and underneath the angel? This mountain peak and all peaks in the tarot represent humanity's attempt to merge with the Divine. It is the greatest height the physical body can reach while remaining on the ground.

VII, The Chariot: The stars upon the Chariot's canopy represent the infinite universe.

VIII, Strength: The sideways figure eight above the female is a lemniscate—the symbol of infinity, ying and yang, and eternal energy flow—and it is also found on the Magician and the Two of Pentacles.

IX, The Hermit: The Hermit carries a six-pointed star in his lantern, created by merging two triangles together. The light emanating from the lantern represents the Hermit shedding his wisdom to all those below.

X, The Wheel of Fortune: The four creatures in the corners of the Wheel of Fortune represent the four elements and suits of tarot. The Magician has the suits upon his table. The Wheel, as it churns in the tenth spot of the majors, carries these symbols as creatures. The four creatures/suits are seen close-up in the last card of the Major Arcana, the World.

XI, Justice: Justice holds a sword and balanced scales. The scales represent positive and negative. The sword pointing upward represents careful attention being paid to the decisions you make.

XII, The Hanged Man: Look carefully at the Hanged Man figure: his pose is the graphic opposite of the dancer pictured on the World card.

THE HERMIT.

XIII, Death: Death carries a flag. The symbol upon the flag is the official symbol of the Golden Dawn.

XIV, Temperance: The circle on the angel's forehead with a dot in the center is the alchemical symbol for gold.

XV, The Devil: The configuration of this card is exactly like the Lovers card but with darker overtones. The Devil's number, 15, numerologically reduces to the Lovers' card number, 6 (1+5 = 6).

XVI, The Tower: The tower is square shaped while the crown being knocked off is circular. This demonstrates the idea that a circle will never fit snugly on a square, and that the knocking off, the lightning bolt, is exactly what was needed. The circle and square never fit together to begin with.

XVII, The Star: The giant star above the female's head represents the star Sirius, associated with the fire element; the bird on the tree represents air; the pool, water; and the ground, earth. These four elements surrounding the female represent the perfect balance of the elements. The five streams of water on the ground remind us of the toughness of fives in tarot and that it will all be balanced out again. Also note that there are five streams of water pouring out of the Ace of Cups.

XVIII, The Moon: The moon on this card is engulfed by a giant sun. This reminds us the moon is dependant on the sun for light, but more importantly, it evokes the need for reconciliation between the subconscious (the moon) and the conscious (the sun).

XIX, The Sun: The feather on the head of the child is the same feather worn by the Fool and Death. The child is the Fool's inner child set free as he moves through the Major Arcana.

XX, Judgement: The red cross on the white flag is a reference to the Knights Templar, who wore this symbol on their chest.

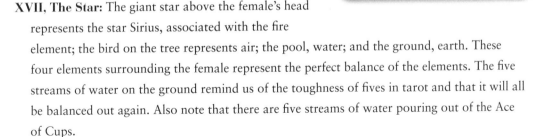

XXI, The World: The wreath around the world dancer forms the symbol zero and connects this card back to the Fool, whose journey shall begin again.

Ace of Pentacles: The gateway leading out of the garden offers a potential path you can follow with this new opportunity.

Two of Pentacles: The juggler on the Two of Pentacles holds two pentacles in his hand—yet eight more pentacles fly above him. This is a reminder of how you can only focus on one thing at a time, no matter how good a multitasker you are.

Three of Pentacles: The three pentacles pictured represent the top triad of the Tree of Life; the Father, Son, and Holy Ghost; the Maiden, Mother, and Crone.

Four of Pentacles: Many people assume this card is the miser card, as the person is clinging tightly to the pentacles. In fact, the figure depicted is embarking on the magical act of manifestation, and the city behind him is representative of the kingdom he is creating.

Five of Pentacles: The pentacles upon the stained glass window are a pictorial representation of the top five places on the Tree of Life.

Six of Pentacles: Notice how the gentleman offering money stands above the two beggars, implying a hierarchy? Look at all of the sixes in the minors. They all depict one person above and people below.

Seven of Pentacles: The tendrils of vegetables coil outward on the ground, suggesting there is more to come. He's reaped his harvest, yet more shall grow.

Eight of Pentacles: The figure on the card indicates a Freemason in clothing and tools. This is a reminder that performing enjoyable work is itself an exercise in magic.

Nine of Pentacles: The snail on the ground depicts energy moving at a slow pace—plenty of time to enjoy the marvelous qualities of this divine card. The trained falcon on her wrist represents the trained mind and loyalty.

Ten of Pentacles: The ten pentacles hang in the card in the form of the Tree of Life, but you can also understand this as your family tree. How do you manifest what you have inherited?

Page of Pentacles: The plowed field behind the page is where she shall plant her pentacle.

Knight of Pentacles: The horse upon which this knight rides is specifically a workhorse and implies hard work.

Queen of Pentacles: The rabbit next to this queen represents pregnancy and fertility.

King of Pentacles: The King of Pentacles is the only king who offers us a peek at his armor; note his foot. This is a reference to the king's strength and resilience.

Ace of Wands: The wand on this card is symbolic of the male phallus. I leave further interpretation to your own fertile imagination…

Two of Wands: The figure upon the Two of Wands holds the world in his hands, and this card connects to the World card. It suggests knowing the potential for success and integration is possible while he plots and plans a way to get this for himself. Remember, if you want to embody the World card, first you must ask for it.

Three of Wands: This card is often understood as waiting for your ship to come in, but it actually implies an opposite visual significance. The merchant is watching his carefully packed ships leave the harbor; he has set something in motion.

Four of Wands: The four wands creating structure represent the four corners, the elements of the known world.

Five of Wands: If the youths place the five wands together, they will create a pentacle.

Six of Wands: Notice the horse is looking backward. This is a reminder that past issues may come into play in the future.

Seven of Wands: Sevens embody risk taking, experimentation, and courage. This figure can be understood as a giant fighting the angered masses. Use it to remind you of your massive strength.

Eight of Wands: The flying wands can be understood as arrows of love.

Nine of Wands: The wand the gentleman holds has opened a passage. You now have a new way to proceed.

Ten of Wands: The Ten of Wands shows us the final act of strength that brings a situation to completion.

Page of Wands: Notice this page is the only character in the wands who pays close attention to the fresh leaves sprouting out of the wand—perhaps the only one who even notices. This represents the fascination with growth and freshness.

Knight of Wands: Notice the horse of our fiery knight? The horse rears upward as if startled. This is a clue to the combustible quality of fire.

Queen of Wands: This queen can be understood as the actress card, embodying emotive, passionate qualities. Look at her sunflower and recall how actresses and performers are given flowers at the curtain calls of their shows.

King of Wands: The King of Wands is the only wand court card without a pyramid in the background. This is because he sits upon the pyramid with ultimate authority.

Ace of Cups: The white dove represents the spirit, while the white communion wafer represents matter. The cup in the mysterious hand is the Holy Grail.

Two of Cups: The two snakes entwining on the caduceus represent the souls of the people entwining.

Three of Cups: The three women on this card may be understood as the Triple Goddess: Maiden, Mother, and Crone, or, in other words, a woman at different stages of her life.

Four of Cups: The hand offering a cup is a mini ace hand emerging from a cloud. Opportunity is offered, but will the figure notice it?

Five of Cups: The bridge symbolizes a gateway between two worlds. Will the figure stay and lament over loss or cross to the safety of his castle?

Six of Cups: See the X in the pillar to the left of the young man? This literally means X marks the spot for pleasure. Pleasure is what this card is all about.

Seven of Cups: The figures and objects floating before the gentleman can be connected to the Major Arcana, but they can also be connected with the seven deadly sins for a more sinister overtone. Connect them for yourself.

Eight of Cups: The figure walking away from the cups can be said to be the Hermit at the beginning of his journey.

Nine of Cups: Like the High Priestess's veil, the veil hanging beneath the cups covers what shall happen as a consequence of getting what you want.

Ten of Cups: The winged lion head is meant to invoke the Lovers card.

Page of Cups: See the fish popping out to speak to the young page? This fish is a reference to psychic and intuitive pops.

Knight of Cups: The Knight of Cups pauses before his horse takes the next step. If you look at his helmet and heels, you will note the wings of Hermes.

Queen of Cups: Note the mermaids engraved upon the Queen of Cups' throne. They are water symbols, and the cliffs behind her are the White Cliffs of Dover.

King of Cups: The rocky waters behind the King of Cups signify this particular king's active imagination in the constant churning of the waters.

Ace of Swords: The sword piercing the crown can be seen as a "hole in one."

Two of Swords: Swords that point up into the air, as the Two of Swords depicts, shows thoughts searching upward are graced with inspiration.

Three of Swords: The pierced heart is the quintessential symbol for being in love; think of Cupid's arrow. The three piercing swords may represent yourself being torn between two lovers.

Four of Swords: The effigy (reclining stone knight) seen on this card stems from the Middle Ages, when effigies played an important focal point in funerals. You can understand this card as an idea that has literally been put to rest. The stained glass window depicts the image of Christ giving a blessing.

Five of Swords: Notice the clouds racing by in the troubled sky above the three figures? Whatever situation is reflected for you in the Five of Swords, its nature is soon to change with the racing wind.

Six of Swords: Note the difference in the water on each side of the boat. The rippled water or the right is a sign of tough times; the still water on the left, a sign of things getting better. Nothing denotes hope and promise as much as a child. Let the child in the boat act as a reminder that great promise lies ahead.

Seven of Swords: Notice the figures in the distant background huddling around a campfire? They take no notice of the man sneaking away with the swords. This refers to the fact that you may be getting away with something, but can you live with the consequences of deception?

Eight of Swords: The bound, floating figure of the woman is upsetting at first glance. But if we take this card and understand her as a person about to be released and bloom, like a caterpillar into a butterfly, we see the metamorphosis implied by this card when we free ourselves of doubt and confusion.

Nine of Swords: The blackness that drapes this sorrowful card is symbolic of the deepest recesses of our unconscious roaming free.

Ten of Swords: When swords are rooted, firmly planted into the ground—or into a man's back, as is pictured on this card—it is a reminder that the thoughts have been completely, utterly nailed down.

Page of Swords: The Page of Swords carries the sword of truth, which can cut through the heart of any situation.

Knight of Swords: The Knight of Sword's horse harness is decorated with butterflies and birds, all symbols of air. You can detect wind speed by observing how the clouds race across the sky and the trees bend under the wind. Reference the winds to remind you the issue at hand carries a rapid energy.

Queen of Swords: The butterflies on this queen's crown and throne represent transformation, as the butterfly has transformed from a caterpillar into a winged creature, a reminder of the chrysalis metaphor drawn on the Eight of Swords.

King of Swords: The King of Swords is the only court card who looks directly at you, engaging you with his gaze. The King of Swords always asks you to confront an issue.

A *Final Word*

THE CHARIOT

This book is a jumping-off point for your journey with the cards. The meditations, spells, visualizations, exercises, and meanings of the cards are endless and infinite, just like you.

Your journey with tarot may have begun here with me or it may have started long ago. Whatever the case, I do hope you find yourself among the cards. An electric field pulsing full of synchronicity, coincidence, and magic surrounds us at all times. It is tickling you even as you read these words. But we won't notice and can't access this field if we aren't paying attention. Tarot teaches us to pay attention. It is up to each one of us to seek, discover, and cultivate the magic of our lives; no one can do this for us. Tarot by itself won't help you unless you let it point you in the right direction.

Remember that divaness, happiness, and joy rest in your hands alone. It is you, not a tarot book, who fills the cards with grace, wisdom, and nuance. I may suggest a spell or meditation into a card, but you are the one who colors it with meaning and substance. It is you who takes the suggestion of the archetype of creativity offered by the Empress and brings it into the world in a way no one else can.

A popular transformational workshop offers the secret to life. The secret to life is (*insert drumroll*) … there is no secret. Life itself is meaningless. It is up to you to create meaning in your life. This secret is wise. In essence, life really is what you make of it. This notion also applies to the art of tarot. Even though this very book is full of secrets ascribed to the cards, it is really up to you to create meaning out of the tarot.

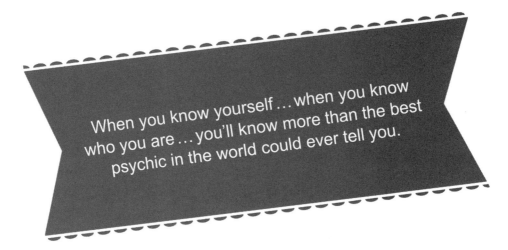

When you know yourself ... when you know who you are ... you'll know more than the best psychic in the world could ever tell you.

You are the secret.

Let tarot guide you.

And remember, if you want to embody the World card, first you must ask for it.

Now, go have your way with the world, diva!

A Diva Dictionary

Adept: A person who has attained a special level of knowledge or skill within a particular organization.

Arcana: The plural form of the word *arcanum*, meaning a deep secret, a mystery. In tarot, the tarot deck is divided into the Major Arcana (twenty-two cards) and Minor Arcana (fifty-six cards).

Archetype: An archetype describes a set of personality traits, an ideal example, or a symbol universally recognized by all people.

BOTA (Builders of the Adytum): A modern mystery school in the Western tradition. BOTA's teachings are based on Qabalah and tarot. BOTA offers a tarot correspondence course; see www.bota.org.

Cartomancy: Fortunetelling using cards. Cards used for fortunetelling could be tarot or any sort of cards, including (but not limited to) regular playing cards, gypsy witch cards, angel cards, and so on.

Crowley, Aleister: Rogue member of the Golden Dawn and controversial figure known in the early twentieth century as "the wickedest man in the world."

Diva: A term describing a successful woman with rare, unusual talent.

Divination: The act of foretelling future events using any number of means, including (but not limited to) astrology, tarot reading, palm reading, tea leaf reading, rune casting, numerology, crystal ball gazing, and so on.

Elementals: Related to or being an element. It is commonly understood the world is composed of the four elements of earth, air, fire, and water.

Earth = Pentacles

Air = Swords

Fire = Wands

Water = Cups

Esoteric: Intended for or understood by a select, small group of people. Confidential. Private. Secret.

The Golden Dawn: The most influential magical group to spring from the nineteenth century. The group who has had the largest impact on modern occultism. Created in England, the Golden Dawn practiced spiritual advancement, magic, and tarot.

Intuition: Quick and ready insight. Instinctive knowledge of or about something without conscious reasoning. A facility available to every single person.

Lemniscate: A symbol meaning infinity and seen as a sideways eight. Pictured in the Magician, Strength, and the Two of Pentacles.

Major Arcana: The Major Arcana is the first twenty-two cards of the tarot deck, numbered 0 through 21. The Major Arcana contains the big archetypes of tarot. The Major Arcana is, in fact, what separates the tarot deck from a normal set of playing cards.

Minor Arcana: Commonly referred to as the minors, or pip cards, the Minor Arcana consists of the aces through tens and court cards of tarot.

Occult: Relating or dealing with supernatural phenomena. Hidden from view, or secret.

Pip Cards: Pip cards are the aces through tens within the four suits of Minor Arcana cards.

Psychic: Sensitive to nonphysical or supernatural forces and influences, marked by extraordinary or mysterious sensitivity, perception, or understanding.

Qabalah: Ancient Jewish mysticism that describes how the universe works. Many tarot scholars apply tarot to Qabalah, as there are twenty-two letters of the Hebrew alphabet and twenty-two Major Arcana cards.

Querent: An old-fashioned term for the person who comes to you for a tarot reading. These days, the querent is almost always referred to as the client.

Reversal: The term used to describe a card that is drawn upside down.

Smith, Pamela Colman: The painter who created the images found on the Rider-Waite deck. She was a member of the Golden Dawn.

Supernatural: Of or relating to an order of existence beyond the visible universe, especially if relating to a god, demigod, spirit, or devil.

Synchronicity: The experience of two or more events having nothing to do with each other yet supposedly meaningful. A coincidence of events that seem to be meaningfully related.

Tree of Life: A mystical concept that explains the universe as described by Jewish mysticism.

Trump Cards: The Major Arcana. The tarot cards numbering 0 to 21. Called trumps because each card is more powerful, or "trumps," the previous.

Waite, Arthur Edward: A member of the Golden Dawn and creator of the famous Rider-Waite deck.

Important Decks Every Diva Should Know

Rider-Waite Deck: The most popular tarot deck in English-speaking countries. The cards were illustrated by Pamela Colman Smith. Ms. Smith took her instructions from Arthur Edward Waite. Originally published in December 1909 by the Rider Company.

Visconti-Sforza Deck: The oldest tarot deck in existence. Italian in origin. Thirty-five cards are in the holdings of the Pierpont Morgan Library in New York City; 26 cards reside at Accademia Carrara, Bergamo, Italy. Check with the institutions before visiting, as the cards are in rotating collections and may not be available for public viewing.

Tarot of Marseille: Marseille tarot refers to decks patterned after French decks created in the eighteenth century. The pip cards are abstract and do not contain pictures like the Rider-Waite but are images of the numbered suit.

Thoth Deck: A tarot deck painted by Lady Frieda Harris. She took her instructions from Aleister Crowley. Neither would live to see this deck published in 1969.

A Diva *Bibliography*

Amberstone, Wald, and Ruth Ann Amberstone. *The Secret Language of Tarot*. San Francisco, CA: Red Wheel/Weiser, 2008.

Bach, David. *Smart Women Finish Rich*. New York: Broadway Books, 1999.

Cameron, Julia. *The Artist's Way*. New York: Penguin Putnam, 1992.

Csikszentmihalyi, Mihaly. *Flow*. New York: Harper and Row, 1990.

Fifield, Kathleen. *Instant Style*. New York: InStyle, 2006.

Gettings, Fred. *The Book of Tarot*. London: Triune Books, 1973.

Gladwell, Malcolm. *Blink*. New York: Little, Brown, and Company, 2005.

Gray, Eden. *A Complete Guide to the Tarot*. New York: Bantam Books, 1970.

Greer, Mary K., and Tom Little. *Understanding the Tarot Court*. St. Paul, MN: Llewellyn, 2004.

Hurley, Judith Benn. *The Good Herb*. New York: Morrow, 1995.

Illes, Judika. *The Element Encyclopedia of Witchcraft*. London: HarperElement, 2005.

Kenner, Corrine. *Tarot Journaling*. Woodbury, MN: Llewellyn, 2006.

———. *Tarot for Writers*. Woodbury, MN: Llewellyn, 2009.

Pajeon, Kala, and Ketz Pajeon. *The Candle Magick Workbook*. New York: Carol Publishing Group, 1997.

Pollack, Rachel. *Complete Illustrated Guide to Tarot*. New York: Gramercy Books, 1999.

———. *Seventy-Eight Degrees of Wisdom*. London: Element, 1980.

Powell, Robert (trans.). *Meditations on the Tarot*. New York: Penguin Putnam, 1985.

Renee, Janina. *Tarot Spells*. St. Paul, MN: Llewellyn, 2004.

Roséan, Lexa. *The Supermarket Sorceress*. New York: St. Martin's Press, 1996.

Telesco, Patricia. *A Victorian Grimoire*. St. Paul, MN: Llewellyn, 1998.

A DIVA *Index*

Eight of Cups, 55–56, 75, 89,
    209, 231, 280, 283–284
Eight of Pentacles, 55, 94, 96,
    182–183, 274, 280, 282, 290
Eight of Swords, 55–56, 75, 92,
    94, 196, 229, 231, 284, 286
Eight of Wands, 55–56, 75,
    89, 92, 251, 282–283
Emperor (Major Arcana card), 13, 31,
    55–56, 74, 86, 108–109, 180, 279
Empress (Major Arcana card), 8,
    13, 30, 54, 73–74, 86, 106–107,
    180, 208, 243–244, 279, 287
Energy, 1–2, 9, 13–15, 23, 25, 30, 32, 34,
    38, 40–43, 50, 53, 61, 63, 71, 82–83,
    85, 87, 90, 92, 98, 101, 104–106, 108,
    110, 112, 115, 117, 119, 123, 125,
    127, 129, 131, 133, 135, 137, 139,
    141, 143, 145, 147–149, 152–153, 156,
    159–166, 168, 176, 180, 185–186,
    190, 193–194, 201, 203, 213–214,
    219, 237–239, 241–242, 245, 253–255,
    258–264, 268–271, 280, 282, 286
Evening check-in, 46, 49–50
Exercises, 1, 5, 10, 22, 37, 43, 45–46,
    50, 141, 148, 166–168, 172, 176,
    179–180, 190, 205, 207, 209, 213,
    215, 217–219, 226, 230–232, 234, 237,
    245–246, 260, 264–265, 282, 287

Fashion, 6, 72, 89, 121–123, 125–126,
    128, 132, 134–135, 137, 142–143,
    180, 189, 207–208, 241, 243, 248
Five of Cups, 55, 57, 74–75, 89, 149,
    200–202, 245, 273, 281, 283–284
Five of Pentacles, 55, 74, 95, 149, 171,
    174, 200–201, 273, 281–282
Five of Swords, 55, 74–75, 93, 149,
    200–201, 222, 226, 273, 284–285
Five of Wands, 55, 74–75, 89, 91, 149,
    200–201, 239, 245, 250, 273, 282–283
Flowers, 35, 41, 45, 47, 106, 204, 247, 284
Fool (Major Arcana card), 13,
    30, 53, 55–56, 69, 73–74, 85,
    97–99, 186, 279, 281–282
Fool's journey, 73–74, 98–99, 281
Fortuneteller, 3–4, 11, 17, 21, 58, 61, 289
Four of Cups, 54–56, 75, 77, 89,
    189, 193–194, 198, 244, 273,
    280–281, 283–284, 289
Four of Pentacles, 54–56, 75, 77,
    95, 167, 172–173, 182, 187, 193,
    273–274, 279, 281–282, 289
Four of Swords, 54–56, 75, 77, 93,
    193, 219–221, 284–285, 289
Four of Wands, 54–56, 75, 77, 91, 193,
    243–244, 248, 273, 282–283, 289
Freemasonry, 59, 195, 280, 282

Golden Dawn, 30–31, 58–60, 94,
    195, 234, 281, 289–291

Magician (Major Arcana card), 8, 13,
    30, 52–54, 70, 74, 85, 101–102,
    208, 243–244, 279–280, 290
Meditations, 1, 3, 5, 9–10, 13, 24,
    38, 45, 110, 180, 188, 215, 217,
    220–222, 230, 234, 246, 287, 294
Modernism, 58
Moon (Major Arcana card), 14, 35, 54, 67,
    70, 75, 87–88, 138–139, 181, 279, 281
Music, 6, 40, 63–64, 76, 78, 80, 91, 155,
    166, 179, 190, 198–199, 203, 230

Nine of Cups, 19, 54, 56, 74–75, 90,
    210, 232, 268, 274, 283, 285
Nine of Pentacles, 54, 74, 94,
    96, 180, 184, 274, 282
Nine of Swords, 54, 56, 74,
    92, 94, 232, 285–286
Nine of Wands, 19, 54, 56, 74, 90,
    92, 253–254, 274, 282–283

Page of Cups, 54–57, 74–75, 90, 151, 153,
    166, 207–208, 211, 274, 283–285
Page of Pentacles, 54–56, 74–75, 94, 96,
    148, 151, 153, 166, 186, 274, 283
Page of Swords, 54–57, 74–75,
    92, 94, 151–153, 284–286
Page of Wands, 54–56, 74–75, 90, 92,
    148, 151–152, 166, 283–284
Pages, 147–148, 150–153
Postmodernism, 61

Power, 2, 4–5, 13–14, 17–18, 30, 32,
    39–40, 43, 47, 50, 52–54, 63, 69–71,
    85, 118, 124–125, 151, 161, 164,
    174, 183–184, 191, 201–202, 215,
    222, 237, 240, 266–267, 271
Power question, 17–18, 183
Psychic, 3–5, 17, 23, 42, 46, 54, 69,
    71–72, 88, 90, 151–152, 159,
    267, 270, 285, 288, 290
Psychic pops, 23, 46, 90, 285

Qabalah, 59–60, 289–290
Queen of Cups, 53–55, 57, 74–75, 90,
    149, 158–159, 161, 283–285
Queen of Pentacles, 53–55, 74, 94,
    96, 149, 158–159, 161, 283
Queen of Swords, 53–55, 74, 92, 94,
    149, 159–160, 212, 284–286
Queen of Wands, 53–55, 74–75, 90,
    92, 149, 159–161, 283–284
Queens, 69, 134, 147–148, 150, 158, 261
Questions, 12–13, 15, 17–19, 64, 72,
    81, 145, 176, 198, 210, 259–260,
    262, 265, 268, 274–275

Reversals, 10, 46, 258, 268
Ritual, 37, 45, 196, 241

Sacred Space, 37–40, 42–43,
    182, 196, 257, 270
Secret symbols, 58, 60, 196–197, 279

Rachel Pollack's Tarot Wisdom

Spiritual Teachings and Deeper Meanings

Rachel Pollack

Beloved by nearly half a million tarot enthusiasts, Rachel Pollack's *Seventy-Eight Degrees of Wisdom* forever transformed the study of tarot. Finally—after thirty years—the much-anticipated follow-up to this revered classic has arrived! Enhanced by author's personal insights and wisdom gained over the past three decades, *Rachel Pollack's Tarot Wisdom* will inspire fans and attract a new generation of tarot students.

Alive with a rich array of new ideas, yet reverent to the history and tradition of tarot, *Rachel Pollack's Tarot Wisdom* is a comprehensive guide for all levels. All seventy-eight cards are explored from fresh angles: tarot history, art, psychology, and a wide variety of spiritual/occult traditions. Pollack also takes tarot reading in new and exciting directions—spanning predictive, psychological, magical, and spiritual approaches. Featuring a wealth of new spreads, anecdotes from the author, and innovative ways to interpret and use tarot, this all-encompassing guide will reinvigorate your practice.

978-0-7387-1309-0

$24.95

7½ x 9⅛

480 pp.

illus, photos, index

An all new approach!

Tarot

For Beginners

A Practical Guide to Reading the Cards

BARBARA MOORE

Tarot for Beginners

A Practical Guide to Reading the Cards

Barbara Moore

Tarot for Beginners makes it easier than ever to learn all you need to know about reading the cards. Award-winning tarot expert Barbara Moore provides a complete foundation in tarot, clearly explaining each aspect while encouraging you to develop your own unique reading style.

Begin with the history and myths behind tarot, and discover the meanings of all seventy-eight cards—broken down into suit, number, and major and minor arcana for simpler learning. You'll also explore symbols, reversals, spreads, interpretation techniques, tarot journaling, and more.

Sample readings of predictive, prescriptive, interactive, and intuitive styles will also help you give insightful and fulfilling readings for yourself and others.

978-0-7387-1955-9

$15.95

5 3/16 x 8

360 pp.

appendices

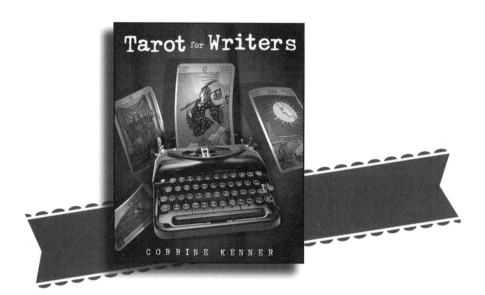

Tarot for Writers

Corrine Kenner

Kick-start your creativity as a writer by calling upon the inspirational powers of the tarot. Used by famous authors such as Stephen King and John Steinbeck, tarot is an excellent tool for unleashing creative thinking and imagination. Applicable to short stories, novels, poetry, nonfiction, and more, this unique guide will enliven your writing at every stage, from fleshing out a premise to submitting a proposal. Breathe new life into an existing project; brainstorm character, dialogue, and plot development ideas; break through writer's block—all with idea-stimulating tarot spreads and card descriptions.

Featuring a clear introduction to all seventy-eight cards in the tarot deck, this down-to-earth guide is fun and accessible for all, from beginners to advanced users. Try your hand at writing prompts and exploratory games that call upon the archetypal imagery and rich symbolism in each tarot card … and let the wellspring of inspiration flow!

978-0-7387-1457-8

$19.95

7½ x 9⅛

384 pp.

Illus.

Each of us has that right, that possibility, to
invent ourselves daily. If a person does not
invent herself, she will be invented. So to be
bodacious enough to invent ourselves is wise.

Maya Angelou